BENDING SPINES

Martin J. Medhurst, Series Editor, *Baylor University*

Rhetoric and Public Affairs Series

BENDING SPINES

THE PROPAGANDAS
OF NAZI GERMANY
AND THE GERMAN
DEMOCRATIC REPUBLIC

Randall L. Bytwerk

Michigan State University Press
East Lansing

∞ The paper used in this publication meets the minimum requirements of ANSI/NISO Z39.48–1992 (R 1997) (Permanence of Paper).

 Michigan State University Press
East Lansing, Michigan 48823-5245

Printed and bound in the United States of America.

10 09 08 07 06 05 04   1 2 3 4 5 6 7 8 9 10

LIBRARY OF CONGRESS CATALOGING-IN-PUBLICATION DATA

Bytwerk, Randall L.
  Bending spines : the propagandas of Nazi Germany and the German Democratic Republic / Randall L. Bytwerk.
    p. cm.— (Rhetoric and public affairs series)
  Includes bibliographical references.
  ISBN 0-87013-709-3 (cloth : alk. paper)
  ISBN 0-87013-710-7 (pbk. : alk. paper)
  1. Propaganda—Germany—History. 2. Nazi propaganda. I. Title. II. Series.
JN3971.A69P8524 2004
303.3'75'094309043—dc22

                                                    2004000275

g green press INITIATIVE Michigan State University Press is a member of the Green Press Initiative and is committed to developing and encouraging ecologically responsible publishing practices. For more information about the Green Press Initiative and the use of recycled paper in book publishing, please visit www.greenpressinitiative.org.

Book and Cover design by Sans Serif, Inc.

Visit Michigan State University Press on the World Wide Web at:
www.msupress.msu.edu

For Robert L. Bytwerk,

who gave me a good start
and who has been a steady help along the way

Contents

Acknowledgments

The research was supported by Calvin College, which provided a sabbatical, other time for travel and research, and an environment conducive to writing because one has something to say rather than because one has to.

The archivists and librarians at the Stiftung Archiv der Parteien und Massenorganisationen der DDR im Bundesarchiv in Berlin oversee a pleasant working environment, and they know their holdings.

Colleagues have taken the time to read drafts of the manuscript and give responses that sharpened my thinking and rescued me from error. Robert D. Brooks, who first prompted my interest in the topic thirty years ago (and it did take some prompting), gave me most helpful counsel. John Rodden did, too. My Calvin colleagues David Diephouse, Barbara Carvill, and Wally Bratt offered good advice. My departmental colleague Quentin J. Schultze gave the penultimate draft a thorough reading that reminded me of what a prince among colleagues he is. The three people who reviewed the manuscript for Michigan State University Press made a variety of suggestions, many of which I took with thanks.

My friends who were once citizens of the German Democratic Republic have stimulated my thinking in many ways. I particularly thank Pastor Wolfgang and Cornelia Gröger, the Kalinkat family, Günter Gießler, and Christa Fischer. They offered friendship and hospitality both before and after 1989.

Sharon and David Bytwerk took the annoyances of a husband and father writing a book in good cheer.

I thank the publishers of the following essays for permission to incorporate parts of them into this book.

- "*Und Ihr habt doch gesiegt:* Rhetorical Aspects of a Nazi Holiday" originally appeared in *ETC: A Review of General Semantics* 36 (1979): 134–146, published by the International Society for General Semantics, Concord, California.
- "The Dolt Laughs: Satirical Publications under Hitler and Honecker" originally appeared in *Journalism Quarterly* 69 (1992): 1029–1038.
- "The Failure of the Propaganda of the German Democratic Republic" originally appeared in *Quarterly Journal of Speech* 85 (1999): 400–416.

- "The Propagandas of Nazi Germany and the German Democratic Republic" originally appeared in *Communication Studies* 49 (1998): 158–171.
- "The Pleasures of Unanimity in the GDR" originally appeared in *After the GDR: New Perspectives on the Old GDR and the Young Länder.* (Amsterdam: Rodopi, 2001) 109–124.

Terms and Abbreviations

ADN: The GDR news agency

Bezirk: One of fourteen GDR districts

DAF: German Labor Front

DEFA: GDR film production company

DSF: Society for German-Soviet Friendship

FDGB: Free German Trade Union

FDJ: Free German Youth

Gau: A Nazi party region

GDR: German Democratic Republic

GPA: German Propaganda Archive

Kreis: Roughly the equivalent of an American county

NSDAP: National Socialist German Workers Party

OKW: Supreme Command of the Wehrmacht

RKK: Reich Chamber of Culture

RMVP: Reich Ministry for People's Enlightenment and Propaganda

RPL: Reich Central Propaganda Office

SA: "Brown Shirts," or Storm Troopers

SAPMO: The repository of East German party and mass organization records, part of the German Federal Archives

SD: Security Service of the SS

SED: Socialist Unity Party of Germany

SS: "Black Shirts," the elite Nazi paramilitary organization

ZK: Central Committee of the SED

Introduction

A pastor who lived through the Third Reich described his meetings with Nazi officials in a way that illuminates life in totalitarian societies: "[O]ne would be pushed further, step by step, until he had crossed over the line, without noticing that his spine was being bent millimeter by millimeter."[1] The Nazis he met with knew that persuasion is a gradual process with many methods.

Just after Nikita Khrushchev's famous speech that revealed some of Stalin's depravity, Johannes R. Becher, author of the GDR's national anthem and minister of culture, wrote a poem that remained unpublished until 2000. It was titled "Burnt Child":

> He who has had his spine broken
> Is hardly to be persuaded
> To stand up straight.
>
> The memory of the broken spine
> Terrifies him.
> Even when the break
> Has long since healed,
> And there is no longer any danger
> Of breaking his spine.[2]

The poem may be a confession. In any event, it was published only long after Becher's death.

National Socialism and Marxism-Leninism put enormous effort into bending, and sometimes breaking, spines—a process for which both found propaganda necessary. The two German systems differ in many ways. One is the mark of vivid evil, the other leaves images of gray old men in colorless cities. The Nazi villain is a regular in film and fiction. Leni Riefenstahl's *Triumph of the Will* (1935) is the quintessential propaganda film. The GDR left nothing that makes evil as striking. GDR writer Volker Braun once called it "the most boring country on earth."[3] Some agree with Margherita von Brentano that "the mere comparison of the Third Reich with the GDR is a dreadful oversimplification. The Third Reich left mountains of corpses. The GDR left mountains of files."[4]

The differences between the systems should not be ignored but neither should the similarities. Both used propaganda to attempt to build new societies in which people were to share almost unanimously a common worldview of religious proportions, what some today call a hegemonic metanarrative, with little room for opposing versions of truth. Both greatly reduced opportunities for open discourse, rendering it difficult and perhaps even impossible for them and their citizens to correct the evils their governments caused. The extent to which the propagandas of two systems close in time and rooted in the same history and culture, yet widely varying in ideology, are similar or different will say something about the larger nature of propaganda in the modern world.

But what is this thing called propaganda? There are about as many definitions as there are writers. F. M. Cornford has my favorite—"The art of very nearly deceiving one's friends without quite deceiving one's enemies"—but that is not a practical definition. Part of the problem is that there are conflicting views of propaganda.[5] Western democracies have feared propaganda and at least in public oppose it. To call someone a propagandist is an insult. Propaganda is seen as a manipulative tool of dictatorships. The foreign propaganda branch of the U.S. government is called the United States Information Agency, and it is prohibited from broadcasting to the United States itself for fear that propaganda masquerading as information could have an untoward effect at home. Propaganda was also suspect in Germany before the Nazi takeover. A scholarly book published in 1924 began with these words: "Even the word propaganda sounds very unpleasant to us Germans."[6] Propaganda was widely seen as something the deceitful Allies had used to deceive honest Germans, a belief encouraged by arguments that Germany lost World War I because it had been "stabbed in the back" by traitors at home.

The great dictatorships of the twentieth century took a different view. To them, propaganda was a necessary and beneficial phenomenon. The Nazis established a state Ministry for People's Enlightenment and Propaganda (RMVP) under Joseph Goebbels. The GDR handled propaganda from party offices. Both, however, built comprehensive systems to influence public opinion and behavior. Social progress depended on new evangelists or social technicians, particularly the propagandists.

The Nazis went so far as to defend the reputation of propaganda by trying to restrict the term to their activities. A 1942 injunction to Nazi propagandists ordered them to guard the word's good name: "The term propaganda should be used only in a positive sense and only for propaganda coming from Germany." The word "agitation" was to be used for enemy attempts to influence public opinion.[7] Regular restatements of the policy suggest its lack of success.[8]

Although the GDR used the term "propaganda" to refer to enemy behavior, it stressed that Marxist-Leninist propaganda was a virtuous activity in contrast to reactionary capitalist propaganda. Following the Soviet distinction, the GDR divided propaganda into two related fields: propaganda and agitation. As the standard GDR dictionary of political terms put it: "Propaganda is a central part of ideological work, the heart of the entire activity of the party."[9] It presented the teachings of Marxism-Leninism in depth to those who then reached the masses with agitation. Agitation was defined as "that part of the political leadership of the society by the party of the working class that brings the word of the party to the masses." According to the Soviet approach, the propagandist conveys many ideas to one or a few persons; an agitator conveys only one or a few ideas but to a great mass of people. As an underground joke in the GDR put it, propaganda provided the scientific foundation for the trip down the broad highway to the bright future of Communism, whereas agitation explained away the detours and potholes.

The approach I use in this book comes from the work of Jacques Ellul. He defines the term broadly: "Propaganda is a set of methods employed by an organized group that wants to bring about the active or passive participation in its actions of a mass of individuals, psychologically unified through psychological manipulation and incorporated in an organization."[10] Ellul sees propaganda not only in its obvious manifestations (for example, mass meetings, newspapers, and posters) but also in the wider social context. It includes education, the arts, public behavior, and the whole panoply of modern technique and method. It is the totality of means by which humans are persuaded to accept the powers that be and depends not only on telling people things but also on securing their cooperation, persuading them to behave in ways that support the system and reinforce desired attitudes.

Ellul views propaganda as more than the mere attempt of political leaders to manipulate followers: "The propagandee is by no means just an innocent victim. He provides the psychological action of propaganda, and not merely leads himself to it, but even derives satisfaction from it. Without this previous, implicit consent, without this need for propaganda experienced by practically *every* citizen of the technological age, propaganda could not spread. There is not just a wicked propagandist at work who sets up means to ensnare the innocent citizen. Rather, there is a citizen who craves propaganda from the bottom of his being and a propagandist who responds to this craving."[11] In other words, propaganda fills needs both for propagandists and propagandees.

Propaganda is an inevitable result of the growing power of technique and method, of an irreversible flow of technology. It helps governments deal successfully with a citizenry made aware of events by modern media. Citizens cannot simply be ignored any longer, but neither can governments provide full information on every subject relevant to their citizens or follow shifting public opinion on a multitude of issues. In the midst of confusion and change, propaganda helps citizens come to satisfying explanations of the world around them.

Ellul argues that all modern propagandas are essentially similar, regardless of their democratic or totalitarian makers. However, totalitarian systems expect far more of propaganda than do democratic societies. Although not expecting instant results, they hope that, with time, propaganda will help them to mold a different type of human being, the prerequisite to the utopian futures they envision.

The word "propaganda" has its origins in religious persuasion. Pope Gregory XV founded the *sacra congregatio christiano nomini propagando* (commonly known as the Sacred Congregation of Propaganda) in 1622. It was charged with spreading Catholicism in the New World and combating Protestantism in Europe. With a considerably different mandate, it exists to this day, and visitors to Rome can walk down Propaganda Street. As this book makes clear, the religious origins of the term are revealing in the context of the twentieth century's seemingly secular modes of propaganda.

In a curious way, both National Socialism and Marxism-Leninism were in the business of propaganda in its original religious sense, a statement the Nazis would agree with more readily than the Marxists. Politics typically deals with a part of life. In contrast, the great religions generally lay claim to it all. Western democracies tend to have weak political parties that make few demands on their members, but the National Socialists and Marxist-Leninists subordinated all areas of life to their worldviews, indeed the lives not only of their party members but of everyone in their societies.

The comparison to religious movements is frequently made in passing by those writing about totalitarian movements, but the analogy can profitably be developed in more detail. The totalitarian movements resemble the Christian faith in Europe before the Peace of Westphalia in 1648 (which generally ended European attempts to compel the adherence of all citizens to the religion of the state) or the practices of some Islamic states today.[12] This variant of religion compels public adherence to an established creed, an adherence that takes varied forms. Some accept the established religion with genuine faith, believing its tenets and seeking to realize them in their lives. These people can do dreadful things with the confidence that they are about good work.[13] Others adopt the creed for pragmatic reasons: their careers or personal security depend on outward adherence. Another large group does not quite disbelieve. That is, the forces of the church, and of the society that seems universally to accept the church, produce acceptance without passion. Citizens go through the motions of adherence, but their faith is lukewarm. Finally, there are heretics and infidels. Heretics share the basic theology but interpret it in ways other than those of the established church. Infidels hold to an entirely different religion. Heretics are worse than infidels, since they demonstrate that the accepted truth is not universally held within the society. A large cadre of priests promotes and enforces public adherence, and church and state are deeply intertwined. The parallels between the old church and modern totalitarian movements are neither few nor trivial.

Western states decided after Westphalia that God was in a better position to judge the beliefs of their citizens than were governments. Too many religious wars had left too many dead. Totalitarian systems, even ones like National Socialism that have a vague religious connection, cannot depend on God. If truth is to be defended, the state or the party must do it. They are compelled inevitably to repeat the mistakes of state religions as a result.

Kenneth Burke's vivid review of *Mein Kampf* saw Nazism as "a bastardization of fundamentally religious patterns of thought."[14] Hitler would have disagreed only with the term "bastardization." In *Mein Kampf* he discussed the importance of religion: "Take away from present-day mankind its education-based, religious-dogmatic principles—or, practically speaking, ethical-moral principles—by abolishing this religious education, but without replacing it with an equivalent, and the result will be a grave shock to the foundations of their existence. We may therefore state that not only does man live in order to serve higher ideals, but that, conversely, these higher ideals also provide the premise for his existence."[15] He is not interested in the truth of religion, rather its pragmatic results. He admired the firmness with which the Catholic Church held to its doctrines and noted: "The great masses of a people do not consist of philosophers; precisely for the masses, faith is often the sole foundation of a moral attitude."[16] He wanted the Nazi Party to provide an equivalent that brought the power of religion to the political arena.

His acolyte Joseph Goebbels, in a speech to party propagandists in 1928, said: "You will never find millions of people who will give their lives for an economic program. But millions of people are willing to die for a gospel [*Evangelium*], and our movement is increasingly becoming such a gospel."[17] We will see in chapter 1 how the Nazis used specifically religious themes in propaganda. For now, it is enough to note that they were building not merely a political system but a worldview that claimed authority over every area of life.

What about the Marxist-Leninists? Seeing an atheistic philosophy as religious seems at the least odd. Yet the early German Marxist Karl Kautsky, writing of the Soviet state, made an explicitly religious comparison: "Like the God of the monotheists, a dictatorship is a very jealous god. It tolerates no other gods."[18] A more vivid description of the "religion" of the GDR written shortly after its demise claimed: "East Germany resembled the huge temple of a pseudo-religious cult. It had all the trappings: godlike veneration of the leader, pictures of 'saints' and quotations from their teachings, processions, mass rituals, vows, and strict moral demands and commandments administered by propagandists and Party secretaries who held priestly 'rank.'"[19] Polish writer Czeslaw Milosz put the point in milder form: "In the people's democracies, the communists speak of the 'New Faith,' and compare its growth to that of Christianity in the Roman Empire."[20]

Though denying religion's claim to truth, Marxism-Leninism's assertions fulfilled the same functions. As one witness during the German Bundestag's hearings on the GDR put it: "Marxist ideology grew out of the loss of a common, compulsory Christian state religion."[21] The language of Marxism, as we shall later see, was often religious in nature, speaking of eternal truths and everlasting friendships, and it promised in Communism a millennial vision of a blessed future state.

I write as a Christian in the Reformed (Calvinist) tradition and see totalitarianism as appealing to fundamentally religious motives and fulfilling an inherent human need. Though it is a poor sort of substitute religion, it partially fills the need for a worldview. As Erich Voegelin wrote: "when God has become invisible behind the world, then the things of the world become new gods."[22] Those who do not share my outlook will, I trust, be able to accept the point that totalitarian systems functioned in ways similar to the great religions.

This book examines National Socialism and Marxism-Leninism as expressed through their evangelists, the propagandists. In the Christian tradition, evangelists are spreaders of the Gospel, of good news, which is an almost exact description of the role of totalitarian advocates. I begin with an overall examination of the worldviews of the systems, which are fundamental to an understanding of their approaches to propaganda. I show how these worldviews addressed the typical concerns of religion and established ideological catechisms for the guidance of adults and youth alike. Following chapters look at the structures and makers of propaganda, the media, the arts, and public life. I conclude that despite all the sound and fury, totalitarian propagandas share inherent weaknesses that assure their eventual failure. Simply put, they cannot in the long term sustain the full range of religious desires, practices, beliefs, and meanings in ways that satisfy human needs.

But why compare Nazi Germany and the GDR? The more obvious comparison is between Nazi Germany and the Soviet Union, between Hitler and Stalin. There are a variety of books along these lines.[23] After all, Marxism-Leninism came to the GDR with the Red Army and ended when Mikhail Gorbachev made it clear that Soviet tanks no longer would maintain it. Germany was the center of Nazism, just as the Soviet Union was the center of Marxism-Leninism. Why compare the sun to the moon? And people don't like the comparison. I received angry responses both from neo-Nazis and Marxists when I noted on a web site that I was working on this book. Neo-Nazis want their system to have nothing in common with Marxism. Former citizens of the GDR (and those Western scholars who had rather hoped the GDR would succeed) prefer to have as much distance between the two systems as possible.[24] The comparison also risks prompting a miniature version of the German *Historikerstreit* of the 1980s, occasioned by the suggestion that Nazism had learned its barbarism from the Soviet Union.

The Nazi-GDR comparison is worthwhile for several reasons. Both systems shared a common history and culture. Both claimed to represent the best of Germany. It should be interesting to see how two different systems attempted to build propaganda on the same foundation. Just how flexible is propaganda? The GDR came into existence as a state in 1949, but its foundations were laid from the first days of the Soviet occupation that immediately followed the collapse of the Third Reich. Can the same methods be used successfully on the same people to promote two quite different systems, with essentially no time between? Second, how much do the two systems have in common? Does the propaganda of the GDR reveal a "kinder, gentler" form of totalitarianism? Did the more humanitarian vision of socialism lead to a propaganda less harmful than that of the

Nazis? These are questions likely to aggravate many, a sign perhaps that there is a stubborn overlap in the nature and consequences of these disparate systems.

Propaganda is an enormous subject. A 2000 bibliography of publications on National Socialism lists over 37,000 items, many of which have at least some bearing on propaganda.[25] The literature on the GDR will never equal that on National Socialism, but it is substantial and growing.[26] This book does not attempt a comprehensive analysis of the content of the propagandas of the two systems. Rather, my goal is to consider larger questions: What role did propaganda play in two great totalitarian systems? What did the propagandas of National Socialist Germany and the GDR have in common and where did they differ? How did they succeed and where did they fail? I refer in the notes to sources that provide more detailed analyses of specific topics.

This book is the result of a long interest in German propaganda. I became interested in Nazi propaganda in 1971 as a graduate student at Northwestern University under Robert D. Brooks. In the early 1980s I began subscribing to East German periodicals (an annual airmail subscription to *Neues Deutschland,* the country's leading daily newspaper, cost $22 at the time). Although the GDR did not encourage independent tourism, it did run courses for foreign teachers of German that were open to those willing to pay a nominal fee. The courses provided an open visa for the country, and the staffs were not overly insistent on attendance, giving me the opportunity to travel through the GDR in the summers of 1988, 1989, and 1990 and meet a variety of East Germans. As an American, some saw me as a "safe" conversational partner whom they quickly trusted. My 1989 visit was particularly interesting. In April 1989 my name appeared in the pen pal column of the mass weekly *Wochenpost.* I had not expected to see my address published. It was the first Western address the magazine had printed since 1949, and I received more than 2,300 letters from GDR citizens eager to correspond with an American. I was able to visit a variety of people as a result.[27] I owe much to my GDR friends and acquaintances, who will not always share the conclusions I drew from our conversations.

There is a virtual appendix to this book, the German Propaganda Archive (GPA), an Internet site providing English translations of propaganda material from the Nazi and East German eras. It also includes many images. Some notes will refer to sections of the GPA that provide translations or images relevant to the matter discussed. The GPA can be found at http://www.calvin.edu/ academic/cas/gpa/.

It is difficult to predict the future of technology. I write in 2003 and trust this book will be read when the present version of the Internet is a historical curiosity. I intend to maintain and add to the archive for the foreseeable future, however, and will work to adjust to opportunities that technology may provide. I will also deposit copies with the Calvin College Library in Grand Rapids, Michigan in whatever electronic forms become available.

1

Secular Faiths

At the last congress of the GDR writers' association in 1987, Jürgen Kucyzinski, the perennial tolerated troublemaker of the GDR, wished for a socialist equivalent of prayer: "I have looked in vain for a substitute for prayer that could remind us, despite all the troubles we have and the barriers we encounter each day, or at least each week, of the greatness of socialism. . . . How do we remind ourselves once or twice a day of what is really important, of the things that influence our lives every day?"[1] In 1940 Joseph Goebbels asked a related question in his diary: "What can one teach the children, when one still has no new religion? The present substitute is only a substitute."[2] Both were searching for ways of secular worship.

In this book I will consider totalitarian propaganda as a quasi-religious phenomenon. This idea encounters two immediate objections. First, the definition, even existence, of totalitarianism is disputed. Second, although viewing totalitarianism as a religious phenomenon has roots going back to Erich Voegelin and recently has been revived in work by Hans Maier, Michael Burleigh, Claus-Ekkehard Bärsch, and others, it remains an unorthodox way to get at the issues.[3]

The arguments against the concept of "totalitarianism" range from charges that it is itself a term of Cold War propaganda to the claim that since no society can in practice be totally totalitarian, the term has little value.[4] I agree that "total totalitarianism" is impossible but find the term "totalitarian" useful since it reflects the goal of the dictatorships of the twentieth century, even if their practice fell short. History has a record of many impossible goals earnestly pursued, and totalitarianism is that kind of goal.

I shall use the term "totalitarian" in its classic sense. A totalitarian state is dedicated to an ideal vision of history and sees its mission as getting the world there. It has a party willing to do everything necessary to reach its goals, a leader chosen either by Providence or the laws of history, a worldview that lays claim to all aspects of life, a confident reliance on mass propaganda, and central control of at least most institutions.[5] This definition does not require that a totalitarian state succeed in being completely totalitarian or that totalitarian states be equally reprehensible.

The idea of totalitarianism as a form of religious expression is also problematic. Although Dostoevsky's "Grand Inquisitor" chapter from *The Brothers Karamazov,* a prophecy of the century that followed, broke ground for the idea and although people of faith recognized that both National Socialism and Marxism-Leninism were competing for the soul as much as the body, religion has not been central to most analyses of totalitarianism. Although there are numerous analogies to religion, they are usually made in passing. I shall develop the analogy at length.

Religions make claims that ordinary political parties do not, and the claims in a sense are "totalitarian." Christianity and other major religions are worldviews. The Christian assertion is that, in the beginning, God created the heavens and the earth. No part of creation is outside of the reach of its creator. Most Christians expect their faith to have something to say about personal behavior, social policy, the arts, the past, and the future. One may not forget the Ten Commandments upon walking out of church. Christian traditions interpret the faith in differing ways, but Christians generally agree, in principle at least, that Christianity applies to all of life, not only its edges.

Western political parties typically have more modest goals. One would not expect an American political party's platform to determine daily activities. A Republican is not obliged to see a Democrat as someone so misguided as to merit imprisonment, torture, or death. Being a Democrat does not compel one to hold a particular opinion of art or to adopt a

Democratic marriage ritual. Party members are not expected to share the same dogmatic view on the nature of language or agree on how the Girl Scouts should conduct their activities. Standard political parties, in short, are groups of people with overlapping but not identical attitudes and interests who do not expect their parties to resolve all of life's questions.

In contrast, the assertion of the totalitarian parties was explicitly total. Both Nazism and Marxism-Leninism claimed to have truth. Lacking a god to stand behind, their truths could triumph only if their adherents fought for them. Christians may assume they have done their duty by acting as their faith commands and that God will act should he wish. Nazis or Marxist-Leninists depended on their own efforts or on those of the party to realize truth. As I noted in the introduction, Nazism and Marxism-Leninism resembled state religions, an intermingling of the secular and the sacred. They made claims not only on party members, but on everyone. No corner of culture or society was in theory exempt. For Christianity, everything is subject to the will of God. For totalitarianism, everything is subject to the human will (that is, all is political). The totalitarian party knows that to permit islands of the nonpolitical is to allow breeding grounds of heresy or apathy.

Totalitarians were therefore explicit in their claim on every aspect of human life. A speaker at a 1938 Hitler Youth leadership gathering made the totalitarian claim forthrightly: "The worldview of National Socialism, having conquered the entire nation, now begins to place its stamp on every area of life. . . . [The goal is] the transformation of every aspect of our life, down to the smallest detail."[6] Many similar statements were made by Nazi leaders.

They meant it. In 1939 the Nazi party's confidential magazine for political leaders carried an article on home decoration. It claimed that it was "the unspoken duty of political leaders, as it is of all National Socialists, to live their personal lives according to the National Socialist idea. . . . A major part of this is our environment, which we ourselves create: in our families, our homes, our ceremonies." The article goes on to explain how one should, as a National Socialist, decorate one's home.[7] If interior decoration falls under the purview of the party, what does not? Totalitarian worldviews suffuse private life within public ideology, leaving few avenues for political apostasy to develop.

The GDR was equally sweeping in its claims. The GDR's approved definition of a worldview is enlightening: "A systematic and complete explanation of nature, society, the role of people in the world, and the formation of rules for the social behavior of human beings. . . . The role of a worldview is to give a person a full orientation for all of his thought, behavior and practical activity."[8] As the book presented to fourteen-year-olds in the *Jugendweihe* ceremony (the socialist equivalent of the Christian rite of confirmation) in the mid-1970s put it: "To keep you from going astray in the world so that the happiness you dream of will largely become reality, you need a compass for your life, an ever-present way of knowing which direction to go, an intellectual framework. In the world-wide battle of our day between the new and the old, between what is coming and what is perishing, between a changing world and one holding stubbornly to the past, between peace and aggression, between truth and lies—in our day of the battle between socialism and imperialism there is only one correct intellectual framework: the worldview of Marxism-Leninism."[9] Consequently, the GDR's worldview provided ways to see education, the family, leisure, and sports from an approved political angle. The front-page editorial in a 1980 issue of *Trommel,* a weekly for children, responded to complaints that it had too much political content: "Nothing against pleasant trivialities, but only he has the right to enjoy them who also is concerned with the main issues of life. That includes politics. That is important. There cannot be too much about politics. It guides all our lives."[10] Everything was political.

Just as Christians maintain that personal salvation is necessary to transform the human soul, Marxism-Leninism insisted on a kind of intellectual salvation, sometimes termed "clarity." A 1958 report from Berlin noted the view that some citizens could become politically active only when difficulties in production and distribution were resolved. Instead, the report argued: "The mistakes and errors can only be remedied when people are clear in their heads."[11] Clarity, in its GDR definition, meant that people had to accept Marxism-Leninism before they could see reality correctly and eventually resolve their problems.

Both National Socialism and Marxism-Leninism, in short, defined themselves as worldviews that claimed every aspect of life. Who determined what that gospel was? What was its content? I shall begin by looking at the "deities" and "scriptures" of the systems, then consider their methods of "worship," and conclude with a summary of their respective "theologies."

"The Führer Is Always Right"

National Socialism resembled a religious cult whose founder still walked among the faithful. There was an aura of the superhuman in the way Nazis presented Hitler. Hermann Göring used the language of papal infallibility in 1941: "We National Socialists declare with complete conviction that for us, the Führer is infallible in all political and other matters that affect the people's national and social interests."[12] Germans believe "deeply and unshakably" in Hitler's divinely ordained mission, he continued. German soldiers and members of the Hitler Youth swore a personal oath to Hitler, pledging absolute obedience, as if professing and confirming their faith before their god and their fellow believers. A common poster during the Nazi years had a towering image of Hitler with the caption: "One people, one Reich, one Führer."[13] A small 1941 book published by the Nazi Party's publishing house can only be called devotional literature. People were asked what the Führer meant to them. In the words of a soldier: "Our Führer is the most unique man in history. I believe unreservedly in him and in his movement. He is my religion."[14] These examples could be multiplied.

An interesting manifestation of the Hitler cult is the thousands of poetic hymns to the Führer. A slim volume titled *The Song of the Faithful* appeared in 1938. It contained twenty-nine short poems by anonymous members of the Hitler Youth organization in Austria before the 1938 *Anschluß*. A typical poem was titled "Our Führer":

> There are so many people who bless you,
> Even if their blessing is a silent one—
> There are so many who have never met you,
> And yet you are their Savior.
>
> When you speak to your German people,
> The words go across the land
> And sink into countless hearts,
> Hearts in which your image long has stood.
>
> Sometimes the vision of you brings life
> To those in the midst of hard labor and heavy obligation . . .
> So many are devoted to you
> And seek in your spirit a clear light.[15]

The language is unmistakably religious, with words like bless, Savior, life, devoted, spirit, and light. It makes sense only if one sees Hitler as a Christ figure, a union of the divine and the human. *The Song of the Faithful* received the German national book award (which Goebbels used to favor books with the correct content). In the dust jacket copy, Goebbels wrote: "We had almost decided to split the award or draw lots for it when a thin

little book of poetry appeared on the market. It made all further consideration pointless. This book fulfills the goals of the our book prize better than
any other."

Such poetry would have been ludicrous if written about Roosevelt or
Churchill, but Nazis did not see Hitler as an ordinary mortal. Although
they had to recognize Hitler's mortality, as did he himself (he sometimes
noted his uniqueness and the importance of accomplishing his goals before
his death), Hitler was presented as the person in whom Germans could
place absolute trust.

Goebbels gave annual speeches on the occasion of Hitler's birthday, 20
April. They are remarkable reading. Even in 1945, Goebbels drew on religious language: "We feel him [Hitler] in us and around us."[16] Earlier
speeches in the series made similar claims.[17] Hitler's spirit was palpable,
omnipresent.

The quintessential Hitler is presented visually in *Triumph of the Will,* Leni
Riefenstahl's film of the 1934 Nuremberg rally. Hitler is seen in ways that
emphasize his extraordinary nature. His plane drifts silently through the
clouds, accompanied by ethereal music. The shadow of his plane, in the
shape of a cross, falls on marching columns of his faithful followers. He en-
ters Nuremberg in a triumphal procession. The camera views him close up
or from below, magnifying his stature. Radiance emanates from him, as,
for example, in the motorcade into Nuremberg, when Hitler's cupped hand
catches the light. Hitler, holding the Blood Banner (*Blutfahne,* the flag carried during the 1923 putsch), consecrates new party standards. Rudolf Hess
announces that Hitler is Germany and Germany is Hitler. These are not images of an ordinary human being.

Hitler's remarkable status is evident from iconographic images. Photographs, paintings, and sculptures were carefully controlled, requiring
Hitler's personal approval.[18] At least 2,450,000 copies of a 1936 album titled *Adolf Hitler: Pictures of the Life of the Führer,* with tributes to Hitler written by Nazi leaders, were printed.[19] People bought the album and pasted in
pictures received as premiums for buying cigarettes. Heinrich Hoffmann
published over a dozen books of Hitler photographs, and they sold in large
numbers. *The Hitler No One Knows,* a collection of "private" photographs, for
example, sold at least 400,000 copies.[20] Rudolf Herz comments that Hitler's
"photographic omnipresence" during the Third Reich "was an integral
means of presenting the charismatic image of the leadership."[21]

The Nazis did not have time to develop a television system, but if they
had, Hitler's image would have filled it as well. As Eugen Hadamovsky, the

Nazi director of broadcasting, said when experimental transmissions began in 1935: "Now, in this hour, broadcasting is called upon to fulfill its biggest and most sacred mission: to plant the image of the Fuehrer indelibly in all German hearts."[22]

As the superhuman figure in the religion of Nazism, Hitler knew the importance of defining the Nazi worldview. Even Hitler's own speeches could be printed only with his approval, according to a 1937 party directive.[23] In 1939 Hitler ordered the texts of speeches that dealt with the Nazi worldview be approved in advance by Rudolf Hess.[24] After Hess flew to England, Hitler personally approved such speeches.

Worldviews have texts of varying degrees of importance. *Mein Kampf* was the bible of National Socialism.[25] George L. Mosse doubts that Hitler's book was a bible in the same sense that the works of Marx and Lenin were to the Communists, since "the ideas of *Mein Kampf* had been translated into liturgical forms and left the printed page to become mass rites of national, Aryan worship."[26] It is true that the ideas of *Mein Kampf* were realized in a variety of ways, but the book remained central to Nazism. It was published in enormous editions (over ten million copies by 1945). City mayors presented elegant editions to newlyweds. The goal was to have a copy in every home and library. Like a family Bible, it was often unread, but its mere presence testified to its importance.

Hitler's speeches had equal canonical authority. They were events of major significance. Just after the war began the party propaganda office in Linz published advice on studying and using Hitler's speeches. It is a remarkable document:

> The Führer's words are seeds in the people's hearts. The party member must care for this seed and see that it bears fruit. He will therefore study the Führer's speech word for word over and over again in order to master the arguments that he will need in face-to-face propaganda. If he is able to rely on the words of the Führer in all his conversations, he will be able to draw on the Führer's powerful authority to reach and silence even the most stubborn complainer. . . .
>
> The task of each propagandist, therefore, is to guard the national experience of each Führer speech, to nourish the flame of enthusiasm, ever to encourage it. He will be able to do this if he gives his full devotion and earnestness to studying each word, letting them work on him each day anew. Then his conversations with citizens will be imbued with a glimmer of the rousing and unifying power that dwells in all the Führer's words.[27]

This is a description of a sacred text, not a political speech. The sacredness of Hitler's words was emphasized in a widely distributed picture titled "In the Beginning Was the Word," not an accidental quotation of the opening words of the Gospel of John. Hitler is seen speaking to a group of rapt early followers.[28]

Just as the Bible is assiduously mined for proof texts, Hitler citations flooded the Third Reich. Enormous numbers of examples could be given. A 1942 biology textbook cited *Mein Kampf* seven times on "The Laws of Life."[29] *Unser Wille und Weg* (the monthly for propagandists) regularly quoted it. The party propaganda office published 300,000 copies of a weekly quotation poster intended for public display, many of which carried Hitler quotations.[30] The one for 4–10 May 1941, for example, quoted Hitler as saying: "No one will take the ground on which the German soldier stands." *Die Kunst im Deutschen Reich,* the party's magazine of the arts, included elegantly printed Hitler quotations, suitable for framing, during the early months of the war.

Some homes had a "Hitler shrine." As Julius Streicher's *Der Stürmer* put it in 1936: "German citizens give expression to their attitude toward the Third Reich by hanging the Führer's picture in their home."[31] The same year, a German children's magazine told its readers how to respond to Hitler's birthday: "All German children think about the Führer on 20 April, his birthday. We want to decorate his picture, which should hang in every home, with a green wreath we have made with our own hands. That is how we show our love to the man to whom we owe so much thanks."[32] Germans had hung pictures of saints and political leaders on their walls before the Nazis. The difference was that reluctance to hang Hitler's picture on the wall now became evidence of disloyalty.

By May 1933 cities and towns were already renaming prominent streets and public squares for Hitler, and soon after for other prominent Nazis as well. Kaiser-Straße became Adolf-Hitler-Straße (and after 1945, Karl-Marx-Straße in the GDR).

Not only did Germans encounter Hitler's image or words wherever they turned, they were expected to add their own voices to the chorus. The most obvious way was through the Heil Hitler greeting, the "German Greeting," as the Nazis called it. It quickly became a ritual of everyday life. Publicly posted signs announced: "Our greeting is Heil Hitler." Television broadcasts ended with the announcer's Heil Hitler.

The greeting was a barometer of Nazi loyalty. An American visitor wrote in 1935: "'Heil Hitler!' is now the nation's greeting, with people of all classes, everywhere."[33] In 1943, on the other hand, a party member gave the greeting to fifty-one people he encountered in the town of Barmen. Two returned it.[34] The worsening war situation made citizens less eager to proclaim their faith in the Führer. Newspaper obituary notices for soldiers who fell in combat were expected to announce that they had died "for Führer, people and fatherland." When the percentage of announcements actually doing so fell to 4 percent in some newspapers by late 1944, the phrasing became obligatory.[35]

Hitler's personal popularity was high. It was, however, dependent on his successes. As a visible deity, Hitler's power rested on his "miracles," a word the Nazis regularly used to describe his accomplishments. Failure of any kind could not be admitted. Hitler was accustomed to appearing at moments of triumph, as, for example, at the spectacular reception in Berlin after the fall of France. As the war went on and those moments grew fewer, his appearances declined as well. Goebbels's diaries regularly note his efforts to persuade Hitler to make public appearances late in the war, something Hitler was reluctant to do absent victory. Churchill began a speech on 4 June 1940 by admitting that what had happened in France was "a colossal military disaster," but Hitler could not say the same about Stalingrad. A deity who loses battles has limited credibility, as Hitler well knew. Even in private conversations with his intimates, he blamed reverses on others, never himself.

The Nazi canon went beyond *Mein Kampf.* Works by Alfred Rosenberg, Rudolf Hess, Joseph Goebbels, Otto Dietrich, Hermann Göring, and Robert Ley also had near canonical authority. They lacked the power of Hitler's words and were not cited as frequently, though Goebbels and Göring were regulars on the "Quotation of the Week" posters.

The Holy Days of the Nazi Year

A religion needs times and places for worship, ways of making visible the invisible. Holidays and ceremonies are important ways of doing that. The Nazis gave major effort to founding and promoting what can reasonably be called religious holidays and rituals. As usual, several Nazis claimed control, primarily Goebbels and Rosenberg, though this was also an area of interest to Hitler.

By 1934 the Nazis had established their liturgical calendar. It began on 30 January, the anniversary of Hitler's assumption of office. The anniversary of the announcement of the party program in 1920 came on 24 February. In

the first years of Hitler's regime, the holiday emphasized the relationship between Hitler and his earliest followers, though during the war it came to
emphasize the faith of early party members, faith that was now needed by
everyone if Germany were to win. Heroes' Memorial Day, honoring war
dead, came in mid-March. The last Sunday in March was Duty of Youth
Day, a rite of passage in which those crossing from youth to adulthood were
reminded of their obligations to the Fatherland. Hitler's birthday on 20 April
was a cause for major celebration (the pinnacle coming on his fiftieth birthday in 1939, for which a remarkable film was made). The Nazis transformed
1 May from the Marxist Labor Day into the National Holiday of the German
People, although it remained a holiday of the worker. Mother's Day came
early in May. Mothers with four or more children received medals. The
summer solstice was particularly celebrated by the Hitler Youth and the SS.
The first part of September saw the supreme Nazi spectacle, the Nuremberg
rally, an event that even those who did not attend participated in through
massive press and radio (even television) coverage and Riefenstahl's party
rally films *Victory of Faith* and *Triumph of the Will*. The rallies grew in size and
pomp until 1938.[36] The 1939 rally, ill-named the "Party Rally of Peace," was
canceled just before the war began, but plans went on into summer 1940
for a rally that year.[37] Work on the monumental buildings on the party rally
grounds continued until late in the war. The Harvest Festival fell at the beginning of October. Hundreds of thousands of farmers gathered on the
Bückeberg, a large hill in southern Germany, to hear Hitler praise the
virtues of agriculture. The most sacred date on the Nazi calendar was 9 November, the anniversary of the 1923 Beer Hall Putsch. Even Christmas, the
last holiday of the year, took on a Nazi rather than a Christian interpretation. By the war years, the party published books on observing Christmas
that had not a single mention of Christ. The German word for Christmas
(*Weihnacht*) made the task easier, since it did not include any direct link to
Jesus Christ.[38]

   The nature of Nazi holidays is clear in the case of 9 November, a
pseudoreligious celebration of the first order. Its eventual significance was
not obvious at its beginnings. In November 1923 Hitler resolved to stage a
putsch. On 9 November, as the band of claimants on state power neared
the Feldherrnhalle, a prominent public monument in Munich, the police
opened fire. Sixteen of Hitler's followers died. Hitler, lightly wounded,
made his escape, subsequently serving a comfortable prison term. He
reestablished the NSDAP in 1925, and at the party rally that year in
Weimar, the blood-soaked flag that had been carried two years earlier

became the Blood Banner, the most sacred treasure in the Nazi reliquary. The day was observed as the "National Day of Mourning of the NSDAP" for the remainder of the Weimar Republic, though no one else paid heed.

In 1933, 9 November became a national holiday. That year, and annually until 1943, Hitler spoke to a gathering of his earlier followers in Munich on the evening of 8 November. Though only the long-term party members (*alte Kämpfer*) attended, the next day's newspapers printed the text of Hitler's speech. On 9 November, ceremonies were held in Munich, the most dramatic of which was a reenactment of the 1923 march. Tall pylons with the names of Nazi dead lined the route, and buildings were draped with flags and black cloth. As Hitler walked past each pylon, loudspeakers announced the name of a Nazi who had died in Hitler's service. Upon reaching the Feldherrnhalle, a moment of silence was observed.

Following years saw ceremonies even more impressive. Munich annually was decked with flags and banners. In 1935 the sixteen dead were moved from their separate graves to a pair of "Honor Temples" in Munich where they took up "eternal watch." It was as if they had been born again. Flags that formerly had flown at half mast were now at full mast. The *New York Times* correspondent observed that Munich was celebrating "not a funeral but a triumph."[39] As the names of the sixteen were called in a last roll call before the Honor Temples, the assembled crowd of thousands answered "here" to each name, not a new technique but a moving one.

The Munich observances were relayed to the entire nation by press and radio, but most towns and schools organized their own rites. They were on a smaller scale then the ones in Munich, but, even so, flag-draped buildings, graveside ceremonies, and solemn meetings prevailed throughout Germany.

A typical such local celebration was held in a carefully decorated room. It began with the ceremonial entrance of uniformed party groups, accompanied by elevating music. The crowd sang the 9 November hymn, "Today a Hundred Thousand Flags Are Marching." An invocation, Hitler's promise that the day would be forever observed in Germany, was followed by more music. A local dignitary then delivered a speech that tried to establish the myths of 9 November and to encourage the audience to follow the examples of devotion set by Hitler's early followers. The local Hitler Youth band played a fanfare, and the chairman said: "We remember the first blood martyrs of the movement." The flag-bearers lowered their flags. "On 9 November at twelve-thirty in the afternoon the following men, in true faith in the resurrection of their people, fell before the Feldherrnhalle and in the court of the former War Ministry in Munich." The names of the sixteen were read, followed by a poem:

You died
Struggling for our Reich.
You had to die
So that we
Could live victoriously.

Your deaths
Were the movement's victory
And your heritage
Is to us eternal obligation.

Other dead of the party and the military were also remembered. The flags were raised, symbolizing the victory of the dead. After more poetry, songs, and praise of Hitler, the meeting closed with the party anthem, the *Horst Wessel Song*.[40]

The Nazis used Christian imagery in abundance. Hitler said in 1934 that "the blood which they shed has become the baptismal water of the Reich."[41] Terms such as blood martyr, sacrifice, holy, resurrection, Golgotha, and pilgrimage were regularly used. The Nazis, here and elsewhere, followed a strategy of infusing old symbols with new meaning, co-opting them for the new faith. A party writer made the point explicitly in 1939, arguing that Christianity had grown by incorporating pagan rituals. An adherent of earlier religions "had not the faintest idea that under the guise of his old customs a new and foreign religion was creeping up on him." Nazism also needed to fill traditional symbols with new ideological meaning, he continued: "National Socialism can consider its ideas secure only when they are anchored in the soul of each citizen."[42]

The holiday contributed to the establishment of a pantheon of Nazi saints. All of those who died in Hitler's cause, the "martyrs" of the movement, enjoyed honor, but the dead of 1923 were at the pinnacle of veneration. Consider a 1935 description of their activities: "Out of the need, out of the agony, out of the baseness, out of the abyss of despair, out of the chaotic gorge of destruction and defenseless slavery, the names of the unknown soldiers thundered through the night of the people's wretched isolation. Revenge for betrayal was the fire that burned within them, revenge forged from pain, molded from sorrow, hardened from honor wounded nigh undo death, enormous, unquenchable revenge."[43] This is not language about ordinary mortals. These were men who were models of virtue for Germany. Biographies of the sixteen presented them as suffering saints in Germany's cause. A 1935 series of biographies began with the observation that "from their life portraits we will receive new courage to struggle for the future of the German people." Of one it was said: "His hero's death before the Feldherrnhalle was the towering culmination of a life that was nothing but a sacrifice for Germany." A second victim "knew nothing higher than the Fatherland."[44]

The dead even won immortality, which came through the Nazi triumph in 1933. The day after taking power, Hitler went to Munich to pay his respects to the dead, saying: "*Und Ihr habt doch gesiegt,*" or "You have won after all." The faithful repeated his words innumerable times on meeting-hall banners, in newspapers, by speakers, even on postage stamps. The holiday was also a popular theme in Nazi art.[45]

Nazi rhetoric suggested further kinds of immortality as well. The spirit of the martyrs somehow lived on. A book on the conduct of ceremonies in schools suggested: "Now they sleep again, quietly and peacefully, in their graves. A great bliss, an eternal joy, has come over them because of the words of praise and thanks by the Führer: '*Und Ihr habt doch gesiegt.*'"[46] The *Völkischer Beobachter* wrote in 1936: "A year ago the heroes of the Feldherrnhalle took up eternal watch. Flags of mourning are now yellowed, tattered and superfluous. The dead have risen. They march once more before us and in us."[47] Many similar comments in the Nazi press proclaimed the immortality of the dead.

The Blood Banner was carried in each year's Munich observances, but it also appeared at the Nuremberg rally. Riefenstahl's *Triumph of the Will* shows Hitler consecrating new party banners by touching the Blood Banner to them. In some mystic way, power flowed from the old flag through Hitler to the new ones. As Robert D. Brooks observes, the ceremony connected past and present seamlessly, endowing the event with the deeds and beliefs of the past. It was a moving ceremony that unified those present, giving them a sense of participating in something larger than self and greater than the moment.[48]

Nazi Faith

The full panoply of Nazism reflected in distorted ways the rituals and ceremonies of a religious faith. As any faith, it used them to give mystic significance to the party's everyday activities and to justify activities that otherwise would have appeared disgraceful. Moreover, these ideological liturgies replaced traditional religious meanings with secular meanings, thereby dampening the lingering impact of competing messages.

Knowing the effects and consequences of Nazism, it is comfortable to assume that its followers were unpleasant people out to do ill. But few Germans became Nazis because they desired to massacre Jews or devastate Europe. While pursuing ignoble ends, Nazism appealed to what many Germans saw to be noble goals deeply rooted in German traditions. Nazism, after all, claimed to be the culmination, not the repudiation, of German history and culture, and it is surely true that many elements of the German past could be made consistent with Nazism. As Robert Gellately observed, the content of Nazi propaganda was "an indicator of what people sincerely hoped to be true."[49]

Consider Helmut Stellrecht's *Faith and Action,* something of a Nazi "book of virtues." Despite the pressures of the war, at least 175,000 copies of an elegant edition were in print by 1944. It has brief chapters on faith, loyalty, bravery, obedience, blood, life, and death. Its words on faith suggest the tone: "Because faith is strength, it can do what seems impossible. It is the foundation of any deed. . . . The highest and most important in a person is not his knowledge and understanding, but his faith. Each is worth only as much as the faith he has."[50] The book's religious intent is clear from a review in the party journal for propagandists: "He who wishes to give his growing children something better than the Jewish stories of the Old Testament or proverbs and psalms that have lost their meaning for us today can reach for this book. In noble form and in clear, powerful language, it is a guide for anyone seeking an understanding of the National Socialist worldview and outlook on life."[51] The passing phrase about Old Testament stories "having lost their meaning" is striking. Stellrecht's book is presented as a new way to explain the meaning of life, as a guide for moral behavior. This would not be possible had it ignored the deeply rooted traditional beliefs and values of its readers.

Jesus said faith was sufficient to move mountains. Stellrecht and the Nazis thought it could win wars. Nothing in the book suggests Auschwitz. War is indeed glorified, but in a way that reinforces virtues most Germans readily accepted. Masses of similar material appeared. A German who did not think too hard or look too deeply could comfortably believe that Nazism stood firmly on the side of familiar virtues.

Religions address the great questions of life, including those of origins, destinations, and purposes. Nazism gave answers that, although perhaps not as satisfying as religious answers, still provided ways for citizens to make sense of the world around them. Nature rewarded strength and punished weakness. Germans had the good fortune to be born into nature's favored race, one whose antecedents stretched back into the mists of time and forward into a glorious future.

The amount of material on this theme was enormous. Take, for example, a poem titled "My Boy," published in 1939 in the *Frauen Warte*, the Nazi biweekly for women:

Now I live in you.
You shall and will live on
In times I will not see.
How wonderful that is!
It is as wonderful as in the old sagas,
When each tribe strove
To ensure its bloodline did not perish.

Still, you are yet small.
How could you know
That you are a branch on a large tree!
But the day will come
When I must tell you
That not only you,
But your fathers too will be judged by your deeds.

No, you do not yet understand that.
You dream and play throughout the day.
But when you understand,
Then I will know
That in each heartbeat in you and me
That keeps us living,
Also flows a drop of eternity.[52]

The poem presented each German as a link in an eternal chain, binding the past to the future.

A racially pure German "heaven" was the goal. It would be an earthly paradise that might take generations to achieve, one that required a transformation in human nature. As Hitler said in 1934, the Nazis were gradually building "a new German individual [*Mensch*]."[53]

Though the party's faithful would not in a literal sense live again to experience that heaven, neither were they truly dead, as the rhetoric of 9 November tried to prove. An elaborate book published in 1938 attempted a comprehensive list of all those who had died in Hitler's service. As the book's introductory poem titled "They Live!" claimed:

> They wander through the land and are not dead.
> They are to us both admonition and warning,
> For we the living are the heirs of great heroes.
> Where their memory shines like fire,
> Our path leads through night and misery to the light.
> They are Germany. Germany will never die!

The Nazi anthem proclaimed that "comrades shot by the Red Front and Reaction march in spirit in our ranks." The book asserted that the song was "the prayer of the Germans."[54]

The dead would in some sense experience the new earth as they lived on in their descendants. In February 1945 Goebbels wrote of a happy future for Germany's children after a Nazi victory in the year 2000: "Our hopes will come true in their world and our ideals will be reality. We must never forget that when we see the storms of this wild age reflected in the eyes of our children. Let us act so that we will earn their eternal blessings, not their curses."[55] Again, there was a large amount of such material. It promised Germans an "eternal" reward for their loyal obedience.

Religions need their devils, or sources of evil. In contrast to the Aryan race, the most developed race and the one on which humanity's future depended, stood the Jew. The Nazis frequently referred to "the Jew" rather than "the Jews," a Satan figure in the literal sense. Julius Streicher's *Der Stürmer* often made the comparison. A 1943 issue, for example, carried a front-cover photograph of a Jew captioned "Satan."[56] Hitler made the same comparison in *Mein Kampf,* as did many other Nazis. The Jews were not simply inferior (as were, for example, blacks in Nazi ideology); they were the embodiment of evil, the antipole to the Aryan German. As Hitler had put it in *Mein Kampf:* "By warding off the Jews I am doing the Lord's work." In fighting the devil, anything goes.

Anti-Semitism was crucial to Nazism as a system, even if it was not central to many Germans. All the major Nazi propaganda claims at least implicitly rested on the argument that Hitler and his party were battling the worldwide Jewish conspiracy. Jews had controlled Germany before 1933, they had driven England and France into war against Germany, they were behind Marxism and its Soviet manifestation, and they organized anti-German forces throughout the world.

In sum, National Socialism presented Germans with a developed, if somewhat murky, worldview that explained where they had come from, where they were going, what they should do to get there, and who stood in their way. It was a worldview anchored in familiar words, names, and values. It provided reasons for daily action and hope for the future. For the Germans who could accept Nazism's outward claims, the world made sense. The ideology they were asked to accept encompassed familiar aspects of German history, German thinking, and German culture.

"The Party Is Always Right"

If Nazism was a cult whose founder was still among the faithful, Marxism-Leninism in the GDR was an established religion with a reasonably settled theology, more Catholic than Protestant in structure. The pope was in "the Third Rome," Moscow, though the Orthodox prelate was replaced by the reigning head of the Communist Party of the Soviet Union. The head of the Socialist Unity Party of Germany (SED) was a cardinal, supreme in his realm yet subject ultimately to Moscow. The authority of Marx, Engels, Lenin, and Stalin had passed to the party, and its word was now sacred.

In the early years of the GDR, however, the Stalin cult was strong. One of the first books published by the Soviet occupation forces in 1945 was a brief biography of Stalin, translated from Russian and so hurriedly prepared that there is no mention of his role in World War II. It presented Stalin as a flawless, almost superhuman figure: "J. W. Stalin is the brilliant leader and teacher of the party, the great strategist of the socialist revolution. He is implacable in facing the enemies of socialism, absolutely true to principle, the union of clear revolutionary perspective and clarity of goal in all his activities, combining them with extraordinary firmness and persistence in reaching those goals."[57] Two pages later, the book stated: "The name Stalin is the symbol of the moral and political unity of Soviet society." The comparison to Hess's words in 1934 is evident ("Hitler is Germany and Germany is Hitler"). Thousands of poems in praise of Stalin, generally translated from Russian, flooded the GDR during its early years.[58] In those years, classrooms had Stalin shrines with his picture surrounded by red bunting, and children recited touching verses like this one:

Fold your little hands,
Bow your little head,
Think for five minutes
On Stalin.[59]

A earlier variant of the poem ran:

> Fold your little hands
> Bow your little head
> Think for five minutes
> On Hitler,
> Who gives us our daily bread
> And helps with our every need.

The cult of Stalin rivaled Hitler's until Stalin's death in 1953.

Early Marxists also received adulation, although never to the extent that Hitler did. The youngest members of the Free German Youth (FDJ) were the Thälmann Pioneers. Ernst Thälmann, the martyred leader of the German Communist Party, was to be their model. There were no books of poetry in praise of party leaders, though occasional poetic outbursts did appear. Consider this 1950s' hymn to Thälmann:

> As if Ernst Thälmann could ever die.
> Thälmann died, yet did not die.
> For that which he, while he lived, taught,
> That for which he, without rest, propagandized,
> Lives as an admonition in millions of hearts,
> Lives as knowledge in millions of brains.[60]

Even here, the emphasis is less on Thälmann the man than on what he taught. Such bombast largely vanished by the GDR's later years.

Although the GDR was never willing to repudiate Stalin (one of the reasons the SED banned *Sputnik,* rather a Russian *Reader's Digest,* in 1989 was its forthright discussion of the evils of Stalin's rule), no subsequent Soviet or GDR leader enjoyed the same veneration. No one thought to write of Erich Honecker in such terms. The adulation of Lenin and Stalin had been somewhat inconsistent, given Marxism's egalitarian rhetoric. It also was hard to avoid awakening memories of the treatment of Hitler. That does not mean later leaders were not honored. Their images filled the newspapers, magazines, newsreels, and television, but those images were of normal people. Walter Ulbricht and Erich Honecker appeared more as kindly grandfathers than mighty dictators.

A comparison of the tribute book for Ulbricht, published in 1968 on the occasion of his seventy-fifth birthday, with *Adolf Hitler: Pictures from the Life of the Führer* is striking. Titled *Walter Ulbricht: A Life for Germany,* the book presents him as wise and capable but not superhuman, a man clearly subordinate to the party.[61] The Hitler dust jacket has a photograph of him shot from below, towering over an unseen audience.[62] The cover of Ulbricht's volume shows an elderly man reading a book.[63] According to the introduction: "Walter Ulbricht was educated by the party of Marx and Engels, of Liebknecht and Thälmann. His teachers were international leaders of the labor movement such as Lenin and Dimitroff, who above all taught him that one can lead the masses only if one has the closest connection to them. We are all witnesses of how Walter Ulbricht discussed all important problems with workers and collective farmers, with scientists and artists, with women and the youth, and how he was able to take the knowledge he gained and make theoretical generalizations that improved our lives."[64] Ulbricht is presented as a product of the party, whereas the NSDAP was a product of Hitler and was indeed synonymous with him. The Communist movement predated Ulbricht. It had formed him, he had not formed it. During World War II, a common Nazi poster announced that "Adolf Hitler is victory."[65] Twenty years later the FDJ used the slogan "Walter Ulbricht—that is what we all are! With Walter Ulbricht we will win!"[66] The focus on Hitler in the first slogan contrasts with the broader focus of the second.

Honecker received less adulation. Standard posters with his image did appear in large editions.[67] He guarded his image, ensuring that dozens of photographs appeared in *Neues Deutschland* when he visited the Leipzig trade fair. When even one of his Politburo colleagues wondered if fifty photographs were necessary in a single issue, Honecker replied that he had either to be shown with all of his conversational partners or none.[68] But again, the pictures were of an ordinary human being. No slogans equated him with victory, no photographs magnified his stature. Unlike Hitler, he looked small in photographs, perhaps most notably when dwarfed by Helmut Kohl during his 1987 visit to West Germany. From the GDR perspective, however, his visit was a diplomatic triumph that overshadowed his physical stature. In photographs of parades, Marxist leaders stood together on the platform. They appeared as normal human beings in gray suits, not towering figures dwarfing ordinary people.

The GDR's leaders were infallible "by omission." There is no post-Stalin GDR counterpart to Göring's statement that Hitler was infallible. Rather, there simply was no mention of their errors. Guided by the party, the GDR's leaders always seemed to make the right decision.

The GDR's leaders were important, but the party was the true source of absolute knowledge. According to the SED's *Concise Political Dictionary*, the collective leadership of the party was capable of making "scientifically exact decisions."[69] The wisdom of the party was as absolute as that of any pope, more so indeed, for the pope only rarely speaks ex cathedra, whereas the party usually did. A 1959 training booklet for the GDR's army, for example, asserted that it was impossible for a socialist army to order its soldiers to behave unethically, since such an army was obeying the unalterable laws of nature when it followed the will of the party.[70] Since the SED said what socialism was, such confidence in the absolute correctness of the socialist army's actions is the equivalent of the Nazi soldier's oath of absolute obedience to Adolf Hitler. In each case, the entity to which the oath was made was infallible.

The role of the party is presented in a 1958 pamphlet published to help party groups celebrate the fortieth anniversary of the founding of the German Communist Party. One section cites Brecht's hymn to the party:

The party—
Is the immorality of our mission.
The party—
Is the only assurance.
The mind of the class,
The meaning of the class,
The strength of the class,
The glory of the class—
That is the party.[71]

Here, too, the language is religious, speaking of immortality and glory. Just as the Christian doctrine of predestination asserts that God not only knows the future but directs it to his ends, so, too, the party was guided by the certain laws of history according to Marxist-Leninist theory. Human action could accelerate or slow down history's flow but never in the long run reverse it. The eventual Communist paradise was sure.

Marxist texts had sacred force, but they needed the party's interpretation. At the GDR's end, scholars were working to complete a full edition of the works of Marx and Engels with all the assiduity of biblical commentators. The GDR canon included not only Marx, Engels, and Lenin but also decisions of party congresses and programmatic speeches by party leaders. Those speeches were intended more for reading and study than hearing—though unfortunate party members did listen to them for hours as they were read (and read they almost always were).

Just as Hitler's words were a necessary complement to books and articles during the Third Reich, so were the obligatory citations from the Marxist canon. Dissertation writers knew how important it was to include an appropriate number of citations of the classics of Marxism-Leninism. A popular GDR marriage manual quoted Marx on the importance of the family.[72] Banners with appropriate quotations were almost as common as advertising in the West.

Ways of Worship

The socialist faith was evident in its recurring festivals. As Gibas and Gries observe: "The GDR had an extraordinarily dense set of official state political holidays."[73] The first festival of the year fell on 15 January, the anniversary of the deaths in 1919 of Karl Liebknecht and Rosa Luxemburg. It was the GDR's equivalent of 9 November. As *Neues Deutschland* claimed in 1986: "Karl and Rosa died martyrs' deaths. But they live in our deeds. They are with us! We are under their red flag!"[74] International Women's Day fell on 8 March. May Day remained the major labor holiday. The end of World War II was commemorated on 8 May. The high point of the year was 7 October, the anniversary of the founding of the GDR in 1949. Major holidays were occasions for mass parades, with citizens encouraged in a variety of ways to march past their leaders carrying flags, banners, and placards.

Then there were the recurring anniversaries, not the occasion of a holiday but of significant press coverage: the births and deaths of Marx, Engels, Ernst Thälmann, Wilhelm Pieck, and Otto Grotewohl. The GDR calendar also featured days set aside to honor specified occupations, for example, metal workers, farmers, construction workers, and chemical workers, but these did not receive major press coverage.

The most significant periods on the GDR calendar were the party congresses. Unlike the NSDAP's annual Nuremberg rallies, party congresses were held at four- to five-year intervals after 1950. Eleven were held in all: 1946, 1947, 1950, 1954, 1958, 1963, 1967, 1971, 1976, 1981, and 1986. The planned 1990 congress was rendered moot by the collapse of the GDR, though preparations were well in motion. Each congress, it was claimed, represented a new stage in the development of socialism in the GDR. Unlike the Nazi rallies, which were celebrations of Nazism rather than decision-making bodies, GDR party congresses were allegedly deliberative bodies at which the course of the coming years would be discussed and, through the collective wisdom of the party, determined. "What the Party Congress decided will be realized," as a common slogan proclaimed. The Nazis published two major volumes each year on their party rallies, filled with dramatic photographs. Such volumes were impossible for the GDR's party congresses, since the primary activity consisted of delegates sitting in a large hall listening to interminable speeches. Instead, thick books with the texts of speeches and decisions appeared. The periods between congresses were marked by plenary sessions of the Central Committee, whose decisions were also published.

The major annual festival was 7 October, the "birthday" of the GDR. The "round" anniversaries, those divisible by five, were the subject of particular splendor. Books were issued for each of the decennials.[75] Each of the forty anniversaries was celebrated with the full resources of the nation. The state usually provided "presents" for the population in the form of increased supplies of scarce consumer goods, but the people were also expected to provide "gifts" for their state in the form of increased production. The press reported numerous commitments by factories or work groups to exceed their quota in honor of the anniversary.

The 1984 anniversary, the thirty-fifth, was typical. Planning, as always, began soon after the previous anniversary. *Neues Deutschland* began mentioning it several months in advance. A survey of articles in the weeks leading up to 7 October suggests its centrality:

- 1/2 September: GDR athletes achieve excellent results in honor of the thirty-fifth anniversary.
- 4 September: The thirty-fifth anniversary logo appears for the first time on page 1.
- 11 September: Production goals met in honor of the GDR's thirty-fifth anniversary.
- 15/16 September: *Bezirk* party sections begin their annual training course under the symbol of the GDR's thirty-fifth anniversary. Workers pledge to do their best to honor the GDR.
- 21 September: Erich Honecker meets representatives of artists in the GDR to review accomplishments in the GDR's thirty-fifth year.
- 27 September: Medals are awarded in honor of the thirty-fifth anniversary.
- 2 October: A Berlin theater is reopened in honor of the thirty-fifth anniversary.
- 4 October: Medals in honor of the thirty-fifth anniversary are awarded to military officers, worthy citizens, and effective collectives.
- 5 October: Honecker speaks to members of the anti-Fascist resistance: "In honor of the thirty-fifth anniversary of the founding of the German Democratic Republic, workers have accomplished outstanding deeds."
- 6/7 October: Fourteen of the sixteen pages focus on the anniversary.

- 8 October: Most of the sixteen pages review the events of the celebrations and carry the texts of speeches.

Only three issues after 30 August failed to give at least one lengthy story to the coming anniversary, and these issues focused on Erich Honecker's visit to Ethiopia in honor of the tenth anniversary of its Marxist revolution.

The festivities reminded citizens of the accomplishments of their state and built in them a sense of obligation to "repay" the state. But the centrality went beyond normal holidays. The weeks of preparation, the massive press coverage, and the vast demonstrations were an attempt to give the nation's anniversary a transcendental significance, to build a "we" feeling to convince citizens that they were part of a great endeavor. It was a significant event in the great "salvation story" of Marxism-Leninism, since each year marked another step of socialist progress.

Another quasi-religious manifestation was the network of what might be called pilgrimage sites. These included places connected with Lenin and the history of the party and the huge Soviet War Memorial in Berlin-Treptow (built in part with the stones from Hitler's Reich Chancellery). Alan Nothnagle describes the significance of the Treptow memorial:

> Like all Communist monuments of this type (and like any cathedral), the Treptow Park memorial was not intended as a mere tourist attraction but as a center of constant pro-Soviet and antifascist ritual. It was the site of thousands of ceremonies, most notably the annual celebrations of the Soviet victory on 9 May and Revolution Day on 7 November. But in between it was used as the backdrop for youth consecrations, the initiation ceremonies of Young Pioneer and FDJ groups, the oath-taking of soldiers and officers, flag consecrations, antifascist rallies, anti-imperialist demonstrations, countless torchlight ceremonies, FDJ-Konsomol meetings, wreath-laying by newly-weds, and many other events.[76]

Nothnagle further notes that Young Pioneers tended nearly 3,000 Soviet memorials throughout the GDR. Visitors often left wreaths or other tributes at the memorials. A 1974 book listed about 5,000 GDR memorials commemorating the history of the labor movement, anti-Nazi resistance, and the like.[77] No one survived schooling in the GDR without numerous visits to such sacred places.

Buchenwald was a particularly mythic location, interesting in that it involved a double manipulation of history. It overemphasized the martyrdom of the Left and concealed the fact that the Soviets promptly used it as a concentration camp themselves for a time after 1945. The forty-page brochure distributed at Buchenwald had four passing mentions of the

Jews. The camp was portrayed as an example of heroic Communist resistance against Nazism: "The first inmates were German anti-fascists. Unyielding, firmly convinced of the justice of their cause and of its ultimate triumph, they did not abandon their struggle. They embodied the better Germany, they saved the honour of the German nation."[78] Buchenwald's significance was strengthened because Thälmann had been killed there. Political prisoners were in fact the major victims of Buchenwald, but even when discussing the concentration camps as a whole, the pamphlet gives no hint of the magnitude of Jewish deaths.

Like the Nazis, the SED tried to develop appropriate rituals of birth, marriage, and death but did not put nearly the energy into them that the Nazis did. Occasional books of texts suitable for such occasions appeared. As one of them published in 1961 observed: "In holidays and ceremonies, workers and their families should above all sense the meaning and content of our socialist life, to comprehend it and be encouraged to contemplate."[79] The GDR lacked the equivalent of *Die neue Gemeinschaft* and produced considerably less material overall on ceremonies. By the end of the GDR, efforts at elaborate socialist marriage and christening ceremonies had largely ended. The *Jugendweihe* was the one exception. To its last days, the GDR put substantial energy into impressive festivities for the youth.

The Socialist Faith

Marxism-Leninism presented a world that followed discoverable laws, laws that if obeyed would lead to a wonderful future. Marxist-Leninist theory explained where human society had come from and where it was headed. Its followers were "on the side of history," proponents of a cause that could not fail. To be a Marxist-Leninist was to be a modern, scientific person whose actions served great goals.

Still, the GDR energetically supported traditional German virtues. Perhaps the most vivid example is Walter Ulbricht's "Ten Commandments for the New Socialist Person," revealed at the V. Party Congress in 1958:

1. You should always work for the international solidarity of the working class and all workers as well as for the unbreakable alliance with all socialist nations.
2. You should love your Fatherland and always be ready to give your whole strength and ability to defend the workers' and farmers' might.
3. You should help to eliminate the exploitation of people by other people.

4. You should do good work for socialism, for socialism leads to a better life for the workers.
5. You should act to build socialism through mutual help and comradely cooperation, esteem the collective, and take to heart its criticism.
6. You should protect and increase the people's property.
7. You should strive constantly to increase your achievements, be economical, and strengthen socialist labor discipline.
8. You should educate your children in the spirit of peace and socialism, raising people with broad knowledge, firm character, and strong bodies.
9. You should be clean, live decently, and respect your family.
10. You should express solidarity with the peoples fighting for their national liberation or who are defending their national independence.[80]

With appropriate modifications, most of Ulbricht's commandments could have been made consistent with the Nazi principle that "the common good comes before the individual good."

A wide variety of similar propaganda throughout the GDR's history promoted traditional German virtues to which few objected. These virtues were presented as contributing to the glorious cause of socialism. As a 1983 book on rearing well-behaved children put it: "For us, good behavior is applied socialist morality, a part of the socialist style of life."[81] Ethical behavior was grounded in the socialist worldview.

The end of socialism was the paradise of Communism, never clearly described and always in the future. A 1976 GDR poster gave an enticing vision: "Communism is the bright future of humanity. Under it all forms of exploitation and oppression are eliminated, and people are free of the scourge of war. Communism is the world of peace, labor, equality and brotherhood. Under Communism, all the nations of the earth and their peoples will be able to develop fully their abilities and talents."[82] Whatever the Communist heaven might look like, its achievement justified the hardships and challenges of the present. It was a goal of such cheering prospects as to make possible enduring the weaknesses of the transitional socialist state. As a 1978 book stated, this also required "a new type of human being," to be formed through the whole process of social life.[83] According to Marxist-Leninist theory, human nature was malleable, more the consequence of the objective environment surrounding it than innate human characteristics. Changing the environment would change human beings.

Capitalism played the role of the devil in Marxism-Leninism. It did not have the same status as the marker of absolute evil as the Jew in Nazism, since Marxism-Leninism saw capitalism as a necessary step in human progress. However, once capitalism's time had passed, it became a force for evil. Thus the eventual triumph of socialism depended on the complete elimination of capitalism. Marxist literature is filled with attacks on capitalism that put the battle between systems in the form of the struggle between good and evil. A typical passage comes from a 1973 booklet for military education: "This struggle [between socialism and capitalism] is a bitter world-wide class conflict. There is no field on which it does not rage. Above all, it is intensifying in the ideological realm, in the battle for the minds and hearts of humanity."[84] As the final edition of the GDR's political dictionary put it, capitalism had become a threat to the existence of humanity.[85] Only after the complete elimination of capitalism would the world reach its final and happy state. The struggle against capitalism justified otherwise inexplicable aspects of GDR policy. The Berlin Wall, the domestic spy system, economic difficulties, all were temporary necessities in the worldwide battle against reactionary capitalism.

Like Nazism, then, socialism rooted its ideas in purportedly eternal scientific laws, encouraged citizens to work and sacrifice for fine-sounding goals that would lead to a blessed future, established pseudoreligious rituals and ceremonies, and saw a world where good fought evil.

Summary

Totalitarianism is a comprehensive phenomenon that aims to influence every area of life. As Václav Havel observed, it "commands an incomparably more precise, logically structured, generally comprehensible and, in essence, extremely flexible ideology that, in its elaborateness and completeness, is almost a secularized religion. It offers a ready answer to any question whatsoever; it can scarcely be accepted only in part, and accepting it has profound implications for human life."[86] Both National Socialism and Marxism-Leninism used propaganda as part of an effort to bring all aspects of life under the influence of the party. Both developed the external characteristics of a religion: eternal forces, absolute truths, sacred texts, ways of secular worship.

National Socialism's ideology allowed it to make specifically religious claims. As we shall see in Chapter 7, that forced on it the same conflict many standard religions face with other religions: to tolerate a competing religious worldview is to weaken one's own. Despite the claim of its party platform that the NSDAP favored "positive Christianity," Christian and Nazi claims to truth were inherently incompatible, a fact realized by leaders on both sides. The only way Nazism could deal with Christianity was to deny its claim to be a worldview. Thus Nazism tried to force the church to limit its activities to cultic ceremonies, to leave matters outside the church door and the individual soul to the party.

The GDR faced a less critical conflict. Its Marxist-Leninist atheistic foundation compelled it to resist the broader Christian claim to truth. Unlike Nazism, it said explicitly that religion was a remnant of the past, inconsistent with the "scientific" principles of Marxism-Leninism. Given the strong cultural hold of Christianity in Germany, it would have been unwise to combat it with the same energy that was sometimes used in the Soviet Union. And at times the church's goals and the party's goals coincided (for example, on peace issues or the Luther anniversary in 1983), allowing Christians to be seen as holdovers of an antiquated system that could still point its adherents in the correct direction. Still, Marxism-Leninism's accommodations with Christianity were clearly just that. It had no need to suggest that the worldviews at their core were compatible. Since history was on its side, it could wait until the flow of history washed its religious adversary away.

Nazism was sectarian. It was not, the Nazis claimed, "an export item" but rather a form of government suited only to the Germans. In practice this meant that Marxist-Leninist propaganda had a much wider audience than National Socialist propaganda. Marxism-Leninism was universal in its claim. Communism could come only when socialism had replaced other forms of government throughout the world. There was no reason at all for someone in Asia or Africa to accept Nazism, whereas Marxism-Leninism promised a secular millennium to all. Marxism-Leninism's universal appeal gave it a considerable propaganda advantage when speaking to world audiences.

Both systems fretted about the faith of the coming generation. The Nazis limited admission to their speaker corps to those who had been members prior to 1933 and worried about the influx of members after 1933 who joined the party for pragmatic reasons. The GDR faced a problem in the 1980s as the founding generation aged and did not trust the younger generation to carry on the struggle with the necessary vigor. Several major purges failed to purify the membership sufficiently.

Both systems confronted a situation that resembled the dilemma New England Puritans faced in the mid-seventeenth century. As the devout aged, they saw the church filling with people sympathetic to the faith but who had not undergone the conversion experience that entitled them to church membership. The solution was the "Half Way Covenant," which permitted the children of such people to be baptized in the hope of an eventual conversion experience. Nazism and Marxism-Leninism worried that the younger generation, blessed with the advantages won by their elders, would not be up to their calling. A Nazi writer in 1942 noted that many in Germany lacked the baptism by fire that steeled the party's older members: "[T]hese citizens (including some party members) accept us intellectually, but in their hearts are still far from the party. Perhaps it is because they lack the great experience of struggle before our takeover. They are like heirs to whom peace, satisfaction, prosperity and happiness have been given without their having to raise a finger, without having had a single challenge to overcome."[87] How could the revolutionary experience of those who had fought for the Nazis before 1933, or for the Communists before 1945, be conveyed to those who had not been there? Could they who had not seen yet believe? National Socialism and Marxism-Leninism established enormous educational systems to train the coming generation, and both expressed confidence that the new generation would carry on the work of the old yet feared that it might not.

Both systems promised secular utopias. Although Nazism used more explicitly religious language and spoke of god, the Nazi heaven was to be realized on earth. Human problems could be resolved by will. Humanity might never be entirely perfectible, but once the Jews and the genetically defective had been eliminated and the inferior races put in their place, the Thousand Year Reich would be as close to a perfect state as was possible. Marxism-Leninism's vision of the Communist future for all was certainly more comprehensive than Nazism's Aryan world, but it, too, was a curious mixture that rejected the divine while still expecting a transformation of the human character.

To get to these new worlds, it was necessary to engineer human nature. A long process of education and changes in social conditions would produce a new type of human being. The vision of that new human being varied, but in both cases it was *one* type of person they wanted, devoted to the reigning ideology, loyal to the community above self, freed of the illusions of the past. Both knew this was a task of generations, not of years, and both considered steady, unrelenting propaganda to be a central tool in making citizens worthy of the state in which they would live. The problem was that the new human beings were to be formed by their old, unregenerate parents. And it turned out to be harder to alter the human character than either system expected.

The passion animating the conflict between National Socialism and Marxism-Leninism indicated the conflict of worldviews. The Nazis despised England and France for being decadent and subservient to the Jews yet could view the two nations as having some virtue. They were still part of the West. But Bolshevism was wholly other, a competing religion. Goebbels discussed the matter in his diary entry for 8 May 1943: "The states based on a worldview have one advantage over the bourgeois states. They stand on a clear spiritual foundation. This worked to our great advantage until the beginning of the campaign in the East. Then we met an opponent who also represented a worldview, even if it was a false one."[88] In occupied Luxembourg, the SS intelligence service reported that people were taking a somewhat different view of the war with Russia that still recognized it as a battle of worldviews: "the anti-Christians against the Antichrist."[89]

The GDR often seemed to be refighting World War II in its struggles with West Germany. Its founding myth was antifascism, treating Germany's loss of World War II as a victory for the better elements of the German tradition. The Berlin Wall was the "Anti-Fascist Protective Wall." The GDR regularly presented West Germany as the direct successor to Hitler's state.[90] Why was it crucial to make the connection? It was hard to justify the GDR as a separate state absent the threat of Nazism. In resisting West German capitalism, the GDR resisted a system doomed theoretically to collapse but which stubbornly out-produced the GDR both in quality and quantity. In claiming the anti-Fascist high ground, GDR propaganda had a way to refocus the argument, asserting that its vision of a Communist utopia was the way to resolve the German dilemma.

Neither system was a religion, but both used propaganda to present themselves in many of the same ways that a religion does. The majority of the faithful of any religion are not philosophers. They are interested not in thick books of theology but in the practical benefit religion provides in making sense of the world, in giving life meaning, in answering that greatest of questions: "Why?"

Milan Kundera wrote: "Totalitarianism is not only hell, but also the dream of paradise."[91] Without that dream, National Socialism and Marxism-Leninism could not have established the hold they had on the human soul. The dream made it possible for their followers to choose to overlook evil and see illusions of good.

Their citizens did choose in many ways to turn their gaze, but it will not do to view them as somehow less morally sensitive, less human perhaps, than those who had the good fortune to be born in places where temptations were less attractive. Hannah Arendt rightly observed that mass support for totalitarian systems was the result neither of ignorance nor brainwashing.[92] The totalitarian illusions *were* alluring. Both systems proclaimed high goals. In their disparate ways, National Socialism and Marxism-Leninism encouraged an interest in the common good, bravery, sacrifice, neighborliness, industry, optimism, loyalty, all virtues capable of bringing much good.

Unlike Milton's Satan who boldly asserted "Evil be thou my Good," totalitarianism presented itself as a force for all that was right and true. It was rather easy for citizens to believe their governments were pursuing noble aims, especially since propaganda ceaselessly said so. As Cornelius Plantinga Jr. observed: "To do its worst, evil needs to look its best. Evil has to spend a lot on makeup."[93] Much of that expense went to propaganda.

2

Doctrines

Although National Socialism and Marxism-Leninism were quasi-religious worldviews with absolute claims to truth, they developed significantly different theoretical approaches to propaganda. Nazism was not fond of theory at all. Convoluted academic books were written on various aspects of Nazi ideology during the Third Reich, but Nazism's leaders were not very interested in them. Although Nazism claimed to be founded on the eternal laws of nature, its leaders put their confidence more in faith and steadfast will than in scholarly elaboration, whereas Marxism-Leninism produced enormous numbers of academic treatises on every topic and expected that some would be of interest and benefit to working propagandists.

The difference goes back to their respective founders. Hitler's *Mein Kampf* makes more sense on propaganda than on most topics it covers, but he was not interested in proposing a detailed theory of propaganda, nor was anyone else within the party. Marxism-Leninism, on the other hand, claimed scientific foundations, though those foundations proved of limited help in developing effective propaganda. I shall begin by looking at what the two systems claimed to be their approaches to propaganda, turning in later chapters to what happened in practice.

There Is No ABC of Propaganda

The Nazis rejected the possibility of a scientific theory of propaganda. Goebbels put it bluntly in a book on his early activities in Berlin. The academic propagandist was useless. "He comes up with an intellectual approach while sitting at his desk and is then amazed and surprised when actual propagandists do not use his methods, or when they are in fact attempted but do not achieve their goals."[1] He repeated this view regularly. Propaganda was a matter of practical action, not of academic discussion. He was only following Hitler's lead. *Mein Kampf* has a great deal to say about propaganda, but Hitler does not there or later give a detailed explanation of how or why propaganda functions. His point was to devise propaganda that worked, not to develop theories to explain what might work.

A writer in the Nazi journal for propagandists in 1934 came closer than most to seeing a role for scientific study but made it clear that it was subsidiary: "Modern psychology . . . supported by psychiatry and neurology, attempts to discover the laws of psychological processes through systematic experimentation and statistical analysis (e.g., logical thinking). These modern methods have led to valuable conclusions, but they are not sufficient by themselves. There are imponderables in the psyche of individuals as well as of the masses that can scarcely be explained. Neither psychological experiments nor statistical techniques can produce laws that the propagandist can apply with mathematical certainty."[2] The best propagandists were those who knew intuitively, from their souls and through experience, how to reach the masses. Study and training were necessary but not sufficient.

Mein Kampf was, used in the way Christians sometimes use the Bible, as a source of "proof texts," a way of indicating one was on the right path.[3] No Nazi treatment of the subject failed to bow toward *Mein Kampf.* Since Nazi propaganda theory never developed much beyond it, it remains the best guide to Nazi thinking on the matter.

Hitler claimed no great originality on the subject. He freely admitted to learning from the Catholics, the Marxists, the Freemasons, and quite a range of other sources.[4] His approach was original in its totality and comprehensiveness, not in particular details. He was willing to borrow a good method from any source, since he viewed the methods themselves as neutral.

What did Hitler think about propaganda? He devoted two chapters to the subject, one titled "War Propaganda," the other "Propaganda and Organization," but the subject appears throughout *Mein Kampf.* He saw it as "public education," as a way of persuading the masses to accept the views of a party or a state. Propaganda was to be integrated into the culture of a people, not restricted to particular media or situations. The cardinal principles in his mind were emotional appeal, simplicity, repetition, force, leadership, and faith.

Hitler's principles follow from his unflattering view of humankind in general and Germans in particular. The masses are "stupid and forgetful."[5] He praised Vienna's mayor Karl Lueger, who "took good care not to consider people better than they are."[6] The masses face a complex world beyond their ability to understand rationally or logically. Any attempt to win them over by complicated argument is sure to fail. Ignorant and forgetful people need all the help they can get to stay on the path to truth.

The masses are moved by emotion, which Hitler did not mean pejoratively. Feelings are a surer guide than the mind. The masses can be misled by reason, but in the long run their instincts might save them: "In political matters feeling often decides more correctly than reason."[7] Goebbels made the same point: "The thinking of the masses is simple and primitive. They love to generalize from complicated facts and from those generalizations they draw clear and uncompromising conclusions. Those are indeed generally simple and uncomplicated, but they usually hit the nail on the head."[8] Hitler and Goebbels flattered the masses by telling them that they did not need to work hard at understanding the complexities of the world around them, because their leaders would make what they would instinctively realize to be the right choices.

Hitler considered it crucial to understand the psychology of the masses. They are not absolutely malleable, able to be manipulated in any direction a propagandist might wish: "A movement with great aims must therefore be anxiously on its guard not to lose contact with the broad masses."[9] To move the masses, one has to build on their existing attitudes and feelings. Hitler claimed that Germany's World War I propaganda failed to understand the masses. For example, it mocked foreign soldiers, disconcerting German troops who afterward encountered a determined foe. They were misled by propaganda from both home and abroad. Even during World War II, Hitler was slower to implement total war measures than the Allies for fear that they would arouse popular opposition.

The closer a method of propaganda is to the masses, the more directly it reaches them, the more powerful it will be. Hitler therefore preferred speaking to writing: "[T]he power which has always started the greatest religious and political avalanches in history rolling has from time immemorial been the magic power of the spoken word, and that alone."[10] His emphasis is on passion, easier to arouse through the direct presence of a speaker than through words on a page. The page wins adherents one by one, and only if the reader has the ability to focus on the argument (which Hitler thought the masses lacked). The spoken word makes the audience an ally of the speaker. The speaker's passion becomes the audience's passion.

Hitler's idea of the "big lie," which he thought more readily believed than a smaller one, is often misunderstood. His point was that a small lie (for example, "The mayor is a convicted embezzler") is less plausible than a larger one (for example, "The Jews are engaged in a worldwide conspiracy"). The smaller lie is readily disproved, the larger one less so. Paradoxically, the broader the lie, the harder it is to disprove. The mayor can prove his innocence by a trip to the courthouse. How could Jews prove that they were not engaged in a vast conspiracy? The less the evidence, the more the proof of the power of the conspiracy in suppressing it. His argument comes in the middle of a discussion of the Jewish press in Vienna: "In this they proceeded on the sound principle that the magnitude of a lie always contains a certain factor of credibility, since the great masses of the people in the very bottom of their hearts tend to be corrupted rather than consciously and purposely evil, and that, therefore, in view of the primitive simplicity of their minds, they more easily fall victim to a big lie than to a little one, since they themselves lie in little things, but would be ashamed of lies that were too big. Such a falsehood will never enter their heads, and they will not be able to believe in the possibility of such monstrous effrontery and infamous misrepresentation in others."[11] Hitler did not advocate lying as a general principle, though he saw it as a sometimes necessary tool. He favored lying by selection rather than fabrication but had no concern about fabrication if selection proved inadequate for his purposes. He was clear that propaganda is a means, always subsidiary to the larger goal. Considerations of humanitarianism or aesthetics are irrelevant.[12] The end justifies the means.

In public, Goebbels was less explicit about the need for deception, even though he generally is blamed more for inventing the "big lie" than Hitler. At the 1934 Nuremberg rally, he praised the truthfulness of Nazi propaganda: "Good propaganda does not need to lie, indeed it may not lie. It has no reason to fear the truth. It is a mistake to believe that people cannot take the truth. They can. It is only a matter of presenting the truth to people in a way that they will be able to understand."[13] He was, of course, making propaganda for propaganda. Still, he was serious about being as truthful as he thought the situation allowed. With a mass of facts to choose from, there were usually ones that were congenial or ones that could be interpreted to be so.

Since the masses are easily confused, propaganda must be clear. It should not confound people with choices or complex arguments. Hitler argued that German propaganda during World War I made the mistake of allowing public discussion of the causes of the war. "As soon as our own propaganda admits so much as a glimmer of right on the other side, the foundation for doubt in our own right has been laid. The masses are then in no position to distinguish where foreign injustice ends and our own begins."[14]

Just as a soap manufacturer claims its product is the best, so, too, a political propagandist must admit no virtue on the opposing side. The masses understand black and white, not shades of gray. Goebbels thought that propaganda should not even attempt to prove its most controversial claims. Discussing *Der Angriff,* the Berlin newspaper he founded in 1927, he noted: "It intentionally assumed what it wanted to persuade its readers of, and then drew its conclusions relentlessly."[15] Such propaganda is a monologue, not a dialogue. It squelches contrary ideas or perspectives. In current jargon, it aims for hegemony, never for a marketplace of ideas.

The masses' limited capacity makes repetition critical. Even the most gifted propagandist faces great challenges in securing the attention, much less the belief, of the masses. Since the masses are of limited intelligence and great forgetfulness, "all effective propaganda must be limited to a very few points and must harp on these in slogans until the last member of the public understands what you want him to understand by your slogan."[16] Hitler did not mean that propaganda had to repeat its points in the same way, as that would quickly become boring. Rather, a point must be made in varied ways and not only until it is grasped. Hitler realized that in politics as in advertising, consistent effort is necessary to maintain even an established product: "All advertising, whether in the field of business or politics, achieves success through the continuity and sustained uniformity of its application."[17]

Power to Hitler was part of effective propaganda. The masses have no respect for a movement that tolerates what its propaganda says is evil. The secret to winning the masses is "will and power."[18] Hitler favored a range of appropriate force or power, depending on the circumstances. He approved of anything that demonstrated power that did not alienate the masses. Mass meetings and marches are invariably powerful. Hitler noted the impact Marxist meetings had even on him: "[A]fter the war, I experienced a mass demonstration of the Marxists in front of the Royal Palace and the Lustgarten. A sea of red flags, red scarves, and red flowers gave to this demonstration, in which an estimated hundred and twenty thousand persons took part, an aspect that was gigantic from the purely external point of view. I myself could feel and understand how easily the man of the people succumbs to the suggestive magic of a spectacle so grandiose in effect."[19] He wrote of the significance of the SA and the willingness of his followers to dic for the movement. The expression of force impressed those who were not yet members.

The state has even stronger weapons at its disposal, and Hitler was direct in describing the centrality of power. Leadership requires the use of power: *"Firm belief in the right to apply even the most brutal weapons is always bound up with the existence of a fanatical faith in the necessity of the victory of a revolutionary new order on this earth."*[20] The masses are impressed by a doctrine that tolerates no rival, that asserts absolute confidence in its ability and right to command obedience.

But force is by itself an unstable foundation, capable of holding the masses only in the short term unless combined with something they can believe in: "Any violence which does not spring from a firm, spiritual base, will be wavering and uncertain." Hitler was absolutely clear on the need for faith: "A man does not die for business, but only for ideals." Although he viewed religion as a competitor that ultimately needed to be supplanted, Hitler repeatedly looked to religion as the model of powerful mass influence: "I consider the foundation or destruction of a religion far greater than the foundation or destruction of a state, let alone a party." He made frequent reference to the Catholic Church, whose central control of the faith he found exemplary: "It has recognized quite correctly that its power of resistance does not lie in its lesser or greater adaptation to the scientific findings of the moment, which in reality are always fluctuating, but rather in rigidly holding to dogmas once established, for it is only such dogmas which lend to the whole body the character of a faith."[21]

Hitler saw the personal commitment religion claims to be necessary for an effective mass movement. Typical political parties make suggestions to their adherents. Religion makes absolute claims. He wrote: *"Political parties are inclined to compromises; philosophies never. Political parties even reckon with opponents; philosophies proclaim their infallibility."*[22] It was that infallibility Hitler required for his movement.

The final characteristic of Hitler's approach to propaganda is his emphasis on leadership. A religious faith generally includes a god. As we have seen, Hitler was in fact spoken of as a deity, though he could not present himself in that guise in *Mein Kampf.* He did stress the importance of leadership. Speaking in 1927, Hitler said: "We deceive ourselves if we believe that the people have a desire to be governed by majorities. No, you do not understand this people. This people has no desire to be dragged into 'majorities.' It has no interest in such plans. It wants a leadership in which it can believe, nothing more."[23] He was speaking to thousands of passionate followers whose cheers proved his point.

Hitler saw leadership as an innate ability: "No more than a famous master can be replaced and another take over the completion of the half-finished painting he has left behind can the great poet and thinker, the great statesman and the great soldier be replaced. For their activity lies always in the province of art. It is not mechanically trained, but inborn by God's grace." Such innate leadership has a direct link to propaganda: *"For leading means: being able to move masses."*[24] In its essence, great propaganda, like great leadership, was a matter of personality, of genius, not of principles that ordinary people could master. The masses would not long tolerate ineffective leadership, according to Nazi thinking—but as long as the leadership did its job, it would have the support of the masses.

From the Nazi perspective, effective propaganda required a single will. As Adolf Raskin, a radio director, put it, a propaganda minister cannot operate by majority rule: "Either such a liberal democratic propaganda minister is a farce, or he becomes the dictator of all parties—and thus ceases to be a democrat and the minister of a democracy."[25]

Hitler saw an effective organization as a hierarchy of dictators. He claimed to give party officials "unconditional authority and freedom of action downward, but . . . unlimited responsibility upward."[26] This greatly simplified matters; one obeyed superiors and commanded subordinates. It also had a certain internal logic. Leadership was demonstrated by ability, so if one became a leader, he by definition had the ability. Hitler himself was the great example. In fourteen years he rose from obscurity to absolute power.

Control of propaganda by a strong leader did not mean that anything was possible. Leaders had to understand that followers have differing levels of commitment. Hitler made a distinction between propaganda and organization, basically a distinction between the passive and active followers of a movement.

The function of propaganda is to attract supporters, the function of organization to win members.

A supporter of a movement is one who declares himself to be in agreement with its aims, a member is one who fights for them. . . .

Since being a supporter requires only a passive recognition of an idea, while membership demands active advocacy and defense, to ten supporters there will at most be one or two members.[27]

Hitler proposed a party whose members must be deeply committed but which welcomes the support and votes of those less passionate.

In sum, Hitler viewed propaganda as a pragmatic set of methods instrumental in reaching a goal. The same methods could be used for disparate causes, as Hitler makes clear as he discusses what he learned from other persuasive movements. The best propagandists were not intellectuals remote from their audiences, rather ones who intuitively knew what should be done even if they could not explain why.

The Nazis had little interest in going beyond Hitler's early thinking on propaganda, nor did Hitler himself. He touched on aspects of propaganda in later speeches and conversations, but never again with the intensity of *Mein Kampf.* His followers published one general book on propaganda, Eugen Hadamovsky's 1933 *Propaganda and National Power,* the only broad treatment of propaganda listed in a 1939 bibliography for propagandists.[28] It includes chapters on power, mass meetings, radio, the press, and culture. Although Hadamovsky develops points in more detail than Hitler does, the book is derivative, adding nothing of significance to what Hitler had written in *Mein Kampf.*[29] Goebbels spoke often on propaganda and discussed it in his collections of speeches and essays but again has little to say that significantly extends Hitler's thinking. There were numerous books demonstrating the alleged power of international propaganda directed against Germany, some of which discussed general principles of propaganda.[30] Textbooks in journalism also considered propaganda, but not in a way likely to be useful to a practicing propagandist.[31] Now as then, one wishing to know what the Nazis thought about propaganda turns to *Mein Kampf.*

Propaganda as a Marxist-Leninist Science

Finding the essence of the GDR's approach to propaganda is a more difficult task. In principle, its propaganda was a science, not an art. The Marxist-Leninists distinguished between propaganda and agitation. Propaganda dealt with ideas in depth; agitation presented those ideas in less depth to the masses, but drawing a sharp dividing line between the two forms of persuasion was difficult. Their fields overlapped, leading Willi Münzenberg, the Marxist master of persuasion, to call agitation "applied propaganda."[32] I shall generally use "propaganda" to refer to both.

Someone interested in the Nazi approach to propaganda turns to *Mein Kampf.* There is no similar bible for Marxist-Leninist propaganda. Marx and Lenin did not speak to the subject with Hitler's focused clarity, though both were accomplished propagandists. The approach had to be distilled from their broader writings. The GDR published a book of relevant sections from Lenin in 1974 titled *On Agitation and Propaganda.* According to the dust jacket: "The collection is an indispensable handbook for party functionaries, agitators, propagandists, journalists and many others involved in ideological work." It is unlikely that many found much practical help from the remarkably varied collection. Some items were simply brief notes from Lenin ordering agitators to be sent to a given area.[33]

GDR propagandists had a long reading list. First, there was the general Marxist-Leninist canon. The scholarly edition of the Marx-Engels corpus runs to forty-three volumes. Lenin's works were available in forty volumes. Thirteen of the planned sixteen volumes of Stalin's work appeared before he fell into disfavor. Then there were the shelves of books by GDR party leaders (Erich Honecker's collected speeches and writings were up to twelve volumes with over 5,000 pages in 1988) and decisions of party congresses and meetings, not to mention the productions of scholarly organizations such as the Institute for Marxism-Leninism in Berlin. This was leadership by bureaucracy, not personality.

Second, there was the professional literature. According to a 1972 Socialist Unity Party of Germany (SED) Politburo decision: "Agitation and propaganda can only be fully effective when they are enriched by social scientific research, when the social scientists themselves actively participate in agitation and propaganda."[34] Unlike the Nazis, who had little expectation that academics had anything useful to say to working propagandists, the GDR actively sought their help.

The major theoretical works were translations from the Russian, consistent with the standard GDR slogan: "To learn from the Soviet Union means to learn victory." As a 1972 Politburo decision on propaganda ordained: "A primary goal is to spread the results of Soviet scientific research [on propaganda]."[35] Propaganda was too important a topic to do independently. One had to follow the Soviets, the source of wisdom.

The SED's publishing house, the Dietz Verlag, published three editions of *Methods of Political Education,* a translation of a leading Soviet propaganda textbook. It was an immediate consequence of the 1972 Politburo decision and remained a standard propaganda textbook until the end of the GDR. The book focused on propaganda from the Marxist perspective, meaning education within the party, but it also was interested in mass propaganda and agitation. It began by asserting a scientific foundation for propaganda: "The methodology of party propaganda is an independent branch of the social sciences and party activity. It is based in and develops from the scientific foundation of Marxism-Leninism and the method of dialectical materialism." That did not mean propaganda was to be coldly rational: "If the right methods are not chosen and used to make people aware of propaganda's content, it can entirely miss its goal. . . . The art of propaganda closely resembles the idea of mastery, which includes certain professional knowledge, accomplishments and capacities."[36] The art, however, was second to the science.

The book then gives more than a hundred pages to the theoretical foundations of propaganda. It begins with a reminder of the primacy of Marxist-Leninist theory, which must be constantly studied. The theory is important because it determines the truth that propaganda must preach. A fourteen-page chapter titled "Social Psychological Factors to Increase the Effectiveness of Propaganda" reviews personality, emotional needs, attitudes, and stereotypes. There are chapters on educational methods and logic as well.

Despite various statements about the scientific nature of propaganda, this book and other Soviet works tended to state principles of propaganda rather than demonstrate them empirically. Soviet scholars even complained that the capitalist world did a better job of studying the psychology of propaganda.[37] Capitalist social psychology found its way into Marxist propaganda, often unacknowledged. For example, American social psychologist William McGuire proposed his Inoculation Theory of developing resistance to persuasion in 1961.[38] It soon emerged in Soviet theory.[39] Like Hitler, the Soviets were willing to "baptize" helpful methods that came from opposing traditions.

The GDR produced little of its own scientific study of propaganda, and what it did produce was not helpful. During a flurry of interest in cybernetics around 1970, Georg Klaus, a leading GDR philosopher, published several books that together were the most detailed approach to propaganda during the GDR's history.[40] His convoluted approach had limited influence, particularly after cybernetics fell into disfavor. The 1967 edition of the party's political dictionary stated: "Human society is a highly complex system. To properly control the social processes in socialism, it is particularly important to make comprehensive use of cybernetics."[41] The 1988 edition dropped the word entirely. As one GDR media personality later commented: "Georg Klaus based his book on logic and semantics. That made the book almost unreadable. Perhaps that is why it was printed?"[42] It certainly had few readers who were practical propagandists.

There was no shortage of domestic material on propaganda, though it never departed significantly from the Soviet model. The SED's Central Committee made regular binding declarations on the subject. Party leaders spoke frequently about propaganda.[43] Every level of the SED hierarchy published material for propagandists and agitators.

Methods fell in and out of fashion, which presented difficulties. A 1972 report from the Institute for Youth Research in Leipzig found weaknesses in propaganda, in part because the propagandists could not depend on a consistent method: "[W]ith the best intentions—we hurry from one idea to another, from one method to another, from one high point another. Tested principles are neglected. The lack of methodological continuity necessarily influences the results of our ideological efforts."[44]

To outline the fundamentals of the GDR's propaganda, then, requires sifting through a wide range of sources, but its fundamental principles are clear. If the Nazi principles were emotional appeal, simplicity, repetition, force, leadership, and faith, the GDR saw propaganda as a scientific method of persuading the masses to act in their own best interests. As a result, it was logically based, emphasizing Marxist-Leninist theory more than leadership, but it still preferred simplicity and repetition and proposed, sometimes in religious language, an atheistic faith.

The GDR stressed the scientific or rational foundation of its propaganda, which to its mind distinguished it from the manipulative emotional appeals of Nazi and capitalist propaganda. The party defined propaganda as "the systematic dissemination and thorough explanation of political, philosophical, economic, historic, scientific, technical or other knowledge and ideas."[45] Agitation did not go into the same depth, but it also rested on scientific foundations: "An important aspect of agitation is to build on the foundations of the Marxist-Leninist worldview the socialist convictions and behaviors that will lead the workers to socialist patriotism, proletarian internationalism and firm class positions in the battle against the enemies of peace and socialism."[46]

Marxist-Leninist propaganda had a difficult task. As I have noted, Nazi propaganda was not committed to truthfulness. Although he did not recommend lying as a general policy, Hitler granted its usefulness. Propaganda was also changeable, since the loose National Socialist ideology depended more on what Hitler thought at the moment than on theoretical principles. The GDR's propaganda, on the other hand, claimed to follow laws that were demonstrable and in theory rejected lying, which was supposedly the method of the enemy. That did not stop the GDR's propagandists from lying—but it did make it awkward.

Hitler did not consider the masses without value but thought that they had little idea on their own of what was good for them. The rhetoric of Marxism-Leninism viewed the masses as more capable. The working class was "the most revolutionary class in the history of humanity, and the driving force in the current era of transition from capitalism to socialism."[47] Klaus claimed: "In contrast to imperialist manipulation, we do not want to produce imaginary feelings that will lead people to 'draw their own conclusions' (which in reality are programmed) and make 'free decisions' (which are in fact expressions of intellectual slavery), rather to create favorable conditions to encourage free thinking, uninfluenced by the forces of manipulation."[48] The masses could be misled by adroit capitalist propaganda that concealed their true interests and deceived them into supporting policies that objectively worked to their detriment, but they were capable of understanding complex issues and of making the correct decisions if given the proper guidance.

Marxist-Leninist propaganda therefore was less emotionally based than that of the Nazis. As a Soviet textbook put it: "The goal of propaganda is to train convinced and active fighters for Communism who do not blindly believe, but base their convictions on scientific knowledge, people who view the theory critically and test it in practice, who analyze their experiences and are capable of arguing persuasively for their ideas."[49] The system rejected uncritical belief while putting blinders on its propagandists, directing their sight only in approved directions—but at least the approved directions seemed rational.

The result was a bias in favor of the written word, which provided a better arena for carefully developed argumentation. In speeches in 1953 and 1954, Politburo member Fred Oeßlner quoted Lenin and Stalin: "As is well known, the press is the party's strongest and sharpest weapon."[50] Oelßner was purged from the Politburo in 1958, and other GDR leaders weren't quite as firm as he was on the primacy of the press, but certainly the GDR depended substantially more on the printed word than did the Nazis. As we shall see later, when using the spoken word the GDR preferred person-to-person or small-group oral agitation rather than public meetings, since the former provided better opportunity for tailored argument.

Despite the greater stated confidence in the masses, the GDR still thought leadership important. Erich Honecker's statement was frequently cited: "The art of leadership is the art of persuasion."[51] His words are close to Hitler's statement cited earlier (*"For leading means: being able to move masses"*), but whereas Hitler focused on the leading through passion, Honecker leaned more toward ostensibly reasoned argument.

The SED also favored simplicity and repetition. As an early brochure for propagandists (translated from Russian) put it: "Clarity, simplicity and ease of comprehension are the primary characteristics of Bolshevist agitation."[52] Soviet textbooks did note that simplicity should not insult the audience's intelligence.[53] The basic purpose of agitation was to put the great issues into a form comprehensible by the masses. Klaus discussed repetition, which he thought important as long as it did not bore the audience.[54] Certainly any reader of the GDR's press was struck by its incessant repetition and by its black-and-white reporting.

Marxism-Leninism was a worldview, not merely a political and economic theory. As a worldview, it claimed absolute truth. The GDR frequently quoted Lenin's familiar comment that the "teachings of Marx are all powerful [*allmächtig*] because they are true." A standard work on Marxism-Leninism, published in 1960, made the claim clear: "The successful study of Marxism-Leninism brings one to a unified worldview—the most progressive worldview of our day."[55] To accept this worldview required a certain leap of faith. Although the SED did not use the word "faith" as much as the Nazis did, it called on its followers to accept more than reason could demonstrate.

Summary

In developing propaganda theory, the Nazis and the SED began from different places, both rooted in German culture. The Nazis were pietistic, the Marxist-Leninists people of the Enlightenment. Nazism drew on a tradition that downgraded the intellect, favoring instead intuition and nature. Such an approach saw little good in developing complicated theories of propaganda. It was a matter more of right intuition than study. A good propagandist knew what had to be done. Marxism-Leninism, drawing on the parallel German rational tradition, was confident that propaganda was as subject to theory as any other area of life. Despite their different starting points, in practice their approaches to propaganda had more similarities than differences.

The Nazis thought the masses were not particularly intelligent and were easily swayed, while the SED claimed they were the moving force of history, but both concluded that the masses needed a great deal of help were they ever to accomplish anything significant. Their insistence that the ability to make effective propaganda resided either with leaders of genius or with the Marxist-Leninist party led to problems.

In the case of Nazism, there was no easy way to settle differences in propaganda policy. As Goebbels and Hitler repeatedly said, the measure of effective propaganda was success. If it worked, it was good; if it did not, it was bad. This is a principle with limited predictive value, as it can be applied only after the fact. If Goebbels and Otto Dietrich disagreed about press strategy, their only recourse was to appeal to Hitler.

GDR propaganda was based on Marxist-Leninist theory rather than personality. The problem was that the theory was broad enough to be vague. Thus cybernetics was a touchstone during one period but entirely forgotten during the next. And since the theory was presumed to be infallible, though not perfectly understood, any failings had to be explained by criticizing the technique rather than the theory. Since the theory was nonfalsifiable, it was also difficult to change. When change did happen, it was the result of action by the leadership, not scholarly discussion.

The rational foundation of Marxism-Leninism led to a much more convoluted approach to propaganda in the GDR. As we shall see later, Nazi propagandists did not have to be particularly well trained. They were told that passion was more important than detailed knowledge. SED propagandists, to the contrary, were expected to study Marxist-Leninist theory in substantial depth. Their propaganda was to reach the mind as much as the heart.

The respective party congresses of the two systems demonstrate the differing views on reason and emotion. The Nazis held six Nuremberg rallies from 1933 to 1938. The SED held eleven party congresses. The Nuremberg rallies were spectacular emotional experiences (although it could get dull standing in formation for hours) that gave the world an image of Nazism that yet endures. They were directed outbursts of energy, not decision-making events. The SED's congresses subjected delegates to interminable speeches. They supposedly made the decisions that would guide the country until the next congress, but the outcome was planned in advance. Even the "discussion speeches" were normally prepared in advance. A socialist Leni Riefenstahl could not have transformed an SED congress into a film with the power of *Triumph of the Will*. That may be a reason why socialist societies produced more satirists than the Nazis. Whatever Nazism was, it was not funny. The staid, bureaucratic, and rigid socialist system begged for the satire of writers like Václav Havel.

Both systems placed propaganda in a rhetorical straitjacket. The principle that the Führer or the party was infallible forced both systems to say things that were not true and that contradicted the direct experience of those who received the propaganda. The constraints were felt less when things were going well than when they were going poorly, but even during smoother periods citizens had little difficulty perceiving that propaganda was determined more by how things ought to be than how they were. This knowledge undermined the theoretical claim that each system was able to explain both where the world had been and where it was going.

3

Hierarchies

On 30 March 1945 Joseph Goebbels was complaining to Adolf Hitler about ineffective propaganda produced by Otto Dietrich and Robert Ley.[1] Goebbels never quite succeeded in persuading Hitler to grant him the full authority he craved. Unlike the GDR's propaganda, which had clear lines of authority, Nazi propaganda displayed organizational confusion. Party and state were intertwined in bewildering ways, with half a dozen or more leading Nazis struggling for influence. I begin with a survey of their respective and overlapping jurisdictions, then turn to the clearer structure of GDR propaganda.

Symphonies and Discords

Control over the Third Reich's propaganda was divided between party and state. Some matters were the responsibility of the party, some of the state; some were shared. This did not mean that there were two approaches to propaganda. The Nazis used state structures but made plain who had the power. The "leadership principle" in practice meant that those who could get power had power as long as Adolf Hitler did not intervene. To understand the Nazi system, one must know who actually had what power when, not in theory.

The major players in Hitler's propaganda system were Joseph Goebbels, Otto Dietrich, Robert Ley, Alfred Rosenberg, Joachim Ribbentrop, Philip Bouhler, and Max Amann. All save Ribbentrop were party *Reichsleiter,* of whom there were sixteen in 1933. Each theoretically had direct access to Hitler.[2] Consistent with Hitler's practice of assigning several people to the same area, their respective areas of authority were shifting and overlapping. The boundaries between party and state were equally unclear. The results are suggested by Table 1.

Hitler could and did intervene in any area, and other leading Nazis sometimes claimed authority as well. In most significant areas of propaganda, at least two leading Nazis had say. Sometimes that say came by virtue of simultaneous party and state positions.

The results of organizational uncertainty were at times almost comical. Goebbels and Dietrich each issued daily directives to the German press. Their directives did not always agree. One day in 1940, each gave a speech that he instructed the press to carry as the lead story, putting editors in an unpleasant predicament.[3] Hitler once locked them together in a railway car with instructions not to leave until they had made peace. They left with an agreement that neither took seriously.[4] The Propaganda and Foreign Ministries each maintained a club for foreign correspondents in Berlin. A Swedish journalist noted that the food and service were better at the Foreign Ministry's club. He also observed that being in the bad graces of one ministry often put one in the good graces of the other, useful for a foreign correspondent who was doing his or her duty.[5] While Goebbels and Ribbentrop were fighting for control of international propaganda, Germany invaded the Soviet Union, and Rosenberg won control of propaganda in the East.[6]

There are good summaries of the intricacies of the Nazi propaganda system, the best being Jay Baird's and Robert Herzstein's.[7] I am interested here in the general structure of the system, not in the full details of the infighting and rearrangements over time. What Michael Balfour writes about the disputes between Goebbels and Dietrich is true of the system as a whole as well: "[T]he relative positions of Goebbels and Dietrich were continually changing, so that no statement can be made about them which is valid for the period as a whole."[8] Nazism viewed the world in Darwinian terms, but its internal politics were only semi-Darwinian. Extinction was difficult (Hitler was usually loyal to his intimates), but fading into relative

TABLE 1. Nazi Propagandists

Area	State Control	Party Control
Newspapers	Goebbels Dietrich Ribbentrop	Goebbels Dietrich Amann
Magazines	Goebbels Ley	Goebbels Amann
Films	Goebbels	Goebbels
Books	Goebbels	Bouhler Rosenberg Amann
Public Meetings and Ceremonies	Goebbels	Goebbels Rosenberg Ley
Foreign Propaganda	Goebbels Ribbentrop Rosenberg	Goebbels
Theater	Goebbels	Goebbels Rosenberg
The Arts	Goebbels	Goebbels Rosenberg
Domestic Radio	Goebbels	Goebbels
Party Education		Goebbels Ley Rosenberg

impotence was a constant threat. However, as we shall see, the infighting did not have a great impact on the nature of the propaganda that actually was produced.

I shall begin with Joseph Goebbels, the central figure who made propaganda almost from the day he joined the party in 1924. Hitler sent him to Berlin in November 1926, where he developed an effective propaganda system that greatly increased both the visibility and membership of the party. The following year he founded *Der Angriff*, a newspaper that quickly developed a lively reputation for scandal-mongering. By 1931 he had become *Reichspropagandaleiter*, the head of the party propaganda apparatus, a position he held until 1945. After the Nazi takeover, Goebbels became head of the RMVP. He was president of the Reich Chamber of Culture, the organization to which all employed in culture had to belong. Goebbels was the single most influential propagandist, but he had substantially more power in some areas than in others.

Goebbels's ministry was the most important propaganda entity. It was an unprecedented organization, which Goebbels saw as the director of the symphony of public opinion and which he boasted was the "most modern ministry."[9] It began with 350 employees in 1933. Though Goebbels's professed goal was to keep it under 1,000, there were more than 1,900 employees by 1942. The forty-two regional propaganda offices by the war years employed another 1,400 people.[10] These were organizationally subordinate to the RMVP but in the peculiar Nazi tangle of party and state had heads who often owed allegiance more to their local party *Gauleiter* (party regional leader) than to Berlin. He was near, Berlin was far away, and proximity to was important in Nazism. Among other duties, the regional offices provided detailed reports on propaganda-related matters to Berlin.

Goebbels probably had the most capable ministry in Berlin (at least until Albert Speer's advent as production organizer). Although 92 percent of the staff were party members, he did not tolerate fools.[11] He wanted people of genuine competence, providing they were willing to grant Goebbels even greater competence. As his diaries demonstrate, he kept careful watch on his subordinates, not hesitating to fire those he thought not up to the job. Herzstein observes: "The best background for a successful career in the Goebbels ministry was a doctorate in the humanities or social sciences, combined with a past history as an old Nazi. If one had these qualifications and was under forty, so much the better."[12] The ministry began in 1933 with five divisions: propaganda, radio, press, motion pictures, and theater. By 1941 there were seventeen divisions, including art, music, periodicals, and literature.[13] The Propaganda Ministry was funded primarily by radio license fees that grew at a pace faster than Goebbels's ministry, making it almost self-supporting.[14] This was a happy side effect of the Nazi policy of manufacturing cheap radio receivers (the "People's Receiver") to make radio ownership feasible even for those with low incomes.

Goebbels's goals were comprehensive from the beginning. Two days after the ministry began its official existence, he spoke to the press: "We have founded a ministry for Popular Enlightenment and Propaganda. . . . Popular enlightenment is essentially something passive; propaganda, on the other hand, is something active. . . . It is not enough to reconcile people more or less to our regime, to move them towards a position of neutrality toward us, we want rather to work on people until they are addicted to us, until they realize, in the ideological sense as well, that what is happening now in Germany not only must be allowed, but can be allowed."[15] Goebbels was making the distinction Hitler had made between propaganda and organization, though changing the terms. For him, enlightenment was to win general support, propaganda was to produce passion.

Goebbels was also president of the *Reichskulturkammer,* the Reich Chamber of Culture (RKK). The RKK was the "professional" organization encompassing nearly everyone with any role at all in culture, whether in performance, production, or management. Established in 1933, the RKK initially had separate chambers for literature, theater, music, film, fine arts, press, and radio. The radio chamber proved superfluous and was eliminated after the outbreak of the war. The ties between the Propaganda Ministry and the RKK were cemented by Goebbels's right as president to appoint the RKK's top officials.

The RKK had significant legal powers. Since no one could work in the arts without being a member and since members could be expelled for any violation the RKK thought proper, the RKK encouraged fidelity to Nazi principles without blatant censorship. It also allowed the state to promote the art and support the artists it wished. Since there were regional offices, RKK activities could be coordinated at the local level throughout the country.[16]

Next, I turn to the party propaganda apparatus. The leading organ was the *Reichspropagandaleitung,* the Nazi Party Central Propaganda Office (RPL), based in Munich. Goebbels was its head, but since he was in Berlin, subordinates handled day-to-day direction. The RPL was divided into five main divisions in 1939: active propaganda, film, radio, culture, and coordination. The busiest was active propaganda. Its tasks included "carrying out propaganda actions at every level, from the mass events with their architectonic structure to membership meetings at the local group or section level. This requires organizing the entire speaker system of the party, its subsidiaries and affiliated organizations. Along with handling the daily questions of politics, it provides the entire speaker system with information and sends all propagandists in the country the monthly *Unser Wille und Weg.* The speaker system also requires the production and distribution of appropriate posters and leaflets, as well as the careful examination of meeting reports from the speakers and propaganda offices."[17] The film section organized film showings, particularly in areas that lacked a movie theater. The radio section encouraged listening, promoted programs consistent with Nazi ideology, and organized hobbyists. The culture section had supervision of artistic matters that somehow impinged on the party. For example, it controlled the use of Nazi symbols and approved music for party gatherings and the architecture of party buildings. The coordination section was responsible for relations with the state and other organizations. The RPL had far less power than the Propaganda Ministry.

Subordinate to the RPL was the *Reichsring für nationalsozialistische Propaganda und Volksaufklärung*, the Reich Circle for National Socialist Propaganda and People's Enlightenment. This structure, with national, regional, and local offices, was established in July 1935 as a way of bringing order to the profusion of groups making propaganda. It was headed by the party's propaganda leaders at the various levels. As its director, Walter Tießler, wrote in 1939: "After the seizure of power, we knew that all areas of party activity, propaganda included, were very decentralized. The various subsidiaries and affiliated organizations of the party, as well as other German organizations with propaganda offices, largely did not see the necessity to follow the party's propaganda directives, rather wanted to go their own way wherever possible. The result was that not only were different problems handled at the same time, they were handled in different ways. That inevitably produces uncertainty and mistrust on the part of the population."[18] Of course, the propagandists at the lower level were only following the example of their leaders, which fact could hardly be admitted.

Still, the Reich Circle did help to coordinate the activities of a wide range of groups, beginning with party organizations such as the German Labor Front (DAF), the student association, the SA, the SS, and the NSDAP Colonial Office. It soon also included representatives from many nonparty organizations. Its stated tasks were numerous:

- Guaranteeing the NSDAP's leadership of the entire propaganda apparatus;
- Establishing general guidelines;
- Distributing the RPL's informative material to all propagandists;
- Organizing unified ceremonies and special events;
- Making subordinate propagandists aware of the RPL's general regulations and guidelines;
- Clarifying and eliminating misunderstandings and conflicts between various propaganda offices;
- Supporting propaganda campaigns;

- Supporting conferences and mass meetings;
- Arranging discussions of propaganda at party conferences;
- Arranging meetings and correspondence encouraging the smooth functioning of the propaganda system;
- Holding a monthly meeting for all propagandists in the Reich Circle's jurisdiction;
- Producing quarterly activity reports;
- Informing the RPL three weeks in advance of conferences at which propaganda will be discussed to allow for its participation.[19]

Fine in theory, the Reich Circle sometimes foundered in the inherent chaos of the Nazi system. As Herzstein observes, party potentates often insisted on their own way despite orders from above.[20] They liked the leadership principle as long as they were giving, not receiving, the orders.

Goebbels viewed propaganda as a whole, with responsibilities assigned to the organization best able to handle them. Speaking to propaganda leaders in 1935, he outlined the system: "Take the control of the press: that we do through the state. For the party *cannot* do that since it lacks both the means and the legal authority. The press obeys me as a minister. If I went to it as Reich Propaganda Leader, it would say: You have no legal authority. Say, however, that we want to fill the Tempelhof Field with people. That is the job of the party. When we want to reach the people with a propaganda campaign through *meetings,* the party is responsible. When we want to do it through the *press,* the ministry handles it. The whole influence over public opinion remains in our hands in either case."[21] From Goebbels's perspective, the problem was that "our hands" were not always his hands. Other Nazis fought hard to have influence.

Otto Dietrich was another early party member who brought with him considerable journalistic experience. Hitler appointed him the party's *Reichspressechef* (Reich press chief) in 1931. He became the chief press officer of the government late in 1937 and Hitler's press secretary. Dietrich was organizationally subordinate to Goebbels as an undersecretary in the RMVP, though he rarely showed up at his office there. As party leaders with the rank of *Reichsleiter,* they were equals. During the war, Dietrich was in Hitler's immediate presence far more often than Goebbels was. Since Hitler was by nature more of an optimist than Goebbels, the propaganda minister regularly was distressed by Dietrich's sanguine releases on the state of the war, releases based more on the Führer's optimism than on the true situation.

Dietrich's influence was primarily limited to the press, but he defended his realm with tenacity, as Goebbels's regular complaints demonstrate. In November 1939, for example, Goebbels wrote: "Dr. Dietrich is stirring up trouble. He wants to be press minister. A bone-head without imagination or understanding."[22] Still, Dietrich had daily direct access to Hitler once the war began and also was chairman of the Deutsches Nachrichtenbüro, the sole national news agency after 1939. To compete with Goebbels's daily press conference in Berlin, Dietrich began issuing daily press releases in 1940, which he sometimes used to needle Goebbels. Goebbels gave a speech in February 1941, for example, to which he instructed the press to give major coverage. Dietrich promptly issued a release that said: "There is reason to mention that the reporting of political meetings should be sufficiently restrained so as to allow for stronger coverage for mass meetings addressed by the Führer."[23] Since Dietrich's directives claimed to have Hitler's direct authority behind them, they had influence, but they went from Dietrich to Goebbels for release at his press conference in Berlin. This put Dietrich at a disadvantage. Goebbels was in Berlin, and he was not.

Robert Ley was the party's *Reichsorganisationsleiter* (Reich organization director) after 1932. That gave him considerable say in the party's educational system. He also headed the DAF. The DAF, which eventually had 25 million members, provided every manner of service, some of them propagandistic in nature. As Reich organization director, Ley had party training under his control. He also established a variety of training courses and schools. He and Goebbels got on rather well. Ley knew better than to disagree with Goebbels often.

Alfred Rosenberg was the Nazi Party's "theoretician," though his books were unreadable, even for Hitler. He headed foreign affairs for the party but despite his wishes did not become foreign minister. Still, in 1934 Hitler gave him the grandiose title of Führer's Deputy for the Entire Intellectual and Philosophical Education and Instruction of the National Socialist Party. His vague responsibilities had to do with ideological education within the party. In cooperation with the RPL, his office published *Die neue Gemeinschaft*, a monthly for those conducting party and state holidays and ceremonies. He also became minister for the occupied eastern territories on 17 July 1941, just after the attack on the Soviet Union. This gave him control of propaganda to the East. Since Hitler had given him authority over ideological matters, which he thought included just about everything, Rosenberg regularly sought to expand his reach. He also had grand plans to found a party university.[24] Goebbels thought him incompetent. He had limited influence on day-to-day propaganda.

Joachim Ribbentrop was foreign minister from 1938 to 1945, which gave him considerable authority over foreign propaganda.[25] He lacked the party base of others (he was not a party *Reichsleiter*) but was willing to do what it took to increase his hold on international propaganda. He had primary control over shortwave broadcasting, for example. Several days before the invasion of the Soviet Union, Goebbels noted in his diaries: "Ribbentrop is getting involved in all sorts of things that do not concern him. I shall now take the offensive against him. People like him are only impressed by impudence."[26] Goebbels was capable of that.

Philip Bouhler, among other assignments, headed the Nazi Censorship Committee for the Protection of National Socialist Literature, which certified that books contained nothing objectionable from the party's standpoint. He had claim to censorship authority over all books published in the Third Reich.[27] Goebbels was not pleased. A June 1941 entry in his diary noted: "Gutterer has talked with Lammers: he shares our views regarding Bouhler and his bizarre censorship committee. It is not to be allowed independent power to ban books."[28]

Max Amann was the head of the Franz Eher Verlag, the party's publishing house. He was also president of the press section of the RKK. Primarily interested in the business aspects of publishing (he managed to secure control of about 80 percent of the German press by 1945), he nonetheless did not hesitate to get involved in editorial matters when he chose. Amann did not have the official authority to appoint editors, but he had the practical ability to do so when he wished.[29] He was not a pleasant man to offend.

In short, Nazi propaganda was made by a confusion of people of varying degrees of competence who sometimes did not like each other very much.[30] Why did such a byzantine system function at all? The critical fact about the system was that it was going in the same general direction, working hard to determine (and influence) Hitler's desires. Whenever battles raged too strongly, Hitler would step in and make some sort of peace, generally not a lasting one.

Ian Kershaw uncovered a statement from 1934 that illuminates what held the system together: "Everyone who has had the opportunity to observe it knows that the Führer can hardly dictate from above everything which he intends to realise sooner or later. . . . [I]t is the duty of everybody to try to work towards the Führer along the lines he would wish. Anyone who makes mistakes will notice it soon enough. But anyone who really works towards the Führer along his lines and towards his goal will certainly both now and in the future one day have the finest reward in the form of the sudden legal confirmation of his work."[31]

Although leading Nazis differed on all kinds of matters and did all they could to increase their power at the expense of their rivals, loyalty to Hitler was as absolute as anything could be in the Third Reich. And under the "leadership principle," their power depended ultimately on his. They might disagree with a particular decision, and certainly they did not always follow the Führer's directions on jurisdictional matters, yet all followed Hitler's fundamental opinions on propaganda, as in other matters. Hitler was clear when he needed to be clear, and the general direction of Nazism was discernable to nearly everyone involved.

The Architecture of Socialist Propaganda

In contrast to the tangles of Nazi propaganda, GDR propaganda was organized and orderly. Lines of authority were known, and although perfect amity did not prevail, it was generally clear who had authority over what. It took time to work out the organizational details, but by the early 1970s the basic structures that remained until 1989 were in place.[32] Throughout the period, the changes were more the result of efforts to find more efficient ways to structure the system than of battles between SED leaders.

The SED controlled propaganda, leaving only a minor role for the state. Theoretically, party authority came from the SED's members. According to the principle of democratic centralism, decisions were to be made at each level with the democratic agreement of the members, after which all were obligated to follow them—but the system was far more centralized than democratic. The real decision-making authority was with the head of the party (Walter Ulbricht from 1950 to 1973 and Erich Honecker from 1973 to 1989), with significant input from the Politburo members.

The full Central Committee (ZK) was more than a rubber stamp, but not much more. Its various departments, each under the supervision of a Politburo member, were loci of real power. ZK department heads were of equal standing with government ministers, but although no minister would make a major decision without first checking with the ZK department, the converse was not always the case. The two primary departments influencing propaganda were Propaganda and Agitation, although the departments dealing with foreign information, foreign relations, bloc parties and mass organizations, women, youth, church matters, culture and education, agriculture, and sport also had influence.

The Departments of Agitation and Propaganda were generally separate, although they were merged from 1957 to 1961.[33] There were corresponding departments at the district (*Bezirk*) and county (*Kreis*) levels. Consistent with the Marxist distinction between propaganda and agitation, the Agitation Department supervised the media, speakers, and visual material. The Propaganda Department controlled party training courses and schools, the area that was predominantly Robert Ley's domain during the Third Reich. In comparison to the Nazi bureaucracies, they were economically staffed. The Propaganda Department had only thirty-three staff members in 1983.[34] Agitation had sixty-nine in 1987.[35]

The Agitation Department was the more significant of the two. It came to have eight sections by 1989. Their respective areas were agitation, visual agitation, *WAS und WIE* (the monthly periodical for agitators), a library and archive, foreign correspondents, the "B-Sector" (concerned with plans for military mobilization), press, and radio/television.[36] Its major figures were its secretaries: Horst Sindermann (1954–1963), Rudolf Singer (1963–1966), Werner Lamberz (1966–1971), Hans Modrow (1971–1973), and Heinz Geggel (1973–1989).

The department was supervised by Albert Norden from 1955 to 1967, followed by Werner Lamberz until his death in a helicopter crash in Libya in 1978 and Joachim Herrmann until 1989. One GDR media figure characterized this trio of Politburo members in these ways: "Norden wanted the media to educate entertainingly and to entertain educationally. Lamberz wanted the content to focus on the image of ourselves, the image of the enemy and the image of the world. Herrmann had only the propaganda of success in mind, and measured to the centimeter the size of Honecker's photograph in comparison to those of other Politburo members."[37] By general agreement of GDR propagandists, Lamberz was by far the most capable of the three, and many hoped he would be Honecker's successor. Some suspected that Honecker arranged for the less able Herrmann to take on the role after Lamberz died as a way of ensuring that no one as attractive could threaten his position.[38]

A final entity was the Agitation Commission, established in the 1950s. It was headed by the responsible Politburo member and included the heads of the Agitation Department, GDR television, and the government Press Office, as well as representatives from industry and agriculture. The task of the Agitation Commission was to plan long-term strategy, whereas the ZK

Departments of Propaganda and Agitation were responsible for more immediate matters. This did not always work out in practice. During Norden's
period, for example, both the Agitation Commission and the Department
of Agitation issued directives to the press.[39]

The state's propaganda role was limited. There was a government Press
Office, headed by Kurt Blecha from 1958 to 1989, but its fifty staff members had little power. It lacked authority to approve reports of even such
routine matters as the introduction of daylight saving time without first
clearing it with the relevant party offices.[40]

The Press Office did have authority over religious periodicals, including
the five Protestant weekly newspapers. The editor of the *Potsdamer Kirche*
describes the process. The church lacked its own publishing plant. On Tuesday, the proofs were read and permission to print received from the publishing house. But it was printed on Wednesday. In between, a copy went
to the Press Office: "There was a double approval. This was not officially
declared. We knew it, however. Wednesday morning between 9 and 10
A.M. a call came from the Press Office. 'Mr. Borgmann, come to the Press
Office.' I had to go there. Depending on the severity of the offense, I might
be given a good dressing down, or treated more or less politely."[41] The
church was sometimes able to win an argument and occasionally published
papers with blank spaces, but the rules were reasonably clear, and the
church generally followed them.[42]

The single official GDR news agency, the *Allgemeiner Deutscher Nachricht-
endienst* (ADN), was a state organization, as were the radio and television
systems, but in practice they were controlled by SED functionaries. This
had disadvantages. Joachim Herrmann complained in a 1988 memo to
SED economic chief Günter Mittag that although the electronic media and
ADN were directly subordinate to the SED political leadership, their location within the government apparatus put them at a funding disadvantage
against party newspapers such as *Neues Deutschland*.[43]

Summary

Nazi Germany survived twelve years, the GDR forty, which gave it significantly more time to build its system. Still, the systems turned out to have
more similarities than differences.

Both developed elaborate bureaucracies with offices at every level from
the local to the national. The leadership principle and democratic centralism had much in common. Both obligated subordinates to follow the

orders of their superiors without question, even if in theory authority was from the top down in Nazism and the bottom up in Marxism-Leninism. Either system fit comfortably into German authoritarian traditions.

The NSDAP system was the looser of the two. Nazi leaders fought to increase their personal power in the field of propaganda, as in every other area. Propaganda was a set of quasi-independent entities heading generally, though not always, in the same direction.

The SED's principle of democratic centralism provided a facade of legitimacy to decisions from the top. Having allegedly participated in making the decisions, one was bound to follow them. One GDR journalist expressed the results in this way: "It was a system designed to produce anxiety."[44] The NSDAP system produced its share of anxiety, but it was easier for a propagandist to get into trouble in the GDR than in Hitler's Germany.

The NSDAP put substantially more control in the hands of state agencies. The Propaganda Ministry and other organs had the clear say as to the content of media. The GDR had no equivalent of Goebbels's Propaganda Ministry. Party offices held the reins.

The Nazi system was more confusing than the GDR's. One generally knew where to go for an answer in the GDR, whereas the convoluted Nazi system of battling party leaders and organizations made getting answers more challenging. In both systems, however, it was clear to the public, and to all involved in the shaping of public opinion, that there was firm control over what was said and done. Every attentive citizen learned early on what could and could not be said. The authorities for what could and could not be said were sufficiently clear, and the relevant offices were sufficiently distributed to make it difficult to escape or ignore them.

4

Evangelists

Both the Nazis and the GDR developed substantial central propaganda bureaucracies that determined the general content of propaganda. These bureaucracies alone could never have maintained thorough systems of control. To do that, both systems depended on large numbers of propagandists at lower levels to carry out their activities. Participating in the system implicated larger numbers of citizens, increasing their commitment to the system (or at least making it more awkward for them to express critical attitudes) and simultaneously provided large numbers of people to make propaganda.

Propagandists were the evangelists of and for the new society. As true believers, they were to bring the message of their parties to every citizen both by word and deed. How did the propaganda systems look to them? What did a Nazi speaker or local group propaganda leader read and do? What was the work of a GDR agitator? As we shall see, at the local level these evangelists personalized the propaganda of state and party just as a parish priest might personalize the faith of a church.

Life as a Nazi Propagandist

The Nazi Party was organized hierarchically. There were forty regional districts (*Gaue*) in 1939. Each was divided into *Kreise*, or counties. *Kreise* consisted of *Ortsgruppen,* or local groups. There were 28,376 local groups in 1939.[1] Larger local groups were subdivided into cells comprised of four to eight blocks. Blocks were supposed to have forty to sixty households. Party officials at the *Gau* and *Kreis* level were salaried, those at the local group level were not (although they sometimes had well-paid government jobs). There were propaganda leaders at the *Gau, Kreis,* and local group levels. They had subordinates responsible for active propaganda (speakers and public meetings), film, culture, radio, and sometimes other areas. There were 14,000 party functionaries in propaganda offices in February 1934, but these were only the official staff.[2] Significant numbers of party members were put to work making propaganda, even if they lacked a title. For example, 25,000 people assisted with party film propaganda alone in 1936.[3]

Several hundred thousand others served as block wardens for the party and its subsidiary organizations, providing a personal link between the individual citizen and the organization.[4] They were supposed to hear the concerns of their neighbors and act as intermediaries when necessary, providing fast and unbureaucratic assistance to citizens with problems, but also to fulfill propaganda functions.

Block wardens were critical in campaigns such as the *Eintopfsonntag* collection, which was part of the Nazi Winter Relief charity.[5] Everyone in Germany (including Hitler) on the first Sunday of the month was to have a dinner of a simple stew or soup prepared in a single pot, contributing the money saved to the charity. Block wardens or others were to visit each home that day to accept contributions. The guidelines for Berlin in 1933 noted that every family was expected to participate and that functionaries would be held accountable for any family that did not contribute. At least the guidelines stated that the collectors were not to inspect the content of pots on stoves to be sure the family actually had a one-pot meal.[6]

The duties could become onerous. A 1939 report from a cell leader in Eisenach who was responsible for about 600 citizens outlined his activities for April and May. In addition to his many nonpropaganda functions, his propaganda-related duties included:

- Attending an educational evening for political leaders;
- Promoting membership in various Nazi affiliates;
- Attending a weekend county training course;
- Selling a book of Hitler's speeches;
- Selling a book of Fritz Sauckel's speeches (the *Gauleiter* for the region);
- Inviting each party member to the local group meeting;

- Delivering written invitations to each household announcing block meetings, as well as posting notices, finding rooms, and arranging for speakers and music (he would have had about six blocks under him);
- Conducting block meetings.[7]

In 1939 party officials in Münster complained that, despite explicit party policies, block wardens were the propaganda errand boys of the movement. During the first four months of the year, they were instructed to sell three booklets of Hitler speeches, an edition of *Mein Kampf*, the special edition of the *Illustrierter Beobachter* (the party's illustrated weekly) on Hitler's fiftieth birthday, and five pamphlets on topics ranging from spies to world Bolshevism. They were handed stacks of tickets for party meetings, sometimes the day before the event, to sell to their neighbors. They were expected to visit everyone in their area regularly and maintain a card file on each.[8] And they were given tasks guaranteed to make them unpopular. Late in 1941, for example, Germans were instructed to hang a small sign from their radio's tuning knob to remind them that listening to foreign stations was illegal. Block wardens were supposed to check to see that the signs were there, something that did not increase their popularity.[9]

This mass of lower-level functionaries was central to the party's effectiveness. The party was to be an example to other citizens, a source of help, advice, and encouragement. These grass-roots officials made palpable the party's claim to universal reach. Goebbels in Berlin could not personally take a citizen to task for grumbling, but a local block warden could (and was supposed to). In a curious way, this even increased the credibility of the national leaders. Citizens complained about the "little Hitlers," the minor party functionaries who kept an eye on them, who benefited from the satisfactions of power. Although these functionaries were in fact doing exactly what the system expected them to do, they were also lightning rods that diverted criticism from their superiors. "If only the Führer knew," Germans often said. At the same time, participation in the system strengthened loyalty of these minions (or at least their public support). A block warden or local group functionary could not publicly express unapproved attitudes. Their behavior over time strengthened their own attitudes as well as influenced those of their neighbors.

Party speakers were another major group of propagandists.[10] The elite were the national speakers (*Reichsredner*), who were authorized to speak anywhere in the country. They included leading party officials, the *Gauleiter*, government ministers, provincial presidents, and about sixty others according to 1936 figures.[11] By 1940 the number had risen to about

500.[12] The *Stoßtruppredner* (speakers in training) could be used during intensive campaigns on the national level. They were a step below the *Reichsredner* and could be promoted to the higher category if their performance justified it.[13] The *Gauredner* were restricted to their region, the *Kreisredner* to their county. There also were expert speakers (*Fachredner*) who spoke on particular themes (for example, agriculture or military matters). They were employed by party affiliates, such as the DAF or the Nazi agricultural organization. Altogether, about 9,800 speakers were certified at some level when the war began.[14]

The Nazis paid considerable attention to the ability of their speakers. Well into the Third Reich, only those who had been active party members before 1933 could be certified as speakers. An article in the party monthly for propagandists explained why those who had become members after 1933 were not allowed to join the speaker corps: "Even though the National Socialist worldview has become the worldview of the German people, it is built on a foundation of struggle. Only those party members who themselves experienced and contributed to that struggle can speak with the proper spirit."[15] Their faith had proved its authenticity. Even the expert speakers of party affiliates were to be party members of long-standing and were expected always to draw a political consequence in their speeches. They were expected to relate their speeches to the Nazi worldview.

The central purpose of the party organization after 1933 was propaganda. The system was capable of remarkable activity. During the first year of the war, the NSDAP claimed to have held 30,000 slide shows and about 200,000 public meetings, in addition to distributing enormous numbers of leaflets, brochures, and posters, despite the fact that many experienced propagandists were serving in the military.[16] These figures include only efforts by the Nazi Party itself. The DAF, the party women's auxiliary, and other groups carried on their own activities. Lower levels often concentrated their energies on intense propaganda campaigns over a brief time period. For example, sixty-two mass meetings were held in Breslau (the city's population was about 630,000) on a single day in March 1939.[17] Such bursts of rhetorical energy were common, rather like camp meetings during an American religious revival. As the war went on, the number of meetings diminished somewhat. According to party statistics, however, even during the period from 1 October 1943 to 30 April 1944, with 3,500 speakers serving in the military, nearly 80,000 meetings were held that attracted 19 percent of the population.[18]

An elaborate and, as usual, overlapping system provided information to propagandists at lower levels. The most widely distributed organ was *Unser Wille und Weg,* published by the *Reichspropagandaleitung.* Its monthly circulation was about 120,000 by 1940. *Unser Wille und Weg* carried a wide range of articles. Although few were in any sense theoretical, some did view propaganda in a larger framework.[19] The twelve issues for 1938 included 380 pages. Some articles provided background material on such topics as the history of the Nazi Party in Austria or reasons why Germans needed to eat more fish. Others provided advice on aspects of propaganda. For example, an article on organizing meetings noted that it was important to be sure that the room was neither over- nor underheated. There were brief book reviews of propaganda-related material.

The RPL also published the *Aufklärungs- und Redner-Informationsmaterial* (Educational and Speaker Information Material) in conjunction with the DAF, which was included with copies of *Unser Wille und Weg.* This came in loose-leaf format that could be organized in a binder by topic. The 1936 issues included 560 pages of material on themes such as housing, labor policy, agriculture, Bolshevism, and the Treaty of Versailles.[20] The material was not confidential, although only speakers were likely to subscribe.

The material provided detailed information that speakers could incorporate in speeches. For example, three pages in the July 1936 edition discussed compulsory military service around the world. Hitler had declared compulsory service in March 1935. The point of the information was to demonstrate that Germany was only following the example of the rest of the world. According to the article, the French were the first to introduce conscription in 1793. Austria had reintroduced it in March 1936, Italy in 1934. Russia introduced the draft in 1874: "The Soviet Union has continued the policy, and intends to use compulsory military service to develop a mass army on the largest scale." Most other leading nations had done the same, a policy clearly justified by the experience of World War I. England and the United States have "not yet" done so. The article ends with these remarks: "Nearly all nations have introduced universal military service, though with differing lengths of active service and reserve duty. The freedom of a people depends on the strength and the extent of its military capacity." Since Hitler had just begun an enormous public campaign to rebuild German military power, the material fit smoothly into the broader propaganda campaign. The speaker information provided common material for speakers to draw on, which was particularly useful during the frequent Nazi campaigns that ranged from a 1934 campaign against grumblers and complainers to the four national plebiscites Hitler called between 1933 and 1938.

As Reich organization director, Robert Ley published two propaganda-related magazines. *Der Schulungsbrief* was intended for all citizens and contained articles on various aspects of Nazi ideology. As the result of an energetic subscription campaign involving lower-level propagandists, its monthly circulation rose from 1.5 million at the beginning of 1937 to 4.5 million in 1939. In 1937 issues included themes such as the role of women in the Middle Ages, the Austrian army before 1914, and antiliberalism in the nineteenth century. Its goal was to provide a Nazi interpretation of German history and culture in a form understandable to a reasonably literate citizen.

Der Hoheitsträger appeared between 1937 and 1943 and was intended for party officials at the local group leader level or above. Its circulation in 1941 was 38,000.[21] Each issue was numbered, and every page was marked "confidential." Readers were ordered to keep it from the sight of unauthorized citizens. Nothing in it, however, was confidential; indeed party leaders were urged to share its contents with their subordinates, although not by citing it directly. Typical articles included advice on how to encourage families to have more children, methods of establishing contact between local groups and German emigrants, and ways to encourage block leaders to function more effectively. There were also obituaries of party leaders, criticism of improper behavior (for example, carrying a suitcase with commercial advertising on its sides while wearing a party uniform), and book reviews. Occasionally an article appeared both in *Der Hoheitsträger* and *Unser Wille und Weg.*

Besides these periodicals, propagandists received a wide range of other material. Ley's office published a mass of training material.[22] *Gau* propaganda offices published monthly newsletters.[23] Goebbels introduced a publication for party leaders called *Die Lage* in 1943. Its goal was "to provide leaders in politics, the army and the economy with the information they need to evaluate the situation and carry out their leadership responsibilities."[24] Party affiliates published their own material for propagandists. For example, the DAF established *Unsere Parole,* a periodical for its propagandists, in 1939. Regular propaganda conferences were held.[25] In short, propagandists received a variety of material to support their efforts, which in typical Nazi fashion came from sources that were not always on the best of terms with each other.

A final way of organizing and supporting local propagandists was through the Reich Circle for National Socialist Propaganda and People's Enlightenment, discussed in the preceding chapter. It had some effectiveness in organizing several dozen disparate entities with varying agendas.[26] The *Gau* Circles published monthly newsletters, generally marked "confidential," though there was nothing particularly revealing in them.

Party members were to be models to their fellow citizens. Ley's 1938 *Organizational Handbook of the NSDAP* laid out the responsibilities of party members, perhaps the twelve commandments of Nazism, stated in typical imperative form:

- The Führer is always right.
- Always maintain discipline!
- Do not waste your time in idle chatter or criticism, rather get to work and do something!
- Be proud, but not arrogant!
- The program is your dogma; it requires your absolute devotion to the movement!
- You are the representative of the party. Bear yourself and behave accordingly!
- Loyalty and selflessness are the highest duty!
- Show that you are a true socialist by being a good comrade!
- Treat your fellow citizens as you would like to be treated!
- In a battle be tough and silent!
- Courage is not shown through rudeness!
- Whatever helps the movement helps Germany, which means it helps your people![27]

Party members received steady injunctions to work harder. A 1943 newsletter to propagandists noted: "The party member who came to us voluntarily must prove himself by selfless service to the people, just as he did during the period of struggle."[28] Party members were urged to set the example, to refuse to tolerate any criticism of the party or government. Above all, they were to believe absolutely in the Nazi message. As Hadamovsky wrote in 1938: "We propagandists are used to believing firmly in what will be tomorrow as if it were already so. Only thus are we able to teach faith."[29]

Despite the legions of local evangelists and the plethora of evangelistic literature, things did not work out as well as the party wished. Citizens failed to grant the party the respect it might have earned if its officials had actually obeyed Ley's injunctions. *Der Hoheitsträger* and *Unser Wille und Weg* carried articles lamenting the shabby treatment propagandists sometimes received from other Germans.[30] Citizens quickly grew tired of attending meetings. They accepted minor shows of loyalty (for example, buying the *Schulungsbrief*) while avoiding time-consuming activities. Party propagandists were often a nuisance and sometimes a threat to their fellow citizens.

Propaganda in the Colors of the GDR

The Nazis began their rule with a large corps of experienced propagandists. The entire party had made propaganda, which Hitler deemed to be the first task of an organization. On 30 January 1933 Nazi propaganda changed from opposition to domination, but it was a flexible system that adjusted readily to the new conditions. The Nazis had the advantage of an existing system of mass media and communication, much of which was at least in general sympathy with Nazi goals.

The GDR's opening situation was different. Twelve years of National Socialism left few experienced socialist propagandists. There was no broad party organization. There was no propaganda literature. The mass media system was in ruins.

The first step was to build the party's organization. As under the Nazis, it included a tight network of party units that reached into every part of the country. The SED, too, was organized hierarchically. It came to have about 60,000 local groups, which could be either workplace or neighborhood based.[31] These reported to *Kreis* offices (264 in 1989), which were subordinate to fifteen district (*Bezirk*) offices. There were people responsible for propaganda and agitation at every level. Finding and training them were the first challenges.

The party leadership's 1950 publication titled "On Improving Party Propaganda" noted weaknesses in the party education system:

- The still inadequate Marxist-Leninist training of party members and candidates;
- The inadequate training of propagandistic and theoretical leadership;
- The often formal training at party schools, divorced from the everyday experiences of party work;
- The superficial, random selection of students.[32]

The system that developed after 1950 included party schools at the national, district, and county levels and similar institutions conducted by other organizations. By the end of the GDR, half of the propagandists conducting the *Parteilehrjahr* (the annual training course for party members) had completed one-year courses at party schools, and 80 percent had postsecondary degrees. Most of the rest had attended a party school for shorter periods.[33] In the 1980s all the professional staff members of the Propaganda Department had university degrees.[34] Such formal education became a primary means of equipping members with the right doctrine and techniques.

Securing qualified agitators was a challenging task. The SED needed more agitators than the Nazis, since it tried to place one in each workplace unit, neighborhood, or apartment building. Because the position was time-consuming and unpaid and often failed to secure the prestige from workmates that Marxist-Leninist theory held it ought to receive, many were not eager to take on the task. Finding diligent neighborhood agitators was a particular problem. In 1955 an article in *Neuer Weg* reported that 13 percent of the 350,000 neighborhood groups had held the expected monthly agitation meeting in March.[35] Only 45 percent of the apartment buildings in the Prenzlauer Berg district of Berlin had appointed agitators in 1963.[36]

Finding agitators in workplaces was easier. In 1986 the Prenzlauer Berg district reported that it had agitators in place for all of its 1,700 work collectives, which seems to have been generally true throughout the country.[37] The goal was to find agitators who had credibility with their workmates. An agitation leader at a 1976 district conference reported on the importance of recruiting good agitators: "Our goal is to choose comrades [as agitators] who have the political and professional qualifications, who have the respect of their collective, and who in general have the best abilities. . . . Once it is clear to the comrade that because of his position and knowledge he is already the collective's agitator, the one to whom colleagues come with questions or when they need advice, then we have won the agitator we need to solve our problems."[38]

But appointing agitators was not sufficient. They had to do something. A 1980 report on a department store in Leipzig, for example, found that "the chosen agitators exist more or less only on paper, since they do not receive any guidance from the party leadership and therefore are not effective with their collectives."[39]

Agitators were not always eager to attend meetings or buy the materials intended for them. In August 1961, just before the Berlin Wall was constructed, a propaganda conference in Brandenburg was criticized: "The greatest weakness of this conference was that, despite relatively good preparation, only 52 of the 192 invited propagandists came."[40] Active propagandists had many demands on their time and were not eager to add another long meeting to the week's calendar.[41] Nor did they always buy the proper books. A 1961 report noted that not enough propagandists had bought the recommended editions of Marx-Engels or Lenin.[42] Many who did buy the books failed to read them. Those who were members of the party for pragmatic reasons understandably were not eager to spend more time on party duties than necessary. Hermann von Berg, who left the GDR, summarized the situation: "I know enough professors and party officials who admit with a smile that they have never read a single line in any of Marx's books, but slid through all the examinations nonetheless. The 'Classics of Marxism-Leninism' are on the bookshelves of every functionary and in every library. They are as compulsory as the speeches of members of the Politburo (written by bureaucrats in the party machine) or Hitler's *Mein Kampf* during the Nazi regime. But they are privately rejected—though of course praised all the more in public."[43]

Keeping propagandists informed was a challenge, given the system's tight control over information. A 1957 proposal from the SED's Agitation Department stated: "As true confidants of the masses, they [party officials] must know more about all areas of politics than the average newspaper reader. But it is still the case that the party secretary gets his information in most cases from the newspapers, just as any other citizen of the republic."[44] Proposals to provide confidential information to propagandists were never implemented. Throughout the GDR's history, propagandists knew little more than their workmates who attended to the media. Publications intended for agitators had such wide circulations that they could not contain confidential information. The GDR's constant concern with bad news leaking to West Germany kept even the more restricted local propaganda material from telling agitators anything they were not already likely to know. More than that, to allow even the propagandists to know that the party leadership was not in accord as to the truth would encourage dissent. If they were not sure of what could be said, the masses would not get a consistent message.

Bureaucracy had its common effects. The various arms of the propaganda apparatus competed to demonstrate success, measured by such things as the number of meetings held and brochures distributed. As in any bureaucracy, counting was the easiest way to demonstrate success. A 1961 report, for example, found that the various organizations were more concerned about demonstrating their effectiveness to superiors by holding numerous meetings than in responding to the actual needs of the population.[45] Similarly, a 1963 report based on conversations with the editors of county newspapers reported that the people's correspondent movement (which attempted to get ordinary people writing for the press) was stagnating. Few of them actually wrote anything, but they were kept on the rolls because a high number, even if many did nothing, looked good in reports to superiors.[46]

Although the GDR never succeeded in winning the economic battle, it had won the battle of agitation organization by the 1960s. By then there were large numbers of trained propagandists and agitators. A 1976 estimate had 10–15 percent of the SED membership (then just over two million) holding appointments as agitators.[47] A 1972 report claimed the SED had well over 100,000 propagandists.[48] Most were not full-time propagandists, however. Large numbers of people also made propaganda for the Free German Youth (FDJ), the Free German Trade Union (FDGB), and other mass organizations. A reasonable estimate is that 500,000 GDR citizens had appointments as propagandists or agitators in the 1980s, an estimate supported by the circulation of the agitators' monthly, *WAS und WIE*, about 450,000 in 1980 and 530,000 in 1989.[49] A quite direct relationship between the circulation of *WAS und WIE* and the agitator corps is suggested by a 1976 report from *Kreis* Weißenfels, which claimed 664 appointed agitators and 701 subscriptions to *WAS und WIE*.[50]

A burst of material served the propagandists and agitators. In the beginning, the GDR turned to the Soviet Union, translating eleven pamphlets in a series titled "The Agitator's Library." A 1951 pamphlet in the series "The Fundamentals of Bolshevist Agitation" included fifty-eight pages of advice, for example, "Clarity, simplicity and ease of understanding are the leading characteristics of Bolshevist agitation."[51]

At the same time, an Agitation Department series titled "Questions and Answers" provided material for agitators to use in daily discussions. One edition suggested ways to handle the lost German territories to the east. To answer the question of why Germans in the region were being removed to areas to the west and north, the answer was: "The German population was expelled from the former eastern territories because they to a great degree had joined Hitler's war of conquest. The existence of German minorities in foreign states was always the occasion of National Socialist propaganda aimed at 'freeing the brothers to the east.' To end this once and for all, a radical, hard but consistent policy of removing all Germans from the eastern territories was carried out."[52]

Neuer Weg, the monthly for party officials, began publication in 1945. It often carried articles having to do with propaganda. Early issues were sometimes lively and helpful for propagandists. A 1949 issue warned propagandists against being too negative with those slow to learn:

> "My dear comrade! Your question proves that you have not yet learned enough." That was the answer a speaker in Chemnitz gave to a question that admittedly may not have been phrased in the best way.
>
> In Augustusburg (Saxony), the then head of the Flöhau party organization dispatched a somewhat dense older comrade with the remark: "One can't do anything about stupidity!"
>
> Individual cases? Not at all! Many functionaries and speakers have the habit of responding in such ways. When a comrade has worked up the courage to ask a question in a party meeting, answers like those cited above are a cold shower that often lead to a silent membership. Can that be in the interest of the party?[53]

Such articles displayed both genuine interest in reaching the masses and confidence that they could in fact be reached by competent agitation.

Neuer Weg got duller as the years went on. In 1962 an internal party report noted: "The lower-level party groups receive too little practical advice and guidance from *Neuer Weg* about the ways and means of ideological work, or on the means and methods of agitation."[54] By the 1980s it was filled with articles in "Party Chinese," of which one example should suffice:

> The decisive area of the political-ideological work of the party is and remains the unity of economic and social policy, the cornerstone of our social strategy. Theoretically, but also concretely tied to the task of every branch of industry, factory and work collective, it is necessary to explain the nature of our social strategy in a way that each worker can see how it relates to his own workplace. It must be clear to each individual that in production, and only there, can we produce what is needed in the social and cultural arenas. Therefore there is no alternative to a substantially higher level of effort through the use of the results of the scientific-technical revolution, though rationalization, through the careful use of material, through effective management.[55]

One sympathizes with average citizens who were asked to digest large amounts of such prose. It was hardly likely to inspire earnest commitment and diligent labor.

The periodical also contained specific information to be used in propaganda. A 1986 issue, for example, carried an article in the series "Answers to Current Questions" titled "State Terrorism—Why and How Is the USA Increasingly Practicing It?"[56] The article pointed out that the United States was out to dominate the world, that it was suppressing struggles for national liberation, and that it faced increasing opposition. The reader learned nothing not otherwise available in the press, but the material was at least reasonably concise.

It took time to develop methods to inform agitators on the correct approach to current affairs. The Agitation Department began publishing the twice-monthly *Notizbuch des Agitators* in 1949.[57] It usually had around seventy pages, with a mixture of theoretical and practical articles. A typical issue in July 1953 included a summary of the Central Committee's recent meeting, supporting material on Soviet food shipments, details on GDR wage and price policies and West German elections, a warning on the importance of watching out for enemy subversion, a discussion of agricultural policy, a report on an agitators' conference, and recommended reading. Nothing was confidential. However, the biweekly publication was unable to serve the large audience of agitators effectively, so the Agitation Department ceased publishing it in September 1955. The district offices were to publish their own versions, which in fact happened for several years, but by 1958 most of these had vanished as well.

The ultimate solution was a new national journal for agitators, *WAS und WIE*, which began in 1975. Each monthly issue had thirty-two pages of detailed information agitators could use. The April 1989 issue included articles on the upcoming GDR communal elections, the importance of education, the superiority of socialism to capitalism, GDR reparations to the Soviet Union, efforts to grow more vegetables, social misery in West Germany, the importance of increasing the GDR's exports, financial problems of West German cities, Latin American social conflicts, and the policies of the Bush administration. None of the articles had anything confidential—a diligent newspaper reader would have found nothing surprising—but they did provide reasonably clear arguments and helpful data. *WAS und WIE* appeared until the GDR's collapse. Unfortunately, the rigidities of the system kept it from giving direct answers to many reasonable questions. The final issue in December 1989 apologized to readers for the failures of the past, noting that it had ignored important issues and published some material that was simply false.[58]

There were also regular publications, newsletters, and pamphlets from the Agitation Commission, the district offices, the mass organizations, and so forth. The military was also active, producing a 1988 *Handbook for*

Political Work in Military Groups and Units, a 500-page guide, and *RADAR,* the monthly for military agitators.[59] The Agitation and Propaganda Departments in Berlin produced many slide shows, film strips, and taped lectures that could be used by propagandists. The total amount of such material is enormous, as anyone working through the SED archives learns.

Although the SED tried to persuade those who already enjoyed the respect of their colleagues to become agitators, the position placed people in a difficult situation. Since they knew little more than their workmates and had to explain away many problems rather than resolve them, their credibility was not always high. As one agitator said in 1961, the farmers he talked with were complaining: "You said things would get better, but we do not notice any improvement."[60] A frustrated agitator wrote to Erich Honecker in 1980, lamenting the difficulties she herself had buying daily necessities and noting the challenge it gave her in agitating with her workmates: "I ask you, how can I in my own desperate situation find the right answers to all these questions when I try to win young colleagues as candidates for the party? And how shall I raise my son, who is daily confronted with these problems?"[61] A twenty-three-page letter from an agitator in 1962 complained: "It is hardly possible to list all the problems we face in our work."[62] He gave it a good try, mentioning lack of money, lazy colleagues, and hindrances from the city. A 1982 report observed that posters often arrived late, even for recurring annual events, and that although taped material was being provided, equipment to play it was lacking and the sound quality was often miserable.[63] Party files have many similar complaints.

Agitators had hard going, particularly in the early years. For instance, one suggested way of getting a conversation started in a household was to discuss the family's problems. But hearing the problems was one thing, doing something about them another. The average household could readily provide a long list of difficulties. What was the agitator to do? As the representative of the party, he or she could either say that these problems would eventually vanish as socialism developed, not a satisfying answer to a frustrated conversational partner, or attempt to do something to resolve the problems. That meant giving up scant free time to wander from office to office with little prospect of solving large numbers of the citizenry's difficulties. In either case, household agitation was unlikely to be persuasive. As Ernst Richert noted in 1958, the party press provided few examples of exemplary household agitation, a sign that such examples were scarce.[64]

Then there was the one-way flow of information. Agitation conferences regularly noted that feedback did not function well, that information went from the top down but not from the bottom up.[65] Those at the bottom were often buried in a flood of directives and orders from their superiors. Fred Oelßner noted at a party conference in 1954: "[W]e carry on too many different campaigns at the same time, or shortly after each other, so that the poor agitators down below often do not know what they should do first."[66] Those at the bottom were expected to master not only thick volumes of party decisions and programmatic speeches by party leaders but also regular urgent instructions to do this or that. One harassed official kept count in 1961: "Between 1 January and 3 March 1961, the district and county offices received 31 decisions of the Central Committee. 15 documents with a total of 90 pages went to the counties, the other 16 (87 pages) to the district offices. The Agitation Commission [of the SED] sent 15 teletypes during January and February with a total length of 47 meters."[67] It is painful to imagine what would have happened if the GDR had survived long enough to implement E-mail.

Summary

Both National Socialism and the GDR depended on ordinary citizens to conduct propaganda. Each system faced similar problems. They had to recruit and train large numbers of propagandists, keep up their morale, and supply them with information and arguments, without revealing anything to them at all confidential or giving them real power.

Involving vast numbers of ordinary citizens in agitation not only got the work done and gave a face to the larger organization, it also implicated ordinary citizens in the system. Unless they wanted to admit hypocrisy to themselves, something most people are reluctant to do, participating in the system made them its accomplices. Participation strengthened their attitudes and forced them to put on at least an outward show of enthusiasm to their fellow citizens.

The two systems put their efforts in different directions. The NSDAP focused on reaching people in groups. The primary way the party used its members to reach the masses was through public meetings, though party members were expected to conduct face-to-face propaganda and there was a well-developed system of block wardens. Film, theater, and the media were also used. When the NSDAP wanted to reach the masses, however, it sent out speakers and depended on its multitude of propagandists to organize and promote public meetings.

The GDR depended less on public speakers. The SED did not ignore the spoken word. It held large numbers of meetings but had nothing like the elaborately organized Nazi speaker system. Instead, it depended most heavily on person-to-person and small group agitation. The goal was to have agitators in every work unit and neighborhood who could, on a one-to-one basis, reach the masses with the SED's message. The result was a more labor intensive system. The circulation of *Unser Wille und Weg* was about 120,000 monthly, and this for a population of about 80 million. *WAS und WIE*'s circulation was over four times greater for a population less than a quarter as large. The circulation densities varied by a factor of about twenty.

The disparate numbers of lower-level propagandists led to different styles of propaganda. The Nazi mass meeting was an arena of passion, of whipping up mass enthusiasm. Nazism did not avoid rational argument, but the public meeting was not an appropriate occasion for careful reasoning. The GDR's emphasis on personal agitation resulted in discussions more than orations. Agitators needed to adjust their responses to the particular person or small group to whom they were speaking. They were hindered, of course, by the necessity of following a carefully established party line that made offering convincing answers to many questions difficult.

The SED's system further demanded greater commitment from propagandists. The NSDAP had nothing like the SED's elaborate party educational system. The NSDAP's schools tended to run brief courses for propagandists, but SED propagandists took lengthier courses, either by correspondence or at party schools. Part of the difference had to do with the nature of the respective systems. Nazism doubted the virtues of the intellect in making propaganda. Faith and passion were the keys, and the *Führerprinzip* instructed subordinates to obey blindly their superiors. The SED in practice demanded an almost identical obedience, but in theory it based its demands on scientific principles, and even its leaders built elaborate theoretical justifications for their policies.

One way to compare the demands on local propagandists is to contrast the propaganda plans both systems developed. The March 1942 issue of the propaganda newsletter for *Gau* Weser-Ems included a propaganda plan for the coming weeks. It briefly outlined the major propaganda arguments to be used but noted: "What these men need to know about political events they can easily learn from the newspapers, the radio and the material provided by the RPL . . . and above all from the articles by the *Reichspropagandaleiter*.[68] It is not critical that they know every detail of the situation or of political events, rather they must display complete conviction that there is no alternative but victory for the German people, and that everything must be done for it, above all that the full efforts of each individual are required."[69] Propagandists were not expected to know anything more than their fellow citizens. Rather, their prime task was to display faith.

The SED expected considerably more than confident ignorance. Consider the 1982 propaganda plan for *Kreis* Rochlitz, a county in Saxony. It says nothing about the convictions of propagandists but instead provides pages of detailed arrangements to ensure that the masses got the message. One section deals with reaching workers:

> In cooperation with comrades from the union, discussions and conversations on the basic issues of our policies must be conducted more consistently. . . .
>
> Comrades will receive specific assignments to meet with young workers, particularly those in youth brigades, to discuss the responsibility of the working class and the role and significance of the party. The goal is to win the best as candidate members for the party.
>
> The mass political work with the working class must focus on such problems as:
>
> - The unity of socialism and peace. The securing of peace and banishing the danger of war—the most important problems for humanity.
> - The general strengthening of the GDR and socialism—the most important prerequisite for maintaining pace.
> - Raising national productivity requires increasing labor productivity, efficiency and quality as the main goal of the workers' mass initiative.
> - The close connection between the advantages of socialism and the results of the scientific-technical revolution.
> - The political strength of the working class—the foundation of revolution.
> - The growing leadership role of the SED in the further formation of the developed socialist society in the GDR.[70]

This is a quite different set of expectations. The SED's propagandists were expected to demonstrate conviction, but that conviction was to be backed by solid knowledge.

For both systems, hundreds of thousands of local propagandists worked with varying degrees of diligence to provide a link between ordinary citizens and the party or state. Their jobs were challenging and difficult, since they had considerable duties and often heard complaints about which they

could do little. Their fellow citizens also saw them, with considerable justice, as minions of the system rather than as sources of real information or
assistance. Still, they gave a human and accessible face to the systems,
which could not have functioned without them. And their public pro-
fessions of faith in their systems worked on them as well as on their
neighbors.

5

Maps of Reality

Grigory Aleksandrovich Potemkin, lover and adviser to Empress Catherine the Great, had a problem in 1787. The empress was to tour an area into which he had sunk considerable sums of her money with limited results. After careful preparation, Potemkin presented Catherine with a facade of success, though he did not build the literal Potemkin villages of legend. The empress left convinced of his abilities. He was an early propagandist. His successors, with the resources of modern media, have surpassed his achievement, persuading whole nations of things that were not so.

The media in totalitarian societies have catechetical functions. Their goal is to present people with convincing accounts of what they cannot know firsthand—the reality beyond their everyday lives. That which is presented must agree with the reigning worldview. If Jews are bad, news of Jews anywhere in the world must be bad news. If capitalism is in its dying days, it will not do to present its successes. And if the news is to serve as an organ of the truth, those who determine what is news must be those who supposedly know that truth themselves.

The news media of both National Socialism and Marxism-Leninism have been extensively studied.[1] I shall not repeat in detail what others have already done. Rather, after a survey of the both systems, I shall turn to case studies of the systems in action.

The Führer's Media

National Socialism came to power with a clear idea of the role of the mass media: they were to serve the state. As Hadamovsky wrote in 1933: "German intellectuals active in forming public opinion should not speak of freedom, rather of self-discipline and responsibility. The supreme value to which they should pay spiritual homage is not the press, but the nation that they serve with their ability and their strength."[2] This did not mean that the media should be directly under state control. In theory the Nazis favored private ownership of the media but in practice worked against it.

Their methods were clearest with regards to the press. Although the socialist and Communist publishing houses were quickly eliminated, other newspaper owners retained possession. This kept them sympathetic even as the NSDAP's own newspapers and magazines became dominant. The *Völkischer Beobachter,* the NSDAP's national daily, became the paper of record. Its circulation rose from 130,000 in 1933 to about 1 million by 1940. As the war effort forced many newspapers out of existence, the *Völkischer Beobachter's* circulation reached 1.7 million in 1944.[3] Party organizations put out a variety of newspapers. Goebbels's daily *Der Angriff* was assumed by the DAF. The SS published *Das Schwarze Korps,* a lively and often nasty weekly read outside SS circles as well. Many nonparty organs either became uneconomic or were absorbed by the Nazi press system. Max Amann, the Nazi *Reichsleiter* for the party press, controlled about two-thirds of the daily newspapers by 1939.[4] There were party magazines for boys, girls, women, teachers, doctors, and so forth.

Press ownership made little practical difference, since the NSDAP rapidly established comprehensive control over newspaper content. News agencies were centralized. All those involved in journalism by law had to be members of the Reich Chamber of the Press. Jews could not be members; a limited number could work for newspapers with exclusively Jewish readers. The Nazis avoided official press censorship through the editors' law of 4 October 1933, which made editors legally responsible for the content of their newspapers. They became de facto censors. Journalists learned that even minor errors could result in summary firing. An efficient system of self-censorship resulted. Most journalists, like most Germans, went along to get along. Hardly any journalists whom the Nazis did not force to resign (for example, Jews, Communists, and socialists) did so of their own volition.[5]

The press received guidance in full measure. Goebbels made his goals clear as he spoke to journalists on 15 March 1933, two days after he assumed office as propaganda minister: "You should obviously get your information here, but you should also get your instructions. You should know not only what is happening but also what the Government is thinking and how you can most usefully explain this to the people. We want to have a press that works with the Government, just as the Government wants to work with the press."[6] It would not be an equal partnership.

The Propaganda Ministry held a daily press conference to provide directives to leading journalists.[7] The directives ranged from trivial to crucial. Several examples:

- "There will be an international dog show in Berlin on Sunday. The dog of Miss Heß, the sister of Rudolf Heß, should not receive special attention." [26 October 1935]
- "Greta Garbo may be covered in a friendly manner." [20 November 1937]
- "With respect to the events of last night throughout the Reich [*Kristalnacht*], Baeckow explained that newspapers could add to this morning's DNB [*Deutsches Nachrichtenbüro*] report examples of individual incidents, mentioning that here and there windows were broken and synagogues burned. He requested that the stories not be played up, above all no headlines on the front page. For the moment he also requested no pictures. There should also be no general accounts covering the entire Reich. Newspapers may naturally mention that there was understandable outrage and corresponding actions by the populace in other parts of the Reich." [10 November 1938]

Frei and Schmitz estimate the total number of such directives at 80,000 to 100,000.[8] The published edition of prewar directives runs seven volumes. It is based on covertly taken notes, since it was officially forbidden to take notes during the conferences.[9]

The surviving notes sometimes reveal how journalists responded. In February 1939, for example, cabaret artist Werner Finck was punished for being too good at his art. Journalists were instructed to applaud the step. In response, they concluded that satire in any form was dangerous. Within three weeks, a loyal satirist wrote to Goebbels to complain that no one dared to publish his work. That led to still more instructions to journalists. As Hans Fritzsche, later a prominent radio commentator, told the journalists: "One would hope culture editors had more backbone."[10] But of course most journalists, who had had their spines bent for six years by then, no longer had a great deal of spine left. There was also the *Zeitschriften-Dienst,* a confidential newsletter that went to editors with examples of good and bad journalism.[11] It scolded periodicals that had carried material to which the government objected and praised those that had set a good example.

Radio news was the one area in which the Third Reich faced competition. German-language shortwave broadcasts reached Germany from a variety of sources. Prewar radio magazines even carried the schedules of international broadcasters. Although listening to foreign stations was promptly banned when the war began (by the end of the war people were being executed for the offense), it was difficult to control.[12] The British Broadcasting Corporation (BBC) estimated that by fall 1944 over ten million Germans were listening to its German-language broadcasts. This forced German radio to respond, though newscasters often could not overtly say that they were responding to the BBC.[13]

Television broadcasting began in Berlin in 1935 and in Hamburg in 1941. Sets were expensive and programming limited. The solution was to set up public viewing rooms. Berlin had ten in 1939. Broadcasting continued as late as 1943, but the beginning of the war put an end to the development of a medium the Nazis would have found valuable.[14]

The newsreel was an established institution by 1933. During the war, newsreels ran twenty to thirty minutes and were shown before the feature film. The Nazis realized the importance of the visual and put substantial effort into newsreels from the beginning. Excellent cameramen secured vivid footage, not surprising perhaps, since nearly a thousand members of the propaganda companies that reported the war were killed or injured.[15] Goebbels viewed each newsreel at least twice before approving its release, once without sound, once with.[16] Until Stalingrad, Hitler also previewed newsreels and sometimes ordered changes. The two did not always agree. In July 1941 Goebbels noted in his diary: "The Führer wants more polemical material in the script. I would rather have the pictures speak for themselves and have the script explain only what the audience would not otherwise understand. I consider this to be more effective, because then the viewer does not see the art in it."[17] By art Goebbels meant propaganda. Properly chosen pictures, he was convinced, led viewers to the proper conclusions. Trusting what it saw, the audience would less likely question images than words.

The importance of newsreels is indicated by the resources the Nazis put into them. In the 1930s smaller theaters (which paid less) got a newsreel months after it was released. During the war, 1,600 prints were made, reaching the smallest theaters within a month.[18]

World War II newsreels and photographs were powerful.[19] Internal morale reports regularly noted what newsreel footage had worked and what had not. Heinz Boberach maintains that only Hitler's speeches had greater public impact.[20] The newsreels had clear propaganda purposes. At the beginning of the war they presented Germany as an irresistible military force, later as an invincible fortress. In 1945 the message was resist to the last or face horror. A March 1945 newsreel, for example, had grisly scenes of civilians murdered by the approaching Russians.

The GDR Media

The GDR's system was simpler. Private ownership of the media was prohibited. With the exception of religious publications, all newspapers and significant magazines were published by the SED, the four bloc parties, or organizations such as the FDJ or the FDGB.[21] The SED published *Neues Deutschland*, the leading daily, with a circulation of about one million. Each of the SED *Bezirk* branches published a daily newspaper. Broadcasting was a state monopoly. Films came from DEFA, a film production company owned by the state.

As under the Nazis, the press was watched with great care. Faced initially with a shortage of trained socialist journalists, the SED moved rapidly to build a trustworthy cadre. No one became a journalist without proving political reliability. The SED organized special conferences for journalists in 1950, 1951, and 1959 to make its wishes clear. The program in journalism at Karl Marx University in Leipzig became the primary training ground for journalists. Its purpose was clear by 1967, when Emil Dusiska became its director. He was not a trained journalist but rather came from the Central Committee. One's politics was more important than one's professional background. A student recalls him telling a group that wanted to investigate the effects of the media: "You know that the party does not want that done."[22] The press was to serve the party.

Unlike the Nazi period, in which both party and state had journalistic influence, the line of authority in the GDR flowed from the SED. The Agitation Department of the Central Committee held a weekly press conference each Thursday that laid out the approach to be taken. The instructions were oral, with note-taking prohibited, but the material was important enough to encourage people to violate the rule.[23] Two examples of the press injunctions suggest their nature.

- On the boycott of the 1984 Los Angeles Olympics: "We ask you . . . to avoid any statement or commentary. Until further notice, nothing can be published without our prior approval. No individual initiatives!" [10 May 1984]
- On coverage of the thirty-fifth anniversary of the GDR in 1984: "The people must always see themselves as the builders of the state. Present this socialist state in the manner it deserves. During this period, no one may spout off about things he does not like, Marzahn [a huge housing development at the edge of Berlin] for example. The complainers had to haul coal for forty years, and now hot water flows from their taps. Complainers are people who do not have any idea that collectives and individuals have accomplished great things." [30 August 1984]

Representatives of the bloc parties were not invited to the Thursday conference but received similar directives from the state press office.[24] The Agitation Department also issued a large number of printed directives and teletypes to journalists.

Not only were journalists carefully chosen and instructed, but they also knew that mistakes could end their careers. An unfortunate newspaper in Halle reported on the KZ of the SED rather than the ZK (that is, concentration camp instead of Central Committee). After considerable investigation, the staff escaped with instructions to spell it out in the future.[25] There were numerous similar incidents.

Unlike other socialist nations, the GDR had no official censor. It did not need one. Erich Honecker claimed that a "sense of responsibility" guided GDR journalists.[26] That was nonsense. The journalist's role was made clear at one of the Thursday press conferences in 1984. Klaus Raddatz, second in command at the Agitation Committee, told the gathered journalists: "We journalists are the front-line soldiers of a party that we joined of our own free will. No one is forced to become a journalist."[27] That was clear enough. Given the choice between writing for a newspaper and working in a factory, journalists censored themselves to keep their positions and avoid unpleasantness.

Broadcasting in the GDR was a state monopoly. Radio service was reestablished promptly after the Third Reich fell. There were four national stations and a number of regional ones. Television broadcasting began officially on Stalin's birthday on 21 December 1952. It remained experimental until January 1956, when 2.2 hours were broadcast daily. The initial audience was tiny, but by 1960 the one millionth GDR television was licensed, the four millionth in 1968.[28] There was one channel until 1969, two thereafter.[29]

GDR radio and television faced challenges unique in the socialist bloc. The flow of foreign print media could be controlled, but the entire country received West German radio, and 80 percent of the population was in range of Western television. There were energetic attempts to discourage listening to West German broadcasts for years, particularly after the Wall went up in 1961. A common approach was to have groups of both parents and children pledge to avoid Western media.[30] Schoolchildren sometimes were encouraged to talk about what they watched at home as a way of gathering information to be used against parents. Groups of Free German Youth members tore down antennas pointed west, though this was of limited effectiveness since many could receive Western television with a room or attic antenna.[31] In the end the GDR gave up. Erich Honecker announced in May 1973 that people were free to watch whatever they wanted, though speaking in public about what they saw still could lead to difficulties. This led to the interesting situation that GDR media sometimes responded to Western media, assuming their audiences had seen or heard them, without being able to make clear that was what they were doing.

Television news was most carefully supervised. As the new medium advanced, the newsreel disappeared, with the advantage that, since people did not pay to watch the evening news, there was less incentive to make it lively. The plan for each evening's news broadcast went to the Agitation Department and came back with direct orders. Instructions sometimes arrived after the program had begun. As late as 6 October 1989 Honecker made last-minute changes.[32] The consequence was generally a dreary broadcast filled with long lists of names and titles. The opening stories of the *Aktuelle Kamera* broadcast for 1 February 1989 are typical:

- Seventy-eight hundred elected bodies will be reviewing their accomplishments over the period 1984–1989 in preparation for the communal elections to be held in May.
- Statistics of progress in *Kreis* Delitzsch.
- The minister president of Schleswig-Holstein visits the GDR.
- GDR teachers meet to discuss how the school year is going.
- A meeting of leaders of the SED and the Czechoslovakian Communist Party.
- A West Berlin court has prohibited a member of the Communist Party from working as a postal employee, a violation of human rights.
- Neo-Nazi groups are active in West Germany.

A further result was that the substantial majority of the GDR audience watched Western news. On average, internal reports found that 7–18 percent of the GDR audience watched the domestic newscast.[33] The ratings were secret, even for most of those involved in producing GDR programming. The ostensible reason was to keep the staff from pandering to mass tastes, but embarrassment is the likelier cause.[34]

How did the news media function in practice? One way to answer the question is to examine how the Nazi and GDR media responded to a critical situation—an anomaly between the official map of reality and reality itself. In the case of National Socialism, the case will be the Battle of Stalingrad, the point at which the war's tide turned. For the GDR, the example will be the building of the Berlin Wall in August 1961. Both events presented the media with unprecedented challenges.

Victory in Defeat

As Joseph Goebbels noted, making propaganda is easy when one is winning. The first two years of the war were favorable, with blitzkrieg victories in Poland, Scandinavia, the Low Countries, and France. Initial German uncertainty about the war gave way to national gloating. Even the campaign against the Soviet Union in June 1941 began so well that internal public opinion reports in August found that citizens were expecting the Russians to collapse. German propaganda made mistakes, but there was room for error amid success.

The winter of 1941–1942 was a shock, as ill-prepared German soldiers who expected to be in warm Moscow dwellings suffered frostbite instead. Spring and summer offensives in 1942 revived optimism, but German progress was insufficient. By October 1942 the Germans had captured 80 percent of Stalingrad, a city at least as important for its propaganda value as for its strategic position, but a Soviet counteroffensive in mid-November surrounded twenty-two German divisions with about 330,000 men. Hitler refused permission to withdraw. By the time the remaining 91,000 freezing, starving Germans surrendered on 31 January 1943, another 147,000 had died.[35] The catastrophe made it clear that Germany could lose the war.

Stalingrad was a challenge in part because it was unexpected. The war had generally gone well. News reports had been optimistic. The weekly newsreels for October and November 1942 had scenes from Stalingrad, suggesting that the city was almost entirely in German hands. The daily military communiqué published by the Supreme Command of Wehrmacht

(OKW) reported until early November that mopping up operations were in progress.[36] A mid-October article on Stalingrad in the leading weekly *Das Reich* concluded: "At Stalingrad the Soviet front is tottering. A symbol smolders in endless fields of ruins. A mighty power has received the decisive blow."[37] Hitler stopped short of claiming Stalingrad was in German hands, but speaking on 8 November to the Old Guard in Munich, he asserted: "I wanted to take it [Stalingrad] and—you know—we are modest, we really have it! There are only a few very small places left there."[38] The newsreel for 18 November also claimed that there were only a few Soviet positions left in the city. The next week's newsreel made no claim of approaching victory, but its scenes of advancing German troops left the casual viewer with the impression that German forces were still winning. The average German citizen had every reason to believe victory was near, and that is what morale reports found. In fact, the significance of Stalingrad was not at all clear to the German public. By mid-November public attention focused on the less critical North African front, where the Allies had landed on 8 November. People thought things had quieted down for the winter in Russia.[39]

Goebbels was more cautious. Trying to build support for a total war effort (and add to his own power in the process), he wanted to remind Germans that the war could be lost rather than console them with easy claims of victory, which demanded more forthright coverage. He had, however, limited control over the press. In his usual self-congratulatory style, his diary entry for 12 December 1942 noted: "The latest reports of the SD and the Reich Propaganda offices were presented to me. In both of these, as well as in the reports of the *gauleiters,* there is very sharp criticism of our news policy regarding the situation at the front. I feel absolutely not guilty of this obvious fizzle. I have always encouraged greater frankness in news."[40] Stalingrad would have been difficult to deal with even if Goebbels had gotten his way, but now German media were left with the difficult task of explaining sudden, drastic, and unexpected defeat, the opposite of what they had been predicting. And it could not be avoided. Hundreds of thousands of German soldiers could not disappear without mention, nor could newspapers simply stop publishing maps showing the German lines running through Stalingrad.

The first and easiest strategy was silence. Stalingrad almost vanished from the media. Newspapers mentioned it only in passing. The newsreels for December 1942 and January 1943 turned their attention to North Africa, U-boats, the occupation of southern France, and Nazi pageantry.

There was material from the Russian front—but it avoided Stalingrad. Viewers saw a train bringing supplies to the Leningrad front in the 2 December newsreel. The 27 January newsreel showed Russian forces being driven back in several locations. Hitler, who approved the final draft of each day's OKW communiqué, consistently removed any mention of Stalingrad.[41] The press took the cue and said little.

Silence was a signal to Germans that things were going poorly. The Nazis did not conceal victory. The SD report for 7 December observed that some people noticed the absence of Stalingrad from the OKW communiqué and concluded that the situation was serious, even that German forces there might be surrounded.[42] Letters from soldiers in Stalingrad carried the message, which quickly spread. But in early January the SD report found that people were only scanning the headlines, since they had concluded that nothing significant was likely to happen in the immediate future.[43] Even Goebbels was not fully informed. His diary entry for 5 January 1943 noted that the situation had become "somewhat worrisome," when in fact defeat was already certain. It wasn't until he visited Hitler's headquarters on 22 January that he wrote: "We apparently have to accept the bitter fact that the 22 divisions in Stalingrad are lost."[44]

Since Hitler forbade a withdrawal and the Germans lacked the strength to break the encirclement, propagandists had to explain a military disaster. Silence was impossible as a long-term strategy. Defeat was inevitable. It had to be transformed into a kind of victory. On 16 January the OKW communiqué admitted for the first time that the troops in Stalingrad were being attacked from all sides. Goebbels persuaded Hitler on 22 January to present a more accurate account of the situation. On 25 January the OKW spoke of the eternal honor German forces had won for their valiant and sacrificial struggle.[45] That clarified the situation. Within a week, the SD reported that people were beginning to wonder not how long it would take to win the war but how long Germany could hold out and still win a favorable peace.[46] The tenth anniversary of the Nazi seizure of power fell on 30 January. Goebbels and Göring gave major speeches, and Goebbels read Hitler's proclamation, but none of the three gave Stalingrad central attention. The next day, the remaining German forces in Stalingrad surrendered.

In his diary entry for 4 February, Goebbels recorded the announcement to the public: "We are forced to inform the German people of the loss of Stalingrad. It is bitter, but necessary. We broadcast the news as a special announcement in the afternoon around 4, and put it in an appropriately heroic form. I work out all the details with the Führer personally, who fully approves my proposals."[47] Goebbels also ordered that theaters and other places of entertainment be closed through the following Saturday.

The daily press directive outlined the line the press would take to announce the defeat to the public:

> The heroic battle for Stalingrad has ended. In several days of mourning the German people will honor their brave sons, men who did their duty to the last breath and to the last bullet, and as a result have broken the back of the Bolshevik assault on our eastern front. The heroic battle for Stalingrad will become the greatest of all the heroic epics in German history. The German press has one of its greatest tasks before it. In the spirit of the special OKW communiqué to be issued later today, the press must report this stirring event, which outshines every feat of heroism known to history, in such a matter that this sublime example of heroism, this ultimate, self-sacrificing dedication to Germany's final victory, will blaze forth like a sacred flame. The German nation, inspired by the eternal heroism of the men of Stalingrad, will demonstrate even more nobly than before those spiritual and material qualities which assure the nation of the victory it is now more fanatically than ever resolved to win.[48]

Since the Nazi worldview hardly allowed for a defeat by the forces of Jewish Bolshevism, the media were to turn a real defeat into a mythic victory.

The press suddenly filled with stories that followed these guidelines. Stalingrad was presented as a necessary sacrifice that held Soviet forces down while the front was strengthened elsewhere. Ignoring the fact that the surviving German soldiers, complete with a large complement of generals, had surrendered, the media first suggested that German forces had fought to the last man. This proved awkward, since the Russians were broadcasting the names of survivors in their German-language broadcasts (listening to which was illegal). One of the most effective articles on the subject of those missing appeared in *Das Reich* in mid-February. Hans Schwarz van Berk, one of Goebbels's close aides, condemned the Soviets for using captured soldiers for propaganda purposes, told Germans that all possible steps were being taken to determine an accurate casualty list, and assured them that the sacrifice of Stalingrad had been worth it.[49]

The most memorable element of the propaganda on Stalingrad was Goebbels's "Total War" speech on 18 February 1943. He had been arguing that Germany's full economic and labor resources should be put under his control in service of the war effort, which Hitler was reluctant to do for morale reasons. He organized a remarkable media event aimed both at persuading Hitler and the German public that resolute action was needed.

The scene was the Berlin Sport Palace, site of many Nazi rallies. Goebbels assembled a carefully selected audience of 14,000 that he claimed was representative of the Reich. It included leaders of the party, the military, the state, the arts, science, and culture but also wounded veterans, workers, and women. The usual flags and banners hung above the audience (for example, "A total war is the shortest war"). Radio carried the speech twice, and newspapers printed its full text. And the cameras were there. Five and a half minutes from the speech led off the newsreel for 24 February.

Early in the speech, Goebbels announced his intent to speak forthrightly: "I want to speak to all of you from the depths of my heart to the depths of yours. I believe that the entire German people has a passionate interest in what I have to say tonight. I will therefore speak seriously and openly, as the hour demands. The German people, raised, educated and disciplined by National Socialism, can bear the truth. They know the gravity of the situation, and their leadership can therefore demand the necessary hard measures, yes even the hardest measures."[50] He was seeking to reestablish credibility and whip up enthusiasm for transforming the economy to a war footing.

The speech culminated in Goebbels's famed ten questions on total war. The faithful crowd answered with passion as Goebbels wished, and the resulting newsreel footage was spectacular, but it was also perhaps too transparent. As the SD report noted: "The last part of the speech had mixed responses. The power of the 10 questions was generally admitted, but citizens and party members from all circles observed that the propaganda purpose of these questions and the answers of the hearers and readers were all too obvious."[51]

It is rarely comfortable to recall defeats; once the German public had the time to adjust to Stalingrad, the battle almost vanished from the media. Hitler made no direct reference to it in his speech of 21 March, Heroes Memorial Day, when one would think a reference to "the greatest of all the heroic epics in German history" would have been in order. Goebbels began a major speech on 5 June 1943 with the sentence "The winter crisis is over." The speech did not name Stalingrad. Rather, it focused on the evils of Bolshevism and the Jews, the need for total war, and the prospects of submarine warfare.[52] As the war went on and German forces retreated growing distances, the argument that Stalingrad had bought time to strengthen German lines lost its effectiveness. The memory of Stalingrad became inconvenient, and the inconvenient did not need to be recalled.

The Anti-Fascist Protective Wall

The Berlin Wall was built of necessity. Nearly 2,700,000 East Germans left between 1945 and 1961. In 1960, 199,180 left, followed by 155,402 in 1961 up to the day the Wall was begun on 13 August. Half of those who left were under twenty-five years of age. This was a disaster both from the economic and propaganda standpoints. It is difficult to run a planned economy when one is unsure of what the workforce will be, but it also was awkward to explain why the "Better Germany" was hemorrhaging citizens, including the young trained citizens it could least afford to lose.

The system was not producing, and citizens were bitter. Shops lacked even essential goods, and there was little prospect of improvement. As a typical late May 1961 party report on morale from the Dresden area stated: "One cannot speak of an optimistic mood at all. The mood is depressed—pessimistic. The primary cause is that the population cannot understand why most basic of life's needs are unavailable. The attitudes range from disbelief, incomprehension and dissatisfaction to irony, hostile statements and even a few instances of strike threats. Even factually correct arguments are no longer believed. . . . The members of our party are confused. The comrades can find no way to persuasively explain the major shortages."[53] Party morale was low. A report at the end of July found that 24 percent of party units had failed to hold the obligatory monthly membership meeting in June.[54] Members did not know what to do or say. Their everyday experiences were in too great a conflict with what their worldview promised.

In the weeks leading up to the construction of the Wall, the media were focused on a coordinated campaign to persuade GDR citizens that West Germany was attempting to lure them west by nefarious means. Typical headlines from *Neues Deutschland* suggest the propaganda line:

- Workers Chase GDR Enemies: Fascist Elements Driven across the Border [5 August]
- Border-Crossers Produce War Material (a GDR citizen who worked in the West is tried for his activities) [5 August]
- Arrest Warrant for Baby Kidnapper (from the West) [11 August]
- Workers Demands to the GDR Volkskammer: Take Effective Measures to Protect the Population [11 August]

The rest of the press mirrored the line.

The SED Agitation Department for the Halle area outlined arguments to be used by agitators at the end of July. It claimed that many had been lured

from East Germany by the same capitalists who used Jews and SS prisoners as slave labor in their factories during World War II. Their wretched victims faced a dreadful fate:

> Those traitors to their socialist homeland who were crazy enough to believe
> that life would be a bed of roses in the Bonn military state are now the vic-
> tims of recruiters for the Foreign Legion and the pimps. That is proven by
> the fact that a large number of the youth who have left the GDR, thereby
> betraying it, have found themselves in the Foreign Legion, there to bleed for
> the interests of the French and West German monopolists in Algeria. Other
> youth are forced into the Bonn North Atlantic Treaty Organization (NATO)
> army, where they are trained to shoot at their parents, brothers and sisters
> in the GDR.
>
> Many young girls who had solid job training on which to base their fu-
> tures in the GDR fell victims to terrible slave traders after they had betrayed
> their homeland.
>
> Now they inhabit West German brothels, wasting their lives to amuse
> and satisfy the Ami [American] occupiers, or they must expose their bodies
> to the greedy gaze of overstuffed capitalists and playboys. That is the much-
> praised "Free World," which uses gangster methods to mislead people or
> forces them with criminal means to betray their homeland and fall into mis-
> ery. Many have already regretted their foolish actions and returned from the
> Western world, healed but shameful. Others cannot make the decision, and
> sink deeper and deeper into the swamp of the Western world.[55]

A great deal of such material was published, broadcast, or spread by
agitators.

The GDR leadership realized that something had to be done, but the
convoluted legal status of Berlin made independent action impossible.
Even though the GDR had proposed building a wall as early as 1952 (a
proposal vetoed by the Soviets), Walter Ulbricht answered a question at an
international press conference on 15 June 1961 by asserting that no one
had the intention of building a wall around Berlin.[56] He was lying, since he
had proposed closing the border at a Warsaw Pact meeting in March 1961,
but his proposal was at first declined. He won approval five months later at
a meeting of Communist Party leaders in Moscow on 5 August.

The building of the Wall in 1961 and its collapse in 1989 caught everyone by surprise. Once it was there, it had to be justified. The obvious conclusion was that the GDR was not sufficiently attractive to hold its citizens.
Such a conclusion was unacceptable. The GDR media began a coordinated
campaign to persuade the citizenry that the Wall was a great victory.

Neues Deutschland set the tone on 14 August 1961. Order and clarity now prevailed. Children were protected from kidnappers, families from those trying to lure their members away, factories from headhunters from the West. The enemy was caught by surprise, the citizens of the GDR were delighted. Numerous statements from GDR citizens claimed satisfaction that the GDR was finally secure.[57]

The media tailored the message for various audiences. *Junge Generation,* aimed at FDJ leaders, wrote: "A major blow has been struck. 13 August 1961 will go down in history as an historic date in the history of the German labor movement. Our victory on 13 August 1961 clearly demonstrated the superiority of socialism in Germany and the world to every young person. The self-inflated Brandt and his oppressive front line city thugs got a painful blow to their dirty paws from the fists and weapons of the workers."[58]

The *Trommel,* a magazine for children, carried a picture of happy boys and girls watching tanks in its first issue after the Wall. The accompanying article stated: "On 13 August they left their workbench and drafting table to stand guard for peace along the Western sector of Berlin. These young soldiers, sons of workers and farmers, came to Berlin with their tanks to show the warmongers and troublemakers the iron fist of our peace-loving state. The den of spies in West Berlin is sealed off, without a shot being fired. We thank you, comrades, for this deed. You have won a great victory."

Frau von Heute, a women's magazine, quoted a physician: "I think our government's actions are wonderful. The provocations from West Berlin have stopped, and life is normal again. Our doctors and nurses are optimistic and happy that our state has finally put an end to the trade in human beings and the kidnapping of children. Attempts to lure away the doctors and nurses that we desperately need have stopped. Life has become easier, particularly for us women. . . . The actions of our government are a contribution to peace."[59]

Eulenspiegel, the weekly humor and satire publication, took a biting tone. The first issue after the Wall carried an article titled: "A Very Open Word to One Standing Next to His Packed Suitcase." The advice was simple: unpack. The "freedom" of the West was a chimera.

That freedom was the freedom to call Anita the call-girl on the table telephone at the Palais de Paris dance hall on Augsburg Street when she had finished her "erotic shadow play." That freedom was your ability to make a little something as a currency crook at the money changers. That freedom was the ability to read trashy newspapers with miserable content and the

horoscope that could not tell you that 13 August was coming. You were surprised like a stupid ox. That freedom was the wild west movies, where you
lost bit by bit the last vestiges of humanity. That freedom was the pitiable
freedom of being a swine among swine.

Now you have to stop being a swine and become once again a decent
human being. You will have to earn your money honestly and spend it rationally. Is that really so bad?

Well, unpack that suitcase. You are needed here and have the freedom
that makes it worthwhile to live and work, because through it we all live
and prosper.[60]

Every major newspaper or magazine, in a way appropriate to its audience,
presented the Wall as a step to safeguard peace that was welcomed by the
vast majority of the population. Named "The Anti-Fascist Protective Wall,"
it was portrayed as a victory, not a defeat.

Stalingrad faded relatively quickly from the German media, but the Wall
was a looming presence that could not be ignored. Throughout the remaining history of the GDR, the media presented the Wall as a major ac-
complishment. On its first anniversary, somewhat overshadowed by a
Soviet space flight, *Neues Deutschland* wrote: "A year later, we can conclude:
The protective wall we built against the aggressors has proved secure and
preserved peace. . . . Our state is stable, strong, unassailable, and the Revi-
sionists in Bonn will not find even among their NATO partners anyone
willing to support them in desperate actions."[61] The same basic line was
followed until 1989, when Erich Honecker made his famous statement that
the Wall might still be there in fifty or a hundred years.

Summary

What Michael Balfour wrote of the Nazi press is equally true of the GDR
press and of the media of both systems in general: "[T]he Party obtained
the worst of both worlds. They did not get the press they wanted and they
did not like the press they got."[62] Goebbels noted in 1943: "Any decent
journalist with any feeling of honor in his bones simply cannot stand for
the way he is handled by the press department of the Reich government.
Journalists are sat on as though they were still in grade school. Naturally
this will have very serious consequences for the future of journalism. Any
man who still has a residue of honor will be very careful not to become a
journalist."[63] Joachim Herrmann, the SED's Politburo member in charge of
the press after 1978, told subordinates in 1987: "We have to get rid of the

uniformity of the media. It should not look as if everything is centrally controlled. Or at least no one should be able to notice."[64] It is difficult for citizens not to notice a uniform news system. After 1989, a GDR journalist described the resulting rather low self-image of the profession: "We had no status either with the population or in the party apparatus. . . . We were seen by the entire party apparatus as ink lackeys, as people to whom one gave orders. We were not taken seriously. People said we were the court fools of the nation."[65]

Despite regular complaints even within the systems, nothing could be done about the situation. Since both systems began with the presumption that the leadership had truth and since both feared that their truths stood on uncertain foundations, journalists could not be allowed to carry out many of their customary functions. They were restricted to finding creative ways to say what they were told to say.

Both systems established remarkably similar media systems. There were differences in outward structure. The Nazi media were supervised primarily by the state, the GDR media by the party. The Nazi system was more convoluted than the SED's. The ideologies underlying the systems claimed vastly different goals, but the results were largely similar.

Both systems made explicit demands on journalists to support the state's worldview under all circumstances. To guarantee adherence to the respective party line, they established daily conferences for leading journalists. They then prohibited taking written notes at them, displaying a peculiar obsession to conceal the means of control in a way that made the journalist's job harder than it already was. In both systems, the importance of what was said led some journalists to violate the injunction and take notes.

Journalists quickly learned that even a minor failing could result in difficulty, even the loss of their jobs. They did not have to be told this daily by the state. Journalists' memoirs from both eras make it clear that stories that might have been publishable were held back on the advice of colleagues who gently reminded them of the risk. The similarities to the past were obvious to the GDR's journalists, who called Heinz Geggel, the SED Agitation Department official in charge of the press, "Dr. Geggels" (an unmistakable comparison to Goebbels) behind his back.

Both systems worked hard to establish a new journalistic ethos. The very word "journalist" was suspect. A 1938 article in the SS weekly spoke of "the type we fought and also defeated, the scribbler of a past era who called himself a journalist." There followed an unflattering portrait: "The journalist is a creature for sale. One can throw him out the front door only to have him creep back in through the back door. The journalist is the scum who says one thing today and other tomorrow. He depends on sensation and indiscretion, swindle, lies, lack of conscience and hollow phrases."[66] The preferred Nazi term for a journalist was *Schriftleiter,* suggesting that a newspaper reporter was leading public opinion from a National Socialist perspective rather than pretending to write from an objective stance. The GDR kept the term "journalist" but with qualifications. In 1969 Harry Tisch, head of the GDR labor organization, complained in a letter of a newspaper reporter who thought he had some independence: "Comrade Fötsch believes that he can go beyond his duty as a factory newspaper editor to act as what you might call an 'independent journalist' who is not obliged to his party secretary or the county leadership. He thinks himself to be a 'journalist,' not a party worker."[67] The journalist in both systems was to be a conscious agent of the ruling ideology—an evangelist.

The dangers of error made official press censorship unnecessary. Neither the Nazis nor the GDR had press censors (though during World War II the military censored reports). They did not need them. The complex system of press directives, careful selection of journalists, party involvement, and the threat of sanctions provided multiple ways to keep the media in line. The vast majority of journalists in both systems made the understandable decision to go along to get along.

One might think that the result was an entirely unbelievable press. It is true that there is abundant evidence that the citizens of both systems failed to trust the press. SD reports regularly note public suspicion of the media. The GDR population attended to West German electronic media. Yet the news media still had considerable persuasive power. Newspaper readership was high under the Nazis. When at the very end of the Third Reich paper shortages forced a decrease in newspaper size, someone proposed publishing newspapers every other day. Realizing the desperate need for information and the danger of rumors, the suggestion was rejected, and newspapers were published daily to the very end.[68] In the GDR, despite the remarkable dullness of much newspaper content, circulations were high. By 1989 there were thirty-nine daily newspapers with a total circulation of nine million. Given a population of under seventeen million, the average household received two newspapers. People still needed information and confirmation of what they believed (however faintly).

Jacques Ellul makes the interesting claim that modern propaganda exists under conditions that render the educated more susceptible to its claims than the uneducated. The educated expect to be informed on events but cannot secure that information directly. They rely of necessity on secondhand opinion, what they receive from the media. The mass of such material is so great that even those who claim to be critical readers have little option but to accept most of what they read. They may be suspicious, but it is difficult to confirm their suspicions.[69] Few are able to doubt everything. Citizens of both systems faced a comprehensive media system that was difficult to disagree with. There was either no competing information in the case of National Socialist Germany or limited information in the case of the GDR (electronic media from West Germany). It simply was not feasible for citizens to analyze in detail the flood of information they received.

The news media of both systems played a critical role in maintaining stability. They presented outlooks on the world that people did not wholly believe, but their inescapable ubiquity, their totality, nonetheless guided people's attention and attitudes. The maps of reality they provided were deficient, but a poor map was better than no map at all. At least newspaper readers had some information, some way to make sense of the world.

6

Arts and Entertainment

People may attend to the news, no matter how influenced it is by propaganda, from an understandable desire to make sense of the world around them. The popular arts are different. Their popularity is influenced by matters of taste, style, and personal preference. Moreover, there are other options for leisure than popular arts. The Third Reich and the GDR learned that heavy propaganda made unpopular radio, film, television, and literature. Both systems therefore sought to use the arts in ways that served propaganda without alienating the audience.

Hitler's Arts

"No people lives longer than the evidence of its culture," Hitler proclaimed at the 1935 Nuremberg rally.[1] Whether in the fine arts or architecture, film or radio, literature or music, the Nazis had ideas, if not always clear ones, on what art should be.[2] As the *Völkischer Beobachter* wrote in 1935: "The only possible criterion of judgment for a work of art in a National Socialist State is the National Socialist conception of culture. Only the party and the state have the right to define standards in accord with the National Socialist conception of culture."[3]

It proved harder to define good art than good news. The Nazis tried hard enough. They established literary and artistic prizes. They maintained a list of party-approved literature. They held major exhibitions of both approved and proscribed art (the latter exhibitions drawing more than the former).

The remarkable 1937 "Exhibit of Degenerate Art" in Munich made clear Nazism's approach. The exhibit presented the works of artists like Marc Chagall, Otto Dix, George Grosz, Ernst Kirchner, Paul Klee, Oskar Koko-schka, and Emil Nolde in an unattractive, crowded, and chaotic setting. The message of the exhibition was that Nazism had saved Germany from Jewish Bolshevist art that glorified perversion and ugliness rather than de-cency and beauty.[4] Then as now, many Germans found much modern art unattractive or incomprehensible. There had been popular attacks on mod-ern art even before Hitler's takeover in 1933, so Nazism was able to present itself as the defender of traditional German culture.

To reinforce that claim, the party publishing house put out an elegant magazine, *Die Kunst im Dritten Reich* (after September 1939, *Die Kunst im Deutschen Reich*). It had two editions. Edition A focused on painting and sculpture. Edition B included everything in Edition A, but added material on architecture.[5] Nazi leaders, notably Hitler, Goebbels, and Rosenberg, made regular statements on art. Hitler presented himself as an almost re-luctant politician who would have preferred a career as an artist.

Architecture was Hitler's favorite pastime. He had strong opinions and a mind for detail. Even during the war, nothing could relax him better than discussing building plans with Albert Speer, his favorite architect. His pas-sion was more than personal. Hitler knew the persuasive power of stone. In *Mein Kampf* he wrote: "[O]ur big cities of today possess no monuments dominating the city picture, which might somehow be regarded as the symbols of the whole epoch. This was true in the cities of antiquity, since nearly every one possessed a special monument in which it took pride. The characteristic aspect of the ancient city did not lie in private buildings, but in the community monuments which seemed made, not for the moment but for eternity."[6] The great buildings of antiquity were of a religious na-ture, buildings for eternity rather than the moment, exactly the point Hitler makes.

Albert Speer discusses Hitler's desire to build buildings that would impress future generations, which Speer encouraged by proposing a "ruin value" ap-proach to architecture in 1934. Speer made drawings of how Nazi buildings might look after the Thousand Year Reich had faded. Hitler's entourage was disconcerted, but Hitler found the idea pleasing.[7] The Nuremberg rally grounds, the new Reich Chancellery in Berlin, and dozens of other buildings were intended to testify to the greatness of the Third Reich for generations. Hanns Johst, a leading Nazi writer, made an explicitly religious comparison: "The buildings of the Third Reich are the catechism of this secular faith put in stone and steel, concrete and iron!"[8] He made a similar religious comparison in his eulogy for Fritz Todt, the man responsible for building the autobahn system: "I call Fritz Todt the Martin Luther of our highways. He nailed the thesis of highways to the gates of the Reich."[9]

Hitler was not interested in architecture (or any other art) for its own sake. He wanted to transform major German cities just as he was transforming other aspects of life. He planned a new Berlin with vast avenues, huge domes, and great spaces. People would come to his Berlin as pilgrims came to Rome, awed and dwarfed by a city that was the seat of empire. His buildings were the secular temples of a secular Reich.

Literature was the least favorite Nazi art. Hitler read widely but preferred Karl May (a popular writer of adventure stories, many set in the American West) to Goethe. The Nazis developed their usual complicated and conflicting set of offices that dealt with literature (for example, in the women's organization, the racial policy office, and the Hitler Youth), and the control was tight. After some prominent authors had left the country, the rest more or less wrote what would keep them out of trouble.[10] There were a variety of novels with strong propaganda content that managed to tell a good enough story to be popular. An example is the 1934 novel *Parteigenosse Schmiedecke,* the story of a man who lost his job before 1933 for being a party member. After 1933, he regains his job but loses it again because his upright National Socialist behavior brings him in conflict with those who have not yet accepted the new order. In the end, his comrades, both wavering and steadfast, come to his aid, and he again regains his job.[11] There were a good number of similar novels. Few sold well.

Theater used the spoken word, which the Nazis preferred to the written. To demonstrate their enthusiasm for culture, considerable resources went into theater. The NSDAP's own contribution to theatrical history, the *Thingspiel,* involved large speaking choruses performing in outdoor theaters filled with mysticism and talk of what bliss it was to burn to death for Germany in World War I. Understandably, these proved less popular than hoped, and they died out as the 1930s went on. The Nazis promoted other propaganda plays that were not vastly popular, but theater directors knew they had better include one in the playbill for the year. As the president of the Theater Chamber wrote in 1939: "Theater is a weapon of spiritual struggle. It is ready for combat at the front lines of the intellectual battle."[12] The majority of theatrical efforts went into often excellent productions of the classics.

Hadamovsky outlined Nazi plans for the radio in his 1934 book titled *Our Radio*. The purpose of radio, he wrote, was to be political. That was best accomplished not by overwhelming the audience with political speeches and sermonizing, rather radio should have a political undertone in all it broadcast.[13] Goebbels made the Nazi goal equally clear in a March 1933 speech to what must have been an uncomfortable audience of radio professionals: "The radio belongs to us, no one else! We will put the radio in our service; no other idea will have a chance to speak. If we do allow another idea to be heard, it will only be to show how it differs from us."[14]

After initial Nazi policy provided radio with too much political content, the focus shifted more to entertainment and information, though political considerations were never ignored. As a Nazi writer noted in 1941: "The National Socialist state viewed radio from [the] beginning as a means of leadership that should serve the state and the National Socialist worldview."[15] The question was not whether the radio was to be guided by propaganda but how that could be done most effectively.

Film was handled differently than the press or radio, in part, perhaps, because there was more at stake.[16] A journalist who made a slip could be fired with at most some embarrassment, but a faulty film involved a large investment. Although film companies remained privately owned, a complicated system of controls ensured that film stayed within clear limits. The Reich dramaturge was housed in the Propaganda Ministry.[17] Scenarios for all films needed his advance approval. In 1936 film censors were added in the Reich Chamber of Film. They approved films before release. Government financing and awards influenced the directions the industry went. Goebbels himself had a particular interest in film and kept careful watch. His diaries have numerous comments on film. In August 1937, for instance, he noted: "A mass of film questions, with new ones every day."[18] His interest in film nearly cost him both his position and his marriage, as it led to an affair with Czech actress Lida Baarova. Hitler finally ordered him to break off the relationship and return to his wife. Goebbels reluctantly obeyed.

There was an initial burst of propaganda films. *Hitlerjunge Quex*, for example, dealt with a boy who dies in Hitler's service during the *Kampfzeit*, the period before the Nazi seizure of power. *Hans Westmar*, a completely mediocre film, glorified the SA. Both appeared in 1933. Propaganda films turned out not to be box office hits. People bought a daily newspaper, even with heavy propaganda content, to get what news they could, but they avoided films that provided more propaganda than entertainment. As a result, most films during the Nazi era had relatively limited political content. The goal was to entertain in a way that subtly reinforced (or at least did not undermine) the propaganda line. There were exceptions, films like the anti-Semitic trio *Der ewige Jude, Jud Süß,* and *Der Rothschilds* of the early war years or *Kolberg,* the last Nazi film, which presented the message that if only one held out long enough a miracle would happen. But as Rentschler notes: "Nazi features are anything but universally proscribed or detested; they are still shown today in many places. Most of the era's films exist and—with a precious few exceptions—remain in circulation."[19] Their very "innocuousness" contributed to their propaganda value. By presenting an optimistic, cheerful attitude toward life, they reinforced in subtle ways the basic themes of Nazi propaganda.[20]

There were a considerable number of short propaganda films, usually produced by the party. These had stronger political content. The *Reichspropagandaleitung* alone made 140 such films in 1935. *Gau* offices released others. The RPL's film section developed motorized units able to bring film shows to villages and towns that lacked a movie theater.[21] In the early years of the war, the system had 900 vehicles that provided 50,000 film showings monthly.

Although the film industry often was not overly sympathetic to Nazism, as in other areas of the media, most went along (although the number of prominent personalities who fled Germany was higher in film than in other media). Given a choice between a concentration camp, which Goebbels did not hesitate to threaten, and wealth and acclaim, most held their tongues in public and limited their opposition to matters that did not outrage the system.

An interesting sidelight to Nazi cultural policy is artistic criticism. The problem was that the restrictions Nazism placed on art often led to mediocre, if professionally done, paintings, books, movies, and plays. It would not do to have that said too often, as it would contradict the propaganda line that art was flourishing under National Socialism as never before. Goebbels had a running battle with the critics, finally attempting to ban criticism altogether. Criticism, he decided, was a "Jewish" phenomenon. "The critic is to be superseded by the art editor. The reporting of art should not be concerned with values, but should confine itself to description." The public would supposedly make up its own mind.[22] When the lack of artistic criticism in newspapers led to criticism, Goebbels announced a ban on criticizing newspapers. As he instructed party offices: "Since I have prohibited the press from criticism, I must also ban criticism of the press. . . . From now on, any public criticism of the press is prohibited."[23] This policy proved beyond his powers to enforce, but the attempt showed how dangerous he believed criticism could be to the Nazi cause.

Socialist Art

The SED also had a great interest in art. Politburo member Kurt Hager oversaw cultural policy from 1963 to 1989. Other party leaders, the Central Committee, and party congresses made regular and long statements on what culture ought to be. These expectations changed over the years as the SED tried approaches that had limited success.

As with Hitler, architecture was a favorite pastime of the GDR's leaders, though they went in different directions. There was some interest in building to impress. Walter Ulbricht spoke in 1951 of "buildings for the centuries."[24] In 1969 he encouraged his subordinates to think big in the reconstruction of Berlin: "The most important thing for the council is to concentrate its energies on the city center. A few years ago, there were tendencies to split the energies. One cannot build a capital city that way. It is very important to concentrate all one's resources for a capital city." At the same meeting, Paul Vernier said: "The monumental art of our time should show the greatness and the accomplishments of the socialist order and its people."[25]

Disproportionate resources were put into Berlin in an effort to make it a showplace. Unfortunately, leaving the center of Berlin even in 1989 quickly brought one to buildings untouched since 1945. This was even more true of cities such as Leipzig or Dresden. Like Hitler, the GDR's leaders wanted a capital city that would impress visitors but lacked the resources to carry out their dreams.

Propaganda also influenced the choice of past buildings to be restored or eliminated. For example, the damaged Prussian Royal Palace in Berlin was torn down in 1950 and was eventually replaced by the Palace of the Republic, which became an East Berlin showpiece of socialist architecture, the meeting place of the GDR's parliament, and the scene of major government receptions. It was an intentional removal of a symbol of the past. The University Church in Leipzig was torn down in 1968 in the face of considerable domestic opposition. "The thing has to go," Ulbricht said, even though it was one of the few major buildings in Leipzig's central city that had survived the war in relatively good condition. The Frauenkirche in Dresden was left in ruins as a war memorial. The Semper Opera in Dresden, on the other hand, was elegantly restored, reopening in 1985. As the "Better Germany," the GDR could dispense with old churches and palaces, but not opera houses.

Under Honecker, the major architectural efforts went into attempting to meet his goal of solving the substantial housing shortage by 1990. The result was enormous housing developments like Marzahn in Berlin or Halle-Neustadt. These were often poorly constructed and aesthetically monotonous, but they included central heating (no small matter to those who formerly hauled brown coal up five flights of stairs) and bathrooms (many prewar buildings had shared hallway toilets). Progress in housing was also a steady element of propaganda, which presented it as proof of socialism's ability to meet human needs. Big new apartment buildings were more visible proof of socialism's progress than were restored buildings from Germany's capitalist past. As a result, many once solid apartment buildings decayed through lack of maintenance, often rotting from the top down as roofs began to leak (there was a perennial shortage of roofing tiles in the GDR).

Literature was the queen of the arts in the GDR. The country prided itself on its self-awarded name *Leseland DDR,* or "The GDR: Land of Readers." The GDR produced about 6,000 books a year, 1,200 of which were nonfiction. A careful system of reviewers ensured that few works that were too controversial appeared while eliminating the need for official censorship.[26]

Unlike the Third Reich, which gave no particular benefits to most writers, the GDR's writers were pampered. They were assured of prestige and benefits. The system encouraged writing at every level. In April 1959, for example, the "Bitterfeld Way" was proclaimed. A gathering of writers, directed from behind the scenes by the party, proclaimed that writers should go into the factories and building sites to write literature that would celebrate the glories of labor. Workers themselves were to create works of art.[27] As Ulbricht said at the time: "Artistic representation must always proceed from ideology."[28] The Bitterfeld Way did not prove notably successful and was retired a few years later.[29] The Johannes R. Becher Literature Institute in Leipzig, founded in 1955, admitted twenty residential students annually and also offered correspondence courses to train future writers. It survived to the end of the GDR and produced a number of successful writers, though none of first rank.

A significant number of leading authors left for the West, but those who remained functioned almost as the real journalists of the GDR. Writers like Christa Wolf and Christoph Hein wrote novels that addressed some of the difficulties of life in the GDR in ways that could not have been done in newspapers. There were clear limits, and authors usually had to accept significant revisions to retain some critical content. Klaus Höpke, the SED functionary responsible for literature, explained his rules: "Well, fleeing the Republic was very touchy. The rule of thumb was that it could be indicated, but it was not allowed to be presented as the norm, even though in real life every East German knew someone who had done it. Then there were certain planks of social policy which were untouchable. You couldn't say that many pensioners lived badly here, or that lots of hospitals were outdated. And you couldn't really touch the army, the state security, or relations with the Soviet Union."[30] Or quite a number of other things. Katja Lange-Müller's criticism of Christa Wolf's novels is not entirely fair but has an element of truth that applies to GDR literature in general: "an attempt to express seven unimportant truths in order to leave an important lie covered up."[31]

The system carefully monitored television programs. The GDR produced a range of interesting and popular television programming, some of which found an audience in West Germany. But there were also examples of heavy propaganda, which generally drew limited audiences. The most visible program with heavy propaganda content was Karl Eduard von Schnitzler's *Der Schwarze Kanal,* the 1,519 episodes of which provided commentary to footage taken from West German television.[32] Programs on areas of general interest often had a tangled path before being broadcast. For example, a 1985 program on technology required the approval of ten bureaucrats, ending with Günter Mittag, the SED's economics expert.[33]

The GDR found, like the Nazis, that films with heavy propaganda content rarely were box office successes. DEFA produced a wide range of films for television and the screen.[34] Television fell under the purview of the Agitation Department, film under the Culture Department, which in practice provided more flexibility, but even so the best directors encountered problems in dealing with matters from an angle not wholly congenial to those responsible for film. The fall of the GDR in 1989 resulted in the long-delayed release of a number of interesting banned films, such as Kurt Maetzig's *The Rabbit Is Me* and Frank Beyer's *Trace of Stones.*

As was true of the Nazis, party restrictions on the arts led to criticism. Since the arts were only meeting clear expectations, the GDR also found itself in the situation of discouraging criticism to a certain degree, though there was nothing similar to Goebbels's efforts to ban the practice entirely. Still, Kurt Hager's discussion of criticism in 1981 is representative. He said there were two kinds of criticism: constructive and destructive. Constructive criticism was allegedly welcome. However, criticism directed against the foundations of socialism was unwelcome: "It always finds a hair in the soup, complains about everything, and therefore contributes to throwing socialism's splendid constructive work in contempt along with the party that is the motor of this socialist state of workers and farmers."[35] The point was that criticism could be directed only at presumed deviations from the socialist order and needed to reinforce the overall system.

Awkward Art: Humor and Satire

Humor and satire are particularly awkward areas for totalitarian cultural policy. On the one hand, humor is part of human life; on the other, it has a nasty tendency to be directed at those in authority. Humor can be, and satire usually is, a form of criticism. The Nazis certainly did not want to appear humorless, but neither did they want to be its target. The dilemma is shown in two entries in Goebbels's diaries in 1940. On 7 December 1940 he wrote: "*Simplicissimus* [a weekly humor periodical] is being checked and censored by too many different authorities. I put a stop to it. One must have room to maneuver in order to make jokes." Two days later, however, he noted: "Put the manager of the Vienna *Werkl*, a local cabaret, in his place. This establishment pleases itself with sly subversion and typically Viennese griping. I make the gentleman aware of the dangers of his activities in no uncertain terms. He will be more careful from now on."[36] I shall consider two examples of totalitarian humor: the cabaret and humor magazines.

Come to the Cabaret

The political cabaret had a prominent role in Germany before 1933. The wit was biting and vivid, with little sacred. The Nazi takeover changed things quickly. Many artists were Jewish, leftist, or both, and left the profession or the country.[37] Goebbels hoped that the urge for self-preservation would keep the remaining performers in line, but that did not turn out to be the case. The more subtle performers became, the more effective their lines could be. The classic example is Berlin's Werner Finck, who after his cabaret reopened after difficulties with a previous show said: "We're not too open, but we're open enough to just barely stay open."[38] As the Nazis saw it, Finck was a master of the art of suggesting as much as possible without getting caught.[39] Goebbels sent loyal party members to Finck's cabaret in 1935, only to find that they reached conflicting conclusions. Some thought the material acceptable, but the majority found audiences too willing to draw conclusions inconsistent with National Socialist thinking. Goebbels considered banning traditional cabaret, replacing it with a National Socialist version.[40]

As Jelavich points out, the Nazis had a contradictory goal that ensured their cabaret would be unsuccessful: "The 'positive cabaret' desired by the Nazis was supposed to attack people who disturbed the homogenous mindset. Of course, those same individuals were being persecuted by the state's repressive apparatuses. Far from defending the underdog, Nazi cabaret was supposed to side with the victorious bully. That fact seriously limited the success of the Nazis' 'positive' cabarets. Audiences found little humor in seeing someone already on the ground being kicked gratuitously."[41] Goebbels finally decided to ban political cabaret entirely in December 1937 but lacked the power to make the ban stick. Cabaret continued, rather nervously, into the war years.

The GDR managed cabaret more effectively. In 1982 cabaret performances attracted 428,000 people.[42] There were fourteen troupes in major cities by 1984. Tickets sold out months in advance. In addition, there were many amateur and student cabarets.[43] The GDR even established a university program to train cabaret artists in 1987.[44]

Every cabaret artist realized that there were boundaries, and not always clear ones. Performers knew that the bulk of their material had to be aimed at the enemy, whether at home or abroad. As Ursula Ragwitz, an official in the Agitation Department, wrote in 1983: "The critical material on everyday life in the GDR may not overshadow the most important questions of the class struggle."[45] Cabaret scripts required advance approval from the relevant party office and often from city officials. Even then, performances were sometimes banned. In 1961 the student cabaret in Leipzig, instead of attacking the class enemy, directed some of its satire toward the socialist camp. A typical line ran: "Why does the LVZ [the Leipzig SED newspaper] print abbreviated versions of speeches by Kennedy and Nehru, but not by Khrushchev? Answer: Well, before you can cut them, you have to read them." Five cabaret members were arrested, two expelled from the party.[46] One was Ernst Röhl, later a longtime staff member of *Eulenspiegel,* the

GDR's sole humor magazine, who spent nearly a year in prison. During 1964–1965 Leipzig's Pfeffermühle cabaret had three shows banned, which was a considerable embarrassment since one fell during the fall trade show that attracted numerous foreign visitors.[47]

Still, cabaret had more room to criticize than *Eulenspiegel.* I attended a Pfeffermühle performance in 1988 that suggested that the GDR's leaders were seeing nothing but little Gorbachevs in their nightmares. Such jokes never appeared in more widely circulated media. The cabaret had a limited audience (the theaters seated several hundred at most), and full performances were almost never broadcast on television (though carefully selected skits appeared at times). West German television reporters regularly asked permission to film cabaret performances, which was always denied. As a GDR report noted in 1983, it would be peculiar to allow West German television to broadcast what East German television could not.[48]

The Dolt Laughs: Satirical Publications

There were a number of satirical publications published during the Nazi era. *Simplicissimus* had a long history, as did the *Lustige Blätter.*[49] The Nazis founded their own *Brennessel* in 1931.[50] Following the Soviet example, the GDR had one publication that had a near monopoly on satire: *Eulenspiegel.*[51] I shall consider both periodicals, using material from *Brennessel* in 1934 and 1935 and *Eulenspiegel* in 1985 and 1986.

Brennessel and *Eulenspiegel* are most similar in the ways they used satire to comment on international events. In both systems, the government controlled what could be said about other nations and insisted that all publications support the official line. As a result, the international satire of both periodicals was predictable, repetitious, and dull. I shall only briefly consider it, since it is the least interesting material in both periodicals.

Brennessel found little to appreciate in the rest of the world. Austria, France, Poland, Czechoslovakia, England, the United States, Lithuania—all these and more were regularly the point of its satire. In 1934 Hitler, for example, conducted a campaign against Austria, culminating in the assassination of Chancellor Engelbert Dollfuß on 25 July. Hundreds of *Brennessel* items, ranging from brief swipes to cover cartoons, from major articles to poems, satirized Austria (though the assassination itself was not mentioned). Dozens of items in 1934 accused other European nations—in particular, France—of armaments-building programs aimed at Germany.

In 1935 Austria was no longer a major concern. Numerous items now attacked the Soviet Union and the League of Nations. By fall 1935 Lithuania was a major target. The 19 November 1935 issue, for example, carried two cartoons and four brief items accusing the Lithuanian government of assorted misdeeds.

Foreign satire was clearly part of a centrally managed campaign. *Brennessel*'s office file copies were liberated by an American soldier who donated them to Dartmouth College, his alma mater, after the war. They sometimes include the censor's corrections, made before the issue was released for printing. The 26 June 1934 issue carried a cartoon titled "Ikarus der Dollfüßige," a pun that does not survive translation, depicting Dollfuß attempting to escape his foes by flying high in the sky, only to collide with the rainbow. A handwritten comment in the margin notes: "5 Uhr kam Druckerlaubnis [Approval to print came at 5]." An anti-Austrian poem in the same issue was cut.

Although *Eulenspiegel* never doubted the wisdom of socialist foreign policy, its writers were aware that repeating old stereotypes was dull and ineffective. Peter Nelken, *Eulenspiegel*'s editor, wrote in 1962: "As important as it is for satire to use artistic means to show the deformation of the human under imperialism and to reveal the hopelessly outdated character of its representatives, not every warmonger looks like an ape and not all monopoly capitalists bite their nails in anxiety. These sorts of clichés do not only minimize the severity of the struggle, they also ignore an important function of satire: to provoke the reader or viewer to thought, to force him to contemplate, to draw conclusions, that will affect his action."[52] His injunctions had little impact.

The major campaign of 1985–1986 was directed against the NATO decision to station intermediate range missiles in Europe. Dozens of items spoke to the topic. Nicaragua was a second frequent theme. Front or back cover cartoons showed Nicaraguan schoolchildren being shot, Contra money flowing to Honduras, Contra soldiers shooting up a milk truck, prosperous Americans worrying that the Nicaraguans wanted to take Disneyland away from them, and so on.[53] The stereotypes were the ones Nelken denounced twenty years earlier.

Neither periodical said anything negative about its nation's allies. The proof copies of *Brennessel* show that even mild Italian jokes were cut. For example, the proof copy of the 14 August 1934 issue included two items mentioning Italy. In one, tourists mistake whirling dervishes for Italian journalists. The proof copy for 25 September 1934 had a cartoon depicting an ignorant Italian farmer holding a copy of Tacitus upside down. The caption read: "He cannot read Tacitus, of course—but he at least comes from the area where he wrote two thousand years ago." None of the items appear in the printed editions. The reaction of *Eulenspiegel* to the Soviet Union can only be described as fawning, with never a suggestion that Soviet policy might in any way be subject to criticism.

Although the two publications' general approach to international issues was similar, there was a major difference. *Brennessel* regularly printed caricatures of foreign statesmen, *Eulenspiegel* rarely did.[54] The Nazis did not particularly care what the world thought of them, whereas the GDR was assiduous in seeking foreign recognition and avoided harsh personal attacks on most foreign leaders. Its caricatures were usually generalized capitalists, generals, or politicians rather than specific foreign leaders.

International satire was seldom even slightly amusing, since it so clearly was part of the general propaganda campaign and since there was so little variety. The satirists had no room to say anything outrageous or provocative. Repetitive international satire vanished from *Eulenspiegel* after the Wall came down and the staff gained greater freedom to choose what to write about.

Although their approaches to international satire were similar, *Brennessel* and *Eulenspiegel* took different approaches to domestic matters. *Brennessel* rejected any domestic criticism, whereas *Eulenspiegel* allowed more room for criticism than any other leading periodical in the GDR, although, as we shall see, that criticism stayed within carefully defined boundaries.

Brennessel spent considerable effort supporting Goebbels's propaganda campaign against Germans who complained about shortages, corruption, or inefficiency.[55] Many cartoons, poems, and articles denounced the *Miesmacher* and the *Meckerer,* those who found the slightest thing to complain about or who lacked full confidence in the Third Reich. A typical cartoon in 1934 was captioned "Those who don't want to see will have to feel." In the first frame, two men complain that nothing is happening, while two other men are at work in the background. In the second frame, one of the workers directs the handle of his shovel at the chin of the complainer, apologizes profusely, and comments in the final frame, "Well, something happened after all."[56] Another cartoon has a complainer entering a shop asking for butter. When the clerk informs him that there is none, he replies: "I knew it. Otherwise, I wouldn't have asked."[57] Many items made the same point. To complain was to be disloyal.

Other items attacked Germans who failed to behave in expected ways. Those less than eager to contribute to the party's annual Winter Relief campaign came under scrutiny. A typical cartoon showed a prosperous couple in a large automobile contributing a penny to the Nazi Winter Relief charity.[58] There were complaints about the 110 percenters, those Germans who discovered an attraction to National Socialism after 30 January 1933. One article took the form of a letter to a bureaucrat who survived the transition to National Socialism by taking on the necessary political coloration but complained that having to spend six months in the labor service would cost him 1,000 marks in lost wages.[59]

The message was that all was well with Germany and that to complain was to exhibit lack of faith in the Führer and Fatherland. Whatever problems there were could be solved by those in authority. There was no need for meddling by the masses.

Eulenspiegel's pages, on the other hand, were filled with complaints about the indignities of life in the GDR. Nelken's 1962 essay outlined the appropriate targets of domestic satire: "What negative things stand in the way of our path to socialism? Above all they are the manifestations of egotism nourished by capitalism that still influence people's thoughts and actions. Absenteeism, the attempt to get as much as possible from society without producing a corresponding amount, hoarding, listening to NATO stations to spread rumors, alcoholism and rowdyism, domineering natures and envy, the mistreatment of women in the family and workplace—all these are damaging remains that need to be eliminated."[60] In contrast to *Brennessel, Eulenspiegel* sometimes suggested that there were problems in the GDR, problems that citizens could appropriately complain about. Domestic satire's goal was to help overcome the growing pains of socialism.

Socialism's growing pains, however, increased as time went on. *Eulenspiegel* had no shortage of topics. One issue complained about the miserable food at railroad station restaurants, the filthy toilets, and the limited hours facilities were open. Cartoons in the same issue depicted toilets closed because of the danger of plague and a station kiosk loaded with alcohol: "Here you can find everything you need to forget the late trains."[61] Other issues revealed the tricks GDR taxi drivers used to extort higher than allowable fares, the difficulties in getting spare parts, and the poor quality of consumer goods.[62] Frequent absenteeism was the theme of a cartoon showing six work stations, five of which are vacant. The supervisor comes by to ask where everyone is. The one worker present replies: "Paula's child is sick, Dieter is getting coal, Max some furniture, Hein is at driving school, and Else is just shopping." The foreman replies: "Have a word with Else. The others don't have a choice."[63] Recognizing the strains of life in the GDR, the cartoon accepted absenteeism for good cause.

Each issue carried articles and cartoons that directly addressed the daily difficulties that GDR citizens faced but rarely saw mentioned in other mass-circulated periodicals. Unlike *Brennessel, Eulenspiegel* expressed people's frustrations. Sometimes specific culprits were mentioned, sometimes it was enough to make a general complaint.

There were also items that dealt with deeper problems of socialism. Gentle fun was poked at the constant citation of Marxist leaders, as, for example, in the following poem:

> I have a burning wish to know
> And so I just ask plainly,
> Whom pray tell
> Did Karl Marx quote?[64]

Anyone familiar with the steady stream of quotations that filled the official rhetoric of the GDR smiled. The need to take creative measures to get spare parts or rare goods was satirized in a cartoon in which a man writes his telephone number on a 50 mark note "in case the part comes in early."[65] Items now and again dealt with the regular practice of stealing material from the workplace for home use.[66]

Even more serious problems were on occasion considered. A back cover cartoon showed crying children looking over the balcony of their apartment as three drunken punks destroyed their playground.[67] Another cartoon had workers standing in the midst of their decrepit factory, with broken windows, a leaking roof, and holes in the floor. Their factory head tells them: "What you need, colleagues, is culture. Go to the opera or to a concert!"[68]

Such items were hardly biting criticism, but they were more forceful than GDR citizens found in other periodicals. They must be compared, however, with the treatment *Eulenspiegel* gave the West, where, it seemed, crime, poverty, corruption, and exploitation were the daily lot of many. The occasional disadvantages of socialism were portrayed as minor annoyances.

The magazine regularly gave the targets of its criticism opportunity to respond. To a building manager who complained about an article, the magazine replied: "If there were no problems, one would not need satire. Positive satire would self-destruct. Please do not expect an 'objective report' from those whose jobs it is to deal with deviations from the norm, and who live by exaggeration."[69] *Eulenspiegel* never suggested that it might be necessary to dispose of socialism to improve the courtesy of shop clerks or the quality of consumer goods.

As an *Eulenspiegel* writer later noted, criticism had to be by "street and house number."[70] Specific indignities at the lower level were open to criticism but not the actions of higher-level leaders. When, for instance, *Eulenspiegel* criticized Manfred Ewald, who headed the GDR sports system, staffers lost their jobs. Even the hint of criticism of the leadership was rejected. An amusing example came in 1963, when *Eulenspiegel* attempted to run the following joke: "As the West German President Lübke was on an African trip recently, he let the public know that he was Germany's representative. A passer-by was heard to remark: "He must be an imposter, for Germany's representative has a beard." This was an ever-so-gentle reference to Ulbricht's goatee. The Agitation Department rejected that punch line. Instead, readers found: "He must be an imposter, since I saw Germany's representative at the FDJ Congress." Editor Peter Nelken wrote to the Agitation Department:

> Do we have to be so nervous and defensive in using such silly, empty phrases in popular agitation literature? Why are we so allergic? Is Comrade Ulbricht's beard ugly?
>
> I have been around long enough to know that there are things one does not write, terms one does not use. But look at the way we dance around the word "Wall." One has to listen to what people say if one is to reach them.
>
> I'm not particularly concerned about Comrade Ulbricht's beard, or even an *Eulenspiegel* joke that did not work. I am concerned about defensive and therefore un-Marxist taboos.[71]

But that was a mild altercation. There were a number of cases in which the *Eulenspiegel* staff was taken to task much more energetically.[72]

Although *Eulenspiegel* was permitted greater domestic criticism than *Brennessel,* neither periodical tolerated any criticism aimed at the fundamentals of the society or criticism coming from other countries. Both gave considerable space to suggesting that criticisms directed toward their countries from abroad were ignorant, stupid, and wrong.

Hitler's Germany received more negative coverage from the foreign press than did Honecker's Germany and did not like it at all. *Brennessel's* general line was that foreign criticism was the work of the Jews or émigré malcontents. In a typical item, one man asks another if he had read an article in an emigrant paper: "I read a bit of the paper, a few articles even, but I don't know which article you mean. Is it the one that was made up, or the one that wasn't true, or the one that's a fraud, or the one that's a pack of lies?"[73]

Dozens of other articles and cartoons made the same point. Each suggested that criticism from abroad was false or absurdly exaggerated.

Other items suggested that although there might be minor problems in Germany, things were far worse elsewhere. A remarkable item in 1934, for example, reported: "The Austrian concentration camps will supposedly get cemeteries and crematories to help them better fulfill their purposes."[74] A later cartoon showed two Englishmen outraged because their German neighbor is beating a carpet in his yard, but in a third house the Russians are shooting people while rats creep under the fence to infest the neighboring house.[75]

Eulenspiegel gave frequent space to similar material. Once a month a page titled "The Other Side" purported to be a Western publication commenting on the problems of the GDR and the joys of capitalism. Each version included a picture from the GDR with a specious explanation. One photo showed a child standing beside a pond feeding ducks, noting that in the GDR children were forced to work to meet the party-dictated plan for livestock.[76] *Eulenspiegel*'s efforts on these lines were more challenging than *Brennessel*'s, since most GDR citizens regularly watched West German television and thus saw (as well as experienced firsthand) that the difficulties of the GDR were rather more serious than *Eulenspiegel*'s satire suggested.

Anti-Semitism was a mainstay of *Brennessel*. A 1935 article discussed the uses of humor in the war against the Jews. Too often, anti-Jewish jokes simply make Jews laughable, the author claimed. Effective humor points out the "satanic nature" of the Jews: "The Philistines who prove their anti-Semitism with cheap Jewish jokes and at the same time strengthen the Jews economically are a plague, for they ignore that which is of deadly seriousness!"[77] Jews were presented as ugly caricatures capable of every manner of evil.

Particular effort was given to denigrating those Jews who had fled Germany. A typical article in 1935 attacked Georg Bernhard, former editor of the Berlin newspaper *Vossische Zeitung*. The writer had recently seen a film with clips of Bernhard from the 1920s, during which he claims the audience laughed, unable to believe that such a fossil had once thrived in Germany: "Your face—we don't really want to talk about it—but look in the mirror at that thing you have to carry around as a face. You didn't do so well there. Your racial characteristics do not come across in an attractive way. On top of it all, the camera man caught you, how shall I put it, from the Tel Aviv side. Not attractive, not attractive at all, Georg Bernhard! And then you begin to speak. It was frightfully comic. Try it yourself, say a few words loudly. Then you will know that your German reeks of Yiddish. Do you have any idea how that sounds to us?"[78] The content of the cartoons and articles was repetitive, unvarying, and tiresome.

The GDR was in an awkward position with respect to Jews. As a part of the Germany that committed genocide, it was ill at ease satirizing Jews, but as part of the socialist bloc it was on the side of Israel's foes. The result was that little was said about Israel or Jews in the GDR press. Jews were an unknown people, Israel an unknown country.

No major articles or cartoons during the period here considered addressed Israel in any detail. There were only occasional brief mentions. A 1985 editorial noted that the world condemned Israeli policy, but the United States supported it.[79] Another item satirized Israel's policy of retaliation: "In a bold strike, Israeli commandos Tuesday night blew up the dome of St. Peter's cathedral after one of the twelve hundred visitors had been observed in conversation with an Arab whose sister-in-law had been frequently observed by the Israeli secret service publicly carrying a black and white PLO banner."[80] In comparison to *Eulenspiegel*'s satire directed against the United States or West Germany, however, this was gentle material indeed, an indication that Israel was a topic the magazine preferred to avoid.

The penultimate issue of *Brennessel* in 1938 announced to its readers that it had fulfilled its purpose and would shortly cease publication. The magazine provided its own obituary:

> It was our *Brennessel* that tens of thousands of National Socialist readers enjoyed during the period of struggle as it gave the sharp and hated blows that gradually wore down the old system.
>
> It was *Brennessel* that after the seizure of power took sure aim at external enemies and at the moaners and complainers at home.
>
> It was *Brennessel* whose scorn inflicted deep wounds on the enemy, that made them the laughing stock of the world, that made them ridiculous.
>
> We thank our readers for their loyalty. They know how much *Brennessel* (a piece of the history of our party) served the idea through sharp attack and resolute defense until its great goal was realized, the goal of its entire struggle: the creation of the Greater German Reich![81]

But *Brennessel* did not cease publication because it had fulfilled its mission. It failed because people did not buy it. In 1933 *Brennessel*'s circulation was about 32,000. It had fallen to 23,000 by its final issues.[82]

Brennessel's competitors did little better. *Simplicissimus* sold 86,000 copies in 1908. By 1939 circulation was down to 19,000 (although the influx of *Brennessel* subscribers raised it temporarily to over 40,000). The Third Reich had little appetite for tame satire. People got enough propaganda in the rest of their activities. Since *Brennessel's* satire hardly relieved the tensions of everyday life, indeed it suggested one was disloyal for having tensions, most Germans chose to spend their 30 pfennig elsewhere.

Brennessel failed because it was too much like everything else in the Third Reich. There were no surprises, no risks taken. Humor is often a way of dealing with the stresses of everyday life, rendering them more endurable through laughter, but *Brennessel* permitted no such release. The complainers, the moaners, the dissatisfied, they were the magazine's enemies, its frequent targets. It suggested that to criticize life's difficulties was to be a traitor. This hardly made for good humor. Even Hitler called *Brennessel* "the dreariest rag imaginable."[83]

Eulenspiegel, on the other hand, sold out issue after issue. Nearly 500,000 copies were printed (given population differences between Hitler's Germany and the GDR, *Brennessel* would have needed a circulation of about two million to equal *Eulenspiegel's*). Even the copies it did print were not enough. New subscriptions were not accepted; issues reaching the kiosks sold out rapidly. The editorial staff estimated that twice as many copies could have sold if sufficient paper (in perennially short supply in the GDR) had been available.

Both magazines attempted to force humor into the constraints of propaganda. Why did the one fail, the other succeed?

Brennessel simply failed to interest its readers. It offered them little they could not get elsewhere, and its humor lacked the bite that makes satire appealing. *Eulenspiegel* addressed some of the real difficulties of life in the GDR. Few read *Eulenspiegel* for international satire, nor were they impressed by its attempts to show "the qualitative differences that the satirist must make between using satire as internal criticism and as a means to reveal the external enemy, imperialism and militarism."[84] Although it had its share of blundering satire, it gave considerable space to at least modest criticism of conditions in the GDR. It avoided badgering its readers to participate in *Mach mit* actions (semivoluntary efforts to clean up an area or perform some other kind of civic work) or scolding them for failing to make a contribution to a solidarity drive. Part of its popularity resulted from being in short supply (since people by nature prefer that which is hard to get to that which is easy to obtain).

The man frustrated because he could not find a spare part for a washing machine, the woman annoyed by the survival of sexism in a society where the conditions necessary for it had supposedly been eliminated, the traveler angry because for the third time in a week the train had been late, the person tired of poor working conditions, these people could laugh, perhaps resignedly, as *Eulenspiegel* attacked their problems. True, the magazine rarely got beyond the specific outrage. It never suggested that perhaps there was a systemic reason for the GDR's problems, but a single issue contained more detailed criticism of life in *real existierende Sozialismus* than a month of *Neues Deutschland*.

After the GDR collapsed, the magazine quickly dropped the heavy-handed satire of the Honecker era and began printing genuinely funny and biting material on life in a transformed Germany. Now a monthly, it still survives, though its satire takes substantially different lines.

Summary

Both the Nazi and the GDR systems viewed the arts as important. Just as a large proportion of European art reinforced the Christian worldview for centuries, so totalitarian art reinforced new worldviews. Both systems had difficulty defining exactly what approved art was, but neither hesitated to try. As usual, the Nazi system was more tangled than the GDR's.

Both systems guided art by controlling admission to the professional organizations that were a prerequisite to artistic life. In Hitler's Germany, only members of the relevant body of the Reich Chamber of Culture could be employed in the arts. In the GDR, only members of the relevant professional organization were likely to find a publisher or a gallery. Those who did not follow the proper paths were expelled from the professional organizations.

Both systems also resisted artistic ambiguity. Approved art had clear messages that echoed the ideological metanarrative. Nazi paintings glorified a vanished pastoral world, the party's leaders and history, great building projects, and the military. Nazism rejected "modern" art either because its meaning was unclear or too clear (for example, antiwar art). Approved socialist art glorified workers and the accomplishments of socialism. Neither liked jazz or other forms of "decadent" modern music.

The SED, for all its artistic twists and turns, allowed more artistic license than the NSDAP. Films and television dealt more directly with the problems of the day. *Eulenspiegel* certainly addressed more of life's daily annoyances than did *Brennessel*.

Art still reinforced both systems. With some exceptions, artists were "bought" by the benefits of cooperation. Robert Von Hallberg's argument about artists in the GDR applies as well to the Nazi era. Most intellectuals were not that difficult to control. They were guided less by explicit censorship (although that was used if necessary) than by the obvious benefits of cooperation. His conclusion is worth citing at length:

> One might think that in a totalitarian society fear of the police would back up the directives and suggestions received by intellectuals, but nothing of the sort seems to have occurred in the GDR. GDR intellectuals—not just literary intellectuals—now often say, "In fact, we could have done a lot more." The reason they did not do so was rarely the threat of imprisonment or torture but, rather, fear of professional obstacles. My claim is not simply that certain professional structures, such as the Writer's Union or the Central Institute for Literary History, enforced particular kinds of conformity. The more interesting phenomenon is that the elaborateness of GDR professional organizations seemed to have rendered intellectual life devastatingly predictable: one knew that one would indeed be read carefully, if only by censorious authorities; one thought one knew what would happen if something in particular were said.[85]

Intellectuals and artists in both systems were generally willing to avoid actions that would endanger their status. This did not make them any different than most citizens, who also wished to avoid trouble, but their visibility and prestige contributed in a significant way to maintaining the system. Their credibility gave credibility.

In both systems, art served valuable propaganda functions. It met the public need for entertainment in a way that supported, or at least did not undermine, the official line. Humor and satire, for example, diverted attention from the real failings and evils of Nazism and socialism to the sometimes real failings of their enemies. Rather than having citizens laugh or scorn their governments, totalitarian societies attempt to divert that scorn in other directions.

Art also added significantly to the international stature of both states. Thus the Nazis encouraged the building of theaters and art galleries, and the SED, despite a general shortage of building capacity, put major effort into restoring theaters damaged during the war or in building new ones. It even maintained two opera houses in Berlin, popular with foreign visitors. Art did not exist for the sake of art in either system; artists who thought differently learned that quickly.

7

Public and Private Life

B ending spines takes steady pressure in every area of life. Jacques Ellul observes: "Propaganda tries to surround man by all possible routes, in the realm of feelings as well as ideas, by playing on his will or on his needs, through his conscious and his unconscious, assailing him in both his private and his public life."[1] I have earlier discussed the quasi-religious nature of claims made on all aspects of life. Both the National Socialist and GDR systems took power knowing that they would never win over the whole of the population. They wanted conviction but settled for outward assent from many citizens who refused or were unable to be true believers. They accepted varying levels of compliance and found ways of dealing with those who would not bend. In this chapter I shall consider the general demand for public unanimity, then examine specific ways in which citizens were persuaded to behave as if they believed things they did not believe.

The appearance of unanimity is critical. An ordinary state does not expect 100 percent agreement. Democratic states, in fact, expect a range of disagreements and even find social benefit in the competition of ideas and opinions. Totalitarian states that make absolute claims of truth cannot allow significant public disagreement. They know that heresy spreads. Goebbels spoke in 1928 of ideas as a gas that moves invisibly from person to person.[2] A better comparison is to a disease. Unless totalitarian societies "quarantine" objectionable ideas, they spread, often rapidly. The solution is to make errant ideas invisible by making the consequences of spreading them sufficiently unpleasant to encourage silence. The sudden collapse of the GDR in 1989 surprised nearly everyone, since the system had succeeded in creating a Potemkin village of public unanimity that concealed, even from its own leaders and citizens, the shallowness of its support.

Unanimity in the Party

Any government prefers to present a united front to its political opponents and the nation as a whole, but for dictatorships with absolute claims such unanimity is crucial. As is often observed, the Nazi leadership squabbled incessantly behind the scenes, but Hitler personally ordered there be no public conflict. A September 1942 directive reminded party leaders that "the Führer has repeatedly said that disagreements between leading party members must under all circumstances be kept from reaching the public."[3] The fact that he said so repeatedly proves a lack of success, but it also suggests the importance a united front had. A party that claims truth cannot have its leaders proposing conflicting truths. The problem is that the more capable the official, the more likely he was to see weaknesses. He either held his thoughts or got into trouble. As Michael Balfour observes about the Nazis, the "scarcity of believers with capacity meant that the replacements tended to be believers with reservations."[4]

Maintaining unanimity at lower levels was relatively easy, given the Nazi "leadership principle." Subordinates owed absolute obedience to their superiors. This did not in practice always prove to be the case, but certainly most Nazis shared the general sense that they were heading in the same direction, "working toward the Führer." Local leaders could present themselves as doing the will of the Führer, maintaining at least the appearance of unity.

The GDR's approach was different, but the goal was the same. Since learning from the Soviet Union was to learn victory, the GDR followed the Soviet model in which pressure for uniformity pervaded every aspect of life. This began at the top. One almost amusing example is indicative. When Konstantin Chernenko was reporting to his Politburo colleagues in 1980, he stressed the fact that "'Central Committee plenums last year [1979] were conducted in a spirit of complete unanimity,' prompting Andropov to remark, 'That is an entirely proper conclusion. The plenums really did proceed in complete unanimity,' and Pelshe to add, 'And their decisions were also adopted unanimously.' And when Chernenko mentioned that fifty-one sessions of the Central Committee Secretariat had taken place and that they had passed 1,327 regulations, Suslov and Andropov together piped up, 'Like the Politburo, the Secretariat also conducted its business in complete unanimity.'"[5] The GDR learned from the masters. Günter Schabowski reports only two lively discussions in the Politburo during his membership (1984–1989), one regarding the firing of Konrad Naumann, the Berlin SED first secretary, the second in September 1989 as things were already crumbling.[6] Otherwise, unanimity prevailed. Erich Honecker even voted for his own removal in October 1989.

Unanimity prevailed in the very language the leadership used. Party leaders generally spoke in a "Party Chinese" packed with Marxist-Leninist jargon and quoted the appropriate sources. In 1961 Honecker sent Walter Ulbricht his comments on a document about to be published. Honecker observed: "By the way, I noticed that the report did not mention even once that the Central Committee under the leadership of its First Secretary had done a great deal to carry out the decisions of the V. Party Congress." Ulbricht underlined the passage and added "!!" in the margin.[7] Party leaders packed their interminable speeches with jargon and standard phrases.

If the leaders practiced unanimity among themselves, the pressure on underlings was even more intense. The SED operated under rules that allowed for little public discussion. It was governed by the Leninist principle of democratic centralism. The final edition of the *Concise Political Dictionary* defined the term clearly: "Leadership of the party by an elected central, periodic election of all leading party organs by lower bodies, collective leadership, periodic reports of the party organs to those who elected them; firm party discipline and the subordination of the minority to the majority; absolute execution by lower organs and members of the decisions of higher organs . . . [and] active participation by party members in their organizations to implement these decisions."[8] Since the lower bodies had little real say in electing the higher ones and since the higher bodies did not report accurately to the lower ones, the result was a system that was centralized but not democratic.

The preamble to the 1975 SED party statute stated: "Any sign of factionalism or group-building contradicts the nature of a Marxist-Leninist party and is incompatible with party membership."[9] Most party members, subject to discipline for any slight deviation from the party line and with numerous examples in mind of the penalties for deviation, knew better than to break rank. As those who questioned the wisdom of the SED's decisions were sometimes told: "Do you think you are smarter than the collective wisdom of the party?"[10] "Yes" was not the expected answer.

Party officials knew that disagreeing with their superiors was not a wise career move, nor was expressing any public doubt. Wolfgang Leonhard, a member of the GDR's founding group who later fled to the West, wrote: "I have often seen it myself, that in conversation with people from the West an official who is wrestling with the severest internal doubts will stubbornly, and apparently with complete conviction, defend the official Party line. His Western interlocutor then leaves him with the firm conviction of having been talking to a 150% Stalinist."[11] With nearly everyone trying to persuade both subordinates and superiors of his or her ideological orthodoxy, there was general uncertainty as to what people really thought.

The system found other ways to emphasize obedience to authority. For example, late in the GDR's history Landolf Scherzer published a small book titled *Der Erste.* It followed the first secretary of the SED *Kreisleitung* in Bad Salzungen as he went about his business and was relatively open (for the GDR) in discussing real problems. The book sold out immediately. Scherzer describes a meeting of party members unhappy to learn that the area will not get the new housing they had requested. The first secretary noted he had shared their hopes: "But I am a party worker and I will therefore not discuss the matter any longer. And I demand of each functionary here that we make this decision our opinion and that we collectively present it as our opinion."[12] The first secretary, portrayed as a dedicated and hardworking man doing his best for the people, saw the will of the party as his first obligation, regardless of his personal preferences. He modeled what was demanded of his subordinates and of all citizens.

Ninety-nine Percent Electoral Victories

That Nazi and SED leaders and members were in at least public agreement is not surprising. But what about the mass public appearance of support? No one doubted in 1939 that Hitler was widely popular, and the scholarly literature has numerous embarrassing statements by leading scholars as late as 1989 who were confident that the GDR had a long and stable life ahead of it, based on its evident ability to maintain public support.

In *Mein Kampf,* Hitler distinguished between the members and the followers of a political organization. The members were those committed to the organization, those willing to fight and die for it. The followers might vote for a party but could not be relied on in times of crisis. In his closing speech at the 1934 Nuremberg rally, he looked to the day when every German would be a National Socialist, but only the best National Socialists would be members of the party. Speaking to those in radio in March 1933, Goebbels made his goals clear. The goal was to win 100 percent of the German people. "Once we have it, radio must help us hold it, defend it; it must so drench them with the spiritual message of our day that no one is any longer able to break free of it."[13]

Both Hitler and Goebbels hint at the dilemma. The Nazis could not expect to win over entirely 100 percent of the population. Not everyone was a true believer. The "best" Germans might be party members, but what about the remaining 90 percent? How could they be kept from breaking through the miasma of propaganda? The solution was to create the impression of overwhelming public support for the regime, one so strong that few with doubts would dare express them in public. As Otto Dietrich said at the 1935 Nuremberg rally: "The public opinion of the German people is National Socialism."[14] That left little room for those who thought differently.

Elections are an illuminating illustration of the drive for unanimity. The Nazis got 37 percent of the vote in the July 1932 Reichstag election. In the manipulated but partially free election in March 1933, they received just under 44 percent of the vote. Eight months later, the party secured 92 percent in the November 1933 referendum. Normal methods of persuasion do not secure such drastic and rapid changes. The official figure for the August 1934 referendum, called after Hindenburg's death, was 88 percent, but in some districts it was under 70 percent. This was an unpleasant surprise. An article in *Unser Wille und Weg* observed: "19 August has proven that 10 percent of the German people are still standing to the side. We may leave no means untried to win the greater part of them for the National Socialist state."[15] The word "win" suggests an honest effort to persuade, with the possibility of losing. But a loss was not acceptable. The party made sure that the 1936 and 1938 referendums produced results of 99 percent. No one believed that almost everyone in Germany thought the same way, but neither could a reasonable person know how many people did not think as Hitler wished. That uncertainty was critical. In the face of uncertainty, people held their tongues.

The GDR was no less fond of electoral unanimity. In sixteen of the seventeen *Volkskammer* (the national parliament) and communal elections, the official figures had over 99 percent of the participants voting for the candidates of the National Front, the SED-approved slate of candidates. The figure was allowed to drop to 98.85 percent in the final communal elections on 7 May 1989.[16] Enormous effort went into encouraging voter turnout. Elections even provided opportunity for ordinary citizens to exert pressure. A hint that one might not vote sometimes moved an otherwise stubborn bureaucracy to respond to a citizen's request.

The election of 17 September 1961, a month after the Berlin Wall was constructed, was particularly interesting. The GDR did everything it could to produce the illusion of mass support. Hundreds of thousands of election meetings encouraged citizens to vote. *Bezirk* Magdeburg alone held 25,072 meetings by 22 August, with 644,326 in attendance, 53 percent of the voting population. These meetings were often targeted to specific groups, such as physicians or Christians. With an average meeting attendance under 30, this was a great commitment of resources to encourage voting.[17] The election results were never in doubt (particularly since the percentages could be manipulated to the appropriate number of digits after 99). The goal was not to win an election but to pressure citizens to make a public ceremony of obedience, to give a vote of approval to the Wall. Although citizens had the right to vote secretly, the expectation was that citizens would publicly cast their votes. As a slogan in Halle in 1961 put it: "He who is not willing to openly cast his vote for the candidates of the National Front votes for war."[18] With that clearly expressed, few GDR citizens took advantage of the secret ballot.

Elections were relatively unproblematic. Voting the wrong way had unpleasant consequences and little gain. The vast majority of those less than enthusiastic about the regimes made pragmatic decisions to avoid unnecessary difficulty. But what about day-to-day behavior? People complained, and often.

Tipping Points

The Nazis produced enormous numbers of reports on public attitudes, with various degrees of accuracy. Reports like this one from the Münster area in 1935 were common: "The mood of the population, especially workers, merchants and laborers, is depressed. A series of indications show that the enthusiasm of the broad masses for the National Socialist movement is not as it was in previous years."[19] The wartime reports of the SD are filled with critical comments from the population. The GDR had its share of similar reports. Dealing with the innate human tendency to complain required complicated mechanisms. Complaining could not be eliminated ("the bowel movement of the soul," in Goebbels's words), but it could be made less visible.

Ellul observes that all modern propaganda systems, democratic ones included, strive for unanimity, which is impossible when many complain in public.[20] The difference is that totalitarian systems need more of it since they claim truths that they assert are beyond dispute. Both the Nazis and the Marxists knew it was necessary to be ever vigilant against any form of public disagreement.

Malcolm Gladwell develops an argument that ideas resemble epidemics.[21] Some ideas, like some diseases, are more "contagious" than others. It is not always possible to predict in advance which variant of the flu or which idea will spread widely. At a certain "tipping point," however, a disease or an idea that has spread sufficiently throughout the population becomes epidemic, often with startling suddenness. The flu and fashion spread in similar ways. They can also be stopped in similar ways. Everyone does not need to be vaccinated for a vaccine to be effective. If enough people are, the disease diminishes rather than spreads. In the same way, if enough people are reluctant to spread an idea, the idea diminishes. Totalitarian leaders recognized that some ideas had to be stopped from spreading. They further realized that reducing the number of people willing to express an idea can lead to the death of that idea in public discourse.

In May 1939 a *Kreisleiter* (Nazi county leader) wrote to the Gestapo about a citizen who had complained in public about Hitler and the party: "I urge you to do all you can to see that this man receives the most severe punishment. . . . Ch. seems to have had an infectious impact on the population of Neukirchen and the area around it."[22] The man was apparently well thought of, and his public comments were influential. The leaders of both systems had what Klaus Höpke, the GDR's "minister for literature," later called a "fear of the word." Words were contagious, the spoken word even more than the written.

Elisabeth Noelle-Neumann's spiral of silence theory of public opinion suggests that we have a fine sense for distinguishing opinions that can be safely expressed from those that cannot.[23] "Dangerous" opinions fade from public discussion. Even bringing them up risks, at the least, unfriendly looks from fellow citizens. We know what may lead to unpleasantness and seek to avoid it. Timur Kuran suggests a better phrase is the "spiral of prudence." People commonly go beyond concealing their true opinions, beyond censoring themselves, to making statements in public that contradict their private beliefs but which they know will bring them advantage or allow them to avoid disadvantage.[24]

Public unanimity was reached in two ways: on the one hand, the systems encouraged desired behavior by various forms of social bribery, and, on the other, they discouraged undesired behavior by intimidation and force. The result, outwardly at least, was mass public support.

Much behavior was encouraged by the rewards it brought or the annoyances it avoided. I have already discussed voting; there was little cost to voting and considerable inconvenience to not voting. The mass organizations are another example. The Nazi Party and the SED were themselves mass organizations. Hitler's goal for party membership, never quite reached, was 10 percent.[25] A sixth of the adult population of the GDR belonged to the SED in 1988. Being a party member in either system put one under party discipline, greatly encouraging conformist behavior. For the majorities who were not party members, there was every manner of other organization, membership in which represented conformity to the demands of the system.

The largest single organization of the Third Reich was the DAF. Ninety percent of German workers were members.[26] The SA, the SS, the Hitler Youth, the Nazi women's organization, and all the other party affiliates managed to include most of the rest of the population. It was inconvenient not to belong to several of them. It got one noticed in places like Julius Streicher's *Der Stürmer,* whose notorious columns sometimes denounced those who were not members of the proper organizations.

The GDR also had a variety of organizations that it was wise to join. Nearly all youth joined the various sections of the FDJ. The Society for German-Soviet Friendship (DSF) had 6.2 million members by 1989 (over half the adult population). It was especially popular because joining gave evidence of conformity at a nominal membership fee and with minimal obligation. Pressure to join the FDGB was equally strong.

Asking too much of citizens generally did not work. For example, in 1952 there was a campaign to get GDR citizens to write millions of letters to friends, relatives, and professional colleagues in West Germany to persuade them of the superiority of socialism. A pamphlet with the entertaining title *Your Letter is a Sharp Weapon of Enlightenment in the Struggle for Unity and Peace* provided both good and bad examples of letters ordinary citizens might write. Letter writing groups met regularly to discuss ways to get an effective message to West Germans. These were organized by the National Front, the coordinating organization for many GDR activities. It claimed there were thousands of such groups already, but that tens of thousands were needed. However, citizens were understandably reluctant to spend much time writing propaganda letters, and the campaign seems to have died out shortly after.[27]

Nearly every GDR citizen was a member of several of the mass organizations, and most served in "leadership" positions over their careers. In 1979 the Bitterfeld chemical concern had 19,000 employees; 97 percent belonged to the FDGB, 84 percent had joined the DSF, 71 percent of the younger employees were still FDJ members, and 24 percent belonged to the SED. More than that, these organizations required large numbers of officeholders. The FDGB alone had functions for two-thirds of its Bitterfeld membership.[28]

It was often not easy to persuade people to take on the tasks that provided little real power at the cost of one's spare time. Gentle or not so gentle pressure persuaded people to accept these often unwanted duties. After all, a post in the FDGB or in the DSF or as an agitator might make a vacation likelier, encourage a promotion, or preserve one from tasks more onerous. One woman who wished to drop her FDGB membership was dissuaded by the fact that a small bonus for her entire work collective depended on 100 percent membership.[29] A school psychologist who had been less than eager to join the DSF testified about the pressure she encountered: "There were arguments that membership showed one's attitude toward the state, toward socialism and the Soviet Union, that membership in the DSF was an essential characteristic of a socialist teacher, and that otherwise the teacher collective could not earn the title 'Socialist Teacher's Collective.'"[30] These arguments gained force because they were made by friends and colleagues. The system punished not only individuals for failing to join the proper groups but also their workmates. Given the importance of the collective in the GDR, it took people of fortitude to do something that brought difficulties on themselves and on their friends.

The very fact that these were mass organizations is significant. Ellul notes that effective propaganda requires the fragmentation of society, the elimination of smaller groups that provide shelter for those of common outlook.[31] The result is that individuals, robbed of the warmth and support of smaller groups, become part of a mass of people who share little, or share nervously. William S. Allen titles a chapter of his study of Northeim during the Nazi years "The Atomization of Society." He describes how the Nazis quickly shattered the existing variety of clubs and groups, merging them into larger groups that no longer served the purpose of social interaction among like-minded people.[32] In the same way, the GDR made independent clubs or organizations difficult. The church was one of the few relatively independent spaces, and even there the GDR worked to reduce its reach. A 1964 report on improving atheistic propaganda, for example, noted that patient and persistent work had to be done to lure participants away from church cultural activities.[33] The person who attended a church concert might be drawn into other involvement.

Education received particular attention.[34] Children from the earliest age learned what was appropriate to say in public. Teachers were carefully selected and textbooks rigidly guided. Membership in the youth organizations was for practical purposes compulsory. A 1959 message to parents made this clear: "The start of your child's education begins an important stage of life: the systematic preparation for a life in service to our socialist community. An important helper in socialist education is the Pioneer Organization Ernst Thälmann, the socialist mass organization for children. . . . It will be most beneficial for the development of your child if you agree to his membership in the Pioneer Organization."[35] It took parents with backbones to resist such messages.

Wilfried Poßner, later head of the FDJ, had an illuminating experience while a student. He and his fellow students had objected to chanting a slogan at the 1967 May Day festivities ("Neither ox nor ass can stop the progress of socialism"), which aroused the ire of the party. They also made a poor choice of songs for public performance (for example, "Where Have All the Flowers Gone"). When they proposed naming their school after Bertholt Brecht, the authorities told them they had opposition and elitist tendencies and that their school would instead be named after a Stalinist-era Soviet writer.[36] This was not a personal catastrophe for anyone involved, but it was educational.

The FDJ's beginnings were rough, and even into the 1950s membership was stagnating at around 35 percent of the age cohort, due in part to determined resistance by the church. By the 1960s the percentages had reached entirely satisfactory levels of near unanimity.[37] Parents who might themselves not be strong supporters of the state got a clear message that their children would be outsiders should they not be members. The pressure worked. One of my GDR acquaintances remembers being one of two members of her school class who did not initially participate. The pressure of being an outsider led her to beg her parents for permission to join.

More than that, there were concrete benefits in participating actively in the mass organizations. The FDGB by the 1980s controlled over 5 million vacation opportunities and dispensed 1.8 million trips within the GDR and 16,000 abroad. The FDJ ran a network of youth hostels and also allocated coveted trips abroad.[38] These did not often go to members who had not demonstrated appropriate loyalty.

These were all efforts to persuade people to behave in the approved ways. There was also enormous pressure on people to avoid behavior that undermined the public facade of unanimity. This pressure was not necessarily oppressive—some hardly sensed it. And it came in many forms.

All citizens became part of the process of gentle coercion. From motives sometimes good, sometimes ill, neighbors worked on neighbors. In Hitler's Germany, one might see a sign upon entering the local pub that announced that the "German Greeting" ("Heil Hitler") was expected. Those who failed to display a flag on the proper occasions heard from concerned neighbors, not all of whom were busybodies. As one woman whose mother was slow to conform later recalled: "People were always coming and saying why haven't you hung out a flag, for Hitler's birthday and so on. . . . You almost went to jail. It was very dangerous if you didn't do it. One person after the other came, rang the doorbell, and said you haven't hung out your flag yet. Finally, my mother bought a real tiny one."[39] Helmut Behrens, a university chemist whose attitude toward the Nazis was hostile, nonetheless warned friends to be cautious of their public statements. Writing of a lab assistant, Behrens recalled: "He was a determined opponent of the National Socialist regime, and I had to warn him repeatedly to be a little more cautious in what he said, particularly with loyal party members."[40]

These were the warnings of friends. There were many less agreeable persons eager to report fellow citizens for a variety of offenses. The Gestapo and the other structures of Nazi power were too thinly spread to uncover every hostile word. They depended on denunciations. Robert Gellately and others have documented large numbers of denunciations to the organs of the state.[41] Streicher's *Der Stürmer* printed denunciations of more than 6,500 named or identifiable individuals for insufficient anti-Semitism between 1935 and the outbreak of the war. Many had simply displayed common courtesy or had commercial dealings with Jews.[42] Other Nazi organizations and publications also printed names of those who did not behave as expected, and the Nazis did not hesitate to arrest and sometimes execute those who violated the rules against public opposition.

The GDR was even more assiduous in protecting the public from infectious ideas. It faced the enormous problem that nearly everyone in the country could receive radio or television broadcasts from the "class enemy" to the west. I have already noted the efforts to discourage listening to or watching West German media, efforts that failed. Still, much was done to at least discourage people from talking in public about what they had learned.

Church leader Hans-Otto Furian observed: "The GDR was after all a state that feared nothing so much as the public."[43] The party and state worked hard to keep a unified public outlook on matters large and trivial. Some instances are amusing. For example, the GDR had a perpetual shortage of consumer goods. One could not blame the system for that, but neither could one pretend it did not exist. In 1980 there was a shortage of inexpensive tableware. A note in the SED files discusses the situation: "The wholesalers report that everything is being exported. The management cannot tell the sales clerks that, nor could they pass it on to the customers. If management here works out its explanation, that does not mean that the same argument is used in other shops in the city. To the contrary, each shop comes up with its own explanation, often the most varied ones at that. At the very least, we have to have the same explanation used in a city!"[44] Truth was less important than consistency. The literature on religious cults talks of "holy lies," lies that are said to be acceptable because they serve the divine good. The GDR had many such "holy lies."

Or consider the example of a worker who in 1962 responded to a special edition of *Neues Deutschland* on a Soviet space flight with the comment that "one can wipe his ass with that rag." A party member overhearing the remark "organized a meeting of the whole work brigade to make the situation clear to him. 'He apologized and said he did not mean it that way.'"[45] His public humiliation made it clear to the rest that ill-advised statements had consequences.

The net of Stasi (Ministry of State Security) informants was far tighter in the GDR than it had been in the Nazi period. About 2 percent of the adult GDR population had some relationship with the Stasi. The network of those willing to report their neighbors was well developed.[46] The GDR had forty years to build a refined system of dealing with dissidents, who faced a calculated mixture of isolation, professional pressure, prison, emigration, or expulsion. Those who gave any indication of hostile views were dealt with firmly, so firmly that the Stasi estimated in the spring of 1989 that there were only 2,500 activists and sixty "hard core" dissidents in the entire country.[47] Their definition is significant. Success generally was measured by the degree to which the citizenry was discouraged from expressing hostile views in public, not by what they thought inwardly. It turned out in the fall of 1989 that the majority of the population was not happy with its state, but only a tiny minority was willing to risk the sanctions that came with public disagreement. That is understandable. Given the GDR's success in controlling public discourse, the average citizen was hard-pressed to sense how widespread opposition attitudes were. Dirk Philipsen quotes a Leipzig dissident speaking of the situation in the mid-1980s. There were dissident groups scattered throughout the country, but they often were unaware of each other. "The really terrible thing about all of this is that nobody knew that these things were going on in other places. Just knowing about it would have made a big difference. Then you wouldn't have felt so alone. It would have encouraged us a great deal."[48]

To ensure the public facade of unanimity, the GDR took all necessary steps. Under GDR law, a gathering of more than three people for an identifiable public purpose required a permit. In 1983, for example, church officials in Leipzig were told they needed a permit for a public gathering where more than three people were to carry candles.[49] The Stasi and other forces guarded against any public demonstration of unapproved ideas. In 1988 a group of about 150 people left the Nikolai Church in Leipzig after a church gathering and walked through the city. The Stasi was present in force. According to the report in the Stasi files: "The participants in the procession carried no banners, symbols or other visible signs with them. . . . The group had no impact on public security and order; it had only slight public visibility."[50] The last point was the important one. Hardly anyone knew what was happening.

Demonstrations could be banned even if they had the right message. In 1983 a group from Weimar wanted to hold a demonstration in Berlin against NATO. The rub was that, although they favored state policy, it was to be an independent demonstration. On the scheduled day, there were about a hundred arrests in Berlin. Ulrich Poppe, a participant, notes: "That is the kind of fear this state had against an independently organized demonstration, independent of its content!"[51] The leadership certainly was conscious of the shaky ground on which its public support rested. Politburo member Günter Schabowski made an interesting statement during the German parliament's hearings on the GDR:

> The SED was a party that—although there may have been some who thought otherwise—never had majority support. We could proceed only by

ignoring whether or not we had a majority. If I have to wait for a majority, I have to choose the path of social democracy, and that we despised.

We lived continually by suppressing the reality that a large part of the population, perhaps the majority, was against us.[52]

The leading West German historian of the GDR, Hermann Weber, made a similar observation: "The fundamental failing of the GDR regime was, from start to finish, the absence of any democratic legitimization."[53] A system that suppresses disagreement faces an insoluble dilemma. It knows that its support may be shallow, but the harsher the methods it uses to enforce public unanimity, the more assiduously citizens conceal their true beliefs and display the approved ones, and the more the system fears its citizens are not behind it.

The Church Invisible

The church (whether Catholic or Protestant) was a particular threat to both the National Socialist and Marxist-Leninist systems, since it had a worldview and a source of authority entirely outside their frameworks and since it was all too visible. Large and ancient churches could not be overlooked. Widespread belief in God predated both systems, and the Almighty still had followers who sometimes placed their religious loyalty above their loyalty to the reigning political system. Neither system felt quite able to abolish the church by force, but neither could they lightly tolerate an institution that stood outside the prevailing orthodoxy.

Unlike the Marxists, the Nazis claimed to promote and defend religion. They aimed at co-opting religion more than eliminating it. Hitler sprinkled polite references to God in his major speeches. The Nazi platform pledged the party's support for a "positive Christianity." National Socialism had clear ideas as to how that positive Christianity should be exhibited. The church was to have nothing whatever to say about politics, limiting its activities purely to the spiritual realm, and Christianity's spiritual claims would be separated fully from believers' secular pursuits. As Hitler said in 1933: "The religions and the Churches will maintain their freedom. But we are in charge of politics."[54] A typical Nazi measure came in 1935: "[A]ll Catholic youth associations in the entire state of Prussia were forbidden to participate in any activities that were not of a purely religious nature. In particular, Catholic youth could no longer wear uniforms, or clothes that resembled uniforms in any way; they could not wear pins or medallions in public that would link them with Catholic associations, nor could they publicly display Catholic flags and banners; they were forbidden to go on marches or to go hiking and camping; and they were forbidden to participate in organized sporting activities of all kinds."[55] Protestant organizations suffered the same treatment.

Acceptable religious activity was to be hidden behind the walls of the church, invisible to all save those in attendance. The Nazis steadily complained about "political clergy," which meant any involvement at all by the church in activities not narrowly ecclesiastical. Large numbers of Christians were imprisoned and sometimes killed during the Third Reich. Essentially, the Nazis were denying the church status as an organization with a worldview. The Nazi Party could speak to everything. The church was to restrict its activity to the "purely spiritual." The SD kept careful watch on the church during the war, noting particularly its efforts to go beyond its "proper" role. The Catholics, for example, organized a nationwide "festival of faith" for the youth on Trinity Sunday in May 1940. The SD reported that the bishop of Fulda had said that the Christian faith was "more valuable than any worldview."[56] Although the Catholics had avoided overtly hostile rhetoric, there was no doubt either to church members or the Nazis about what that meant.

The Nazis' goal was to make the church as invisible as possible, to eliminate it as an alternate organization with a powerful and all-encompassing worldview. A 1942 newsletter for propagandists ordered party speakers to avoid religious questions entirely in public meetings: "Difficulties with religious matters have surfaced most of all where speakers let themselves be provoked and led into a discussion of such matters. This gives the church what it wants: a public discussion."[57] State organs kept careful watch over the church and fretted when surveillance was inadequate. Party files from Baden, for example, complain that the more people were involved with the church, the less they were involved with the party and that many meetings occurred behind the "hermetically sealed doors" of the Catholic parsonage, where no one reported on what was said and where there was no possibility of influence.[58]

Church membership remained high, although participation was not always strong. Even in 1939, 95 percent of the German population maintained church membership, including a majority of party members.[59] The hold of the church was clearest with regard to religious ceremonies. Despite attempts to establish party rituals, in many areas the party had less than 1 percent of the "market" for rituals of birth, marriage, and death.[60]

People might say "Heil Hitler," but when it came time to be buried they preferred a priest to their local group leader.

One must recall that for many Germans, membership in the church was nominal, a matter more of traditionalism than strong faith. In the country-side, the hold of the church was often strong, but in cities the story was different. In Berlin, for instance, 70 percent of the population were members of the church (they paid their church tax), but only about 9 percent had taken communion even once during 1932.[61] Still, even for those who were not convinced of the Christian faith, the church provided a refuge, a source of grounding for beliefs outside Nazi ideology. This was not acceptable.

Hitler and other Nazi leaders looked forward to a reckoning with the church once the war was won, but until then they were forced to tolerate its presence while working to limit its influence as much as possible. This was generally a calculated decision that taking forceful action would help the church more than harm it. For instance, Bishop Galen of Münster was outspoken in denouncing Nazi policies (for example, abolishing religious schools and euthanasia). He enjoyed enormous popularity in the heavily Catholic region. The party feared him but concluded that arresting him would cause real problems. As the propaganda leader for the area wrote to Goebbels in 1941: "Police measures against the bishop of Münster are hardly likely to be successful. Were he to be arrested and convicted, the church would see the bishop as a martyr and other bishops and priests would take up his assertions."[62] Many less prominent priests and pastors were arrested, but that generally occasioned only local protest.

The GDR benefited from the damage to the church's credibility resulting from its often inadequate response to Nazism. As a professedly atheist en-terprise, the SED could hardly favor religion. The official GDR position was that the "development, transformation and gradual disappearance of reli-gion follow the inevitable processes of human life."[63] Like the state, Marx-ism predicted that religion would fade away over time, but the church did not diminish as rapidly as the SED had hoped. The SED tried to hurry the process along by a concerted campaign.[64] The efforts took interesting direc-tions. One churchman remembers receiving a biographical dictionary of world history at the beginning of the 1960s that somehow avoided any mention of Jesus Christ.[65]

Like the Nazis, the SED attempted to restrict the church to purely "spir-itual" activities. Stasi head Erich Mielke wrote in 1956: "The existing churches in the GDR have lost a significant part of their influence on peo-ple by the separation of church and state, and will be more and more compelled to limit their activities to purely church matters."[66] Churchman Ehrhart Neubert noted the GDR's success in limiting the church's role in public: "The churches had no opportunity to express themselves independently and freely in public (e.g., in the media). They could only express their views on certain matters 'within the church,' as the regulations said. Even church-owned newspapers, magazines and publishing firms were subjected to strict censorship. Critical public statements and even hints of the same were immediately banned. The distribution of church newspapers was frequently blocked." The result was self-censorship on the part of the church.[67] Fearing to lose what little public say they had, religious leaders generally avoided saying things that would offend the party.

The GDR did try to "socialize" the church in a variety of ways. The GDR Christian Democratic Union was one of the four permitted non-SED parties. With a membership of about 140,000, it provided a way of incorporating Christians into the political structure. Late in its life the SED even discovered a slight affection for the church. The SED gave enthusiastic support for the 1983 Luther Year.[68] *Bear One Another's Burdens,* a surprisingly sympathetic film released in 1988, presented the struggle between a young Lutheran clergyman and a Communist, both patients at a tuberculosis sanitarium. They begin as determined foes but warm to each other as the film progresses. As Kurt Hager observed in a memo to Erich Honecker, the film's message was that "people have to work together for peace and socialism."[69] Many more examples could be given. They were attempts at directing religious energy in approved directions but also consistent with the larger goal: restricting the church to the spiritual realm. Outside of that, the church was to be as inconspicuous as possible.

The church unsettled the SED by providing shelter to some who were attracted more by the safety it provided than by its theology. As John Burgess observes, the church came to have "greater significance as a political than as a religious force."[70] I visited the *Statt-Kirchentag* in a Leipzig church in July 1989, an alternative gathering with a heavy ecological emphasis held during the Evangelical *Kirchentag* (church congress). Much there was far more open than one expected to find in the GDR. Of course, things were already beginning to move, but the experience confirmed what Wolfgang Gröger, the church's youth pastor in Leipzig in the early 1980s, told me of his visits to city hall to secure permission for various church activities. "You can do anything you want as long as it is inside the walls of a church," he was sometimes told. That was not strictly true, since the state's organs kept careful watch on what happened inside as well as outside the walls, but there was more flexibility if things happened where they could not be seen.

Despite the SED's success in keeping the church as invisible as possible, the church remained a problem throughout the GDR's history. In part, the SED simply did not understand it. As Mary Fulbrook notes: "The main miscalculation on the part of the SED here . . . was to assume that the Church operated according to the same hierarchy of command—in other words, that it was essentially characterized by the same democratic centralist structures—as the SED itself. To the SED's dismay, it discovered too late that it could not rely on the leadership of the Church to contain unruly spirits below; that 'turbulent priests' had greater leeway in the Church than did their secular counterparts under the iron hand of communist party discipline."[71]

Still, church membership steadily dropped. Once the SED adopted the policy of making church membership increasingly uncomfortable (but not impossible), those wishing a quiet life decided it was not worth the trouble. The GDR had 82 percent Protestant membership at its beginning. By the mid-1980s it was 30–40 percent. Only 7 percent of East Berliners claimed any church affiliation in 1987. In the new satellite towns (often built with no churches), membership was as low as 3 percent. The SED expected membership nationwide to drop to 20–25 percent by 2000.[72]

Sharp Swords

Goebbels observed that a "sharp sword" stood behind effective propaganda. The GDR Ministry of State Security advertised itself as the "shield and sword" of the party. Everyone knew that force stood behind propaganda. The knowledge that there were consequences for undesired behavior was not usually at the forefront of people's thinking, but they did not forget. As one socialist observer wrote in 1936: "The workers fail to take even those actions that require only a little courage."[73] Ehrhart Neubert asked: "Who in the GDR back then admitted that he was afraid? Only a few, and only in private. It is important that we understand that. Fear was instrumentalized and used by the system."[74] This is easy for those living in more open societies to forget or underestimate. Citizens of both systems knew that dissent risked rapid and severe punishment.

Yet few in Hitler's Germany or the GDR lived in steady fear. Both systems were generally "rational" in their use of terror. With some exceptions, those who got into trouble were not surprised. Most others, knowing the consequences for dissent, allowed their spines to bend, justifying their acquiescence in ways that were psychologically comfortable. There is the human tendency to assume that the universe is fair, that one gets what one deserves. The poor "deserve" to be poor, those arrested "deserve" to be arrested. This relieves the fears of most citizens. Both systems worked to persuade people that only those who deserved it were punished by the state.

Nazi Germany and the GDR were entirely willing to use force, sometimes terror, but generally as a last rather than a first persuasive method. As Hadamovsky noted in the chapter of his book titled "Propaganda and Force [*Gewalt*]": "Propaganda and force are never absolute opposites. The use of force can be a part of propaganda. Between them is every degree of effective influence over people and masses, beginning with the sudden winning of attention or the persuasion of the individual to thundering mass propaganda, from the loose organization of the converted to the creation of half-governmental or governmental institutions, from individual to mass terror, from the legitimate use of force by the stronger rank, class or state to forcing obedience and discipline by military force through martial law."[75] The sliding scale should also be somewhat undefined, leaving the audience unsure of the boundaries of "safe" conduct. They will err on the side of safety. In 1936, for example, people in Hamburg received a letter from the NSDAP local group urging them to display the flag on holidays. It ended with this sentence: "We hope that you will need no further reminder."[76] The letter makes it clear that something could happen to recalcitrant citizens but leaves it to their imagination what it might be.

Werner Best, a high Gestapo official, was clear on the Nazi willingness to use force in 1936. He wrote that the Gestapo was charged with eliminating any challenge to the Nazi worldview. He put it in medical terms:

> Each attempt to promote another political outlook, or even to maintain one, is viewed as a manifestation of disease that threatens the healthy unity of the indivisible national organism that must be eliminated, without regard to the subjective desires of its bearer. . . .
>
> Fulfilling this task is made more difficult by the fact that, since the National Socialist revolution, all outward signs of enemy activity have been eliminated, but their human bearers still exist and to a large degree still pursue their goals in new secret or concealed ways. To find these enemies of the state, to watch over them, and to render them harmless at the proper moment is the prophylactic task of a political police.[77]

Best was worried that he could not see into people's souls and knew that many were only going through the motions. His Gestapo had the medical task of keeping an infection from spreading. He was concerned not about overt action but rather about detecting ideas that, though hidden, could lead to public action.

A remarkable 1943 article in the *Schwarze Korps,* the SS weekly, made clear the sword behind propaganda. It told the story of a soldier home on leave after being wounded at Stalingrad. While visiting friends, the conversation turned to an old woman who had complained about the war effort. People suggested she was not quite right in the head and did not need to be taken seriously. Reporting her might send her to prison or even the gallows. The *Schwarze Korps* was of a different opinion. It noted that there was only "a small percentage of criminals and racial trash in Germany" who opposed the war effort but that they could weaken the resolve of the soldiers at the front: "It therefore goes without saying that we must treat these few outsiders with the same determination and harshness that we show toward the enemy, regardless of how stupid and innocuous we find them. This a war for our very survival. He who does not want our victory wants our defeat. He who wants our defeat wants our death." Those who did not report such people, the article concluded, were cowardly traitors.[78] The article suggested that opponents were few and despicable, buttressing the facade of unanimity while at the same time suggesting that the punishment for failing to support the state, even by an old woman not in full command of her faculties, could be death.

During the twilight of the GDR, Erich Mielke led a Stasi staff meeting. He asked what the mood was in the factories and was told: "That is naturally a very complicated question at the moment, Comrade Minister." Mielke's response: "That is a very simple question. It is a question of power, nothing else." Later in the same meeting he asked if there was the prospect of another 17 June 1953 (the uprising suppressed by Soviet tanks). His subordinate assured him there was no such threat: "That will not happen tomorrow. After all, that is why we are here."[79] The GDR's citizens remembered what happened in their own country in 1953, and Hungary in 1956, and Czechoslovakia in 1968, and Poland in the 1980s.

A person considering robbing a bank may be discouraged by the knowledge that the police are likely to intervene and may be frustrated by the knowledge but not terrified. Totalitarian systems exert a similar pressure. The vast majority of their citizens, knowing at least some of the sliding scale of state measures that awaited unpopular actions, choose to avoid trouble. Propaganda does not hesitate to suggest the power that is hidden behind it. But people are unlikely to tell themselves that they have refrained from a given action through cowardice. They reduce the dissonance by gradually changing attitudes; an action once considered but rejected is less likely to be considered the next time.

Furthermore, it is hard to summon the resolve to resist. In democratic societies, one presumes a certain amount of controversy. In the United States, for instance, Democrats expect Republicans to disagree with them. The sanctioning of disagreement makes it easier to disagree. Totalitarian societies resist and punish most forms of public disagreement while at the same time presenting a facade of certainty. This puts citizens in a difficult position. They are uncertain in the face of certainty. They know that supporting a worldview other than the prevailing one may result in drastic penalties. Yet it is also hard to chip away at a wall of orthodoxy with cautiously stated critical arguments that must presume the fundamental validity of that very orthodoxy. That is, citizens of the GDR had to argue from the basis of socialism in their attempts to change it, yet the SED defined attempts to change socialism by individuals or groups as unacceptable, since only the collective wisdom of the party was able to determine where the party should go. Citizens of Nazi Germany faced a similar wall of orthodoxy that forced those who dissented to use weak arguments to attack an apparently absolute case. What is one against the many, the unsure against the sure? By making many arguments impossible, totalitarian states left the remaining arguments weak.

The Price of Unanimity

Both systems put enormous effort into achieving the illusion of unanimity, which was the foundation of effective propaganda. Whether in elections where 99 percent apparently voted the correct way, in the media, in the schools, or in ordinary public discourse, the goal was to impose an edifice of approved opinion. An extended passage from Václav Havel describes the result:

> The manager of a fruit and vegetable shop places in his window, among the onions and carrots, the slogan: "Workers of the World, Unite!" Why does he do it? What is he trying to communicate to the world? Is he genuinely enthusiastic about the idea of unity among the workers of the world? Is his enthusiasm so great that he feels an irrepressible impulse to acquaint the

public with his ideals? Has he really given more than a moment's thought to how such a unification might occur and what it would mean?

I think it can safely be assumed that the overwhelming majority of shopkeepers never think about the slogans they put in their windows, nor do they use them to express their real opinions. That poster was delivered to our greengrocer from the enterprise headquarters along with the onions and carrots. He put them all into the window simply because it has been done that way for years, because everyone does it, and because that is the way it has to be. If he were to refuse, there could be trouble. He could be reproached for not having the proper "decoration" in his window; someone might even accuse him of disloyalty. He does it because these things must be done if one is to get along in life. It is one of the thousands of details that guarantee him a relatively tranquil life "in harmony with society," as they say.[80]

Havel notes the importance of obedience, of doing the "right" thing in public, and ends with the importance of ideology, or secular faith. The greengrocer surely took the sign out of his window after Czechoslovakia's "Velvet Revolution" moved Havel from prison to the presidency, but even so small a step as putting a sign in a window helped to firm up his unenthusiastic support of the state. The greengrocer may never have been a fervent Communist, but neither was he likely to join with other greengrocers to make a revolution if, as it seemed, nearly everyone else favored the way things were. His faith in the ideology was dim but present. Only when other greengrocers began removing the signs from their windows was he likely to remove the one from his.

Both systems were populated by a relatively small number of "true believers," often those who had risked their lives fighting for a National Socialist or Communist vision, by a much larger group of lukewarm citizens who went along to get along, and by a few who were willing to express public opposition. In that sense, both Nazism and Marxism-Leninism were successful in their persuasive goals. But both knew their support was fragile. Nazism enjoyed more genuine popularity than the GDR, but despite Goebbels's campaigns against grumblers and complaining, an enormous amount of it went on, and once the mixture of propaganda and force vanished in 1945 Germans rapidly relinquished "eternal National Socialist values" in favor of what came next—parliamentary democracy in the West, Marxism-Leninism in the East. The citizens of the GDR, who had the misfortune to lose the war "twice," found themselves with a new and imposed secular faith. By 1970 or so they had adjusted to it, but its shallow hold was revealed in 1989 when, to the surprise of many intellectuals who still saw in the vision of socialism hope for the future, the bulk of the nation's citizenry made it clear that they had no wish to carry on the facade any longer. Just as a religion fails in its goals when it wins outward compliance but not inner conviction, a system of enforced unanimity may seem to rest on broad support but in the end finds it rests only on force.

Summary

Both the National Socialist and GDR systems extended propaganda to every area of public life. Through a comprehensive system of measures using both the carrot and the stick, spines gradually bent. It does not take fear of prison or other catastrophic sanctions to bend spines. In Havel's words from 1975: "[I]t is not the absolute value of a threat which counts, so much as its relative value. It is not so much what someone objectively loses, as the subjective importance it has for him on the plane on which he lives, with its own scale of values. . . . Everyone has something to lose and so everyone has reason to be afraid."[81] Attitudes generally do not change instantly, rather step by step. One step makes the next easier, and it is hard to turn back. Each time a person gives in to the pressure, each time one's spine bends a little more, the next step becomes easier. It is uncomfortable psychologically to admit what is happening, so people in general do not.

The Holocaust could not have occurred in 1933. The Nazis themselves were not ready for it. But after eight years of relentless propaganda and energetic state measures, few were ready to stand by the Jews. I disagree with Daniel Goldhagen's argument that Germany was filled with willing executioners, but surely most Germans did not care much for the Jews and were willing to ignore the signs of barbarism plain to those who wished to see.[82] Only when things happened suddenly were they jolted to awareness and then only for a little while.

The GDR was spared the worst excesses of Marxism-Leninism, which after all is responsible for the deaths of as many as 100 million people over its not-yet-finished existence.[83] Had the Soviets decided to march west, however, who doubts that the GDR would have joined in? Spines bent over the years in ways small and large. Christians in the GDR fought the introduction of the *Jugendweihe* in the 1950s. By 1980 most Christian parents allowed their children to participate. Citizens grew used to holding their tongues and doing the expected things.

Each step of submission was one-way, difficult to reverse. As propaganda molded behavior, attitudes followed. Jesus said that those who can be trusted in small things can be trusted in great things (Luke 16:10), but the converse is also true. Those who bend on small things will bend in time on larger ones. By the late war years, many Germans had the uneasy feeling that the war had to be won because, as morale reports noted, they knew that dreadful things had happened in the East and feared Jewish revenge. Once they had had moral qualms. Now they feared revenge. Citizens of the GDR had nothing as horrifying to fear, but they, too, had grown used to "living the lie," and behaviors that once grated had become taken for granted. Neither system successfully won the full loyalty of its citizens— but both established a sufficient degree of public uniformity through a combination of propaganda and force to make citizens behave as if they had.

8

The Failure of Propaganda

The propagandas of the Third Reich and the GDR failed. Both had as their goal better and lasting worlds populated by new kinds of human beings. The Third Reich survived twelve years, the GDR forty. Both collapsed absolutely, the Third Reich by military force, the GDR through a gradual decline that became suddenly evident when its citizens realized their leaders were no longer prepared to maintain their rule by the bullet. Neither system, despite talk of eternal values and scientific laws, produced adherents who were eager to restore them after they were gone. Nazism's latter-day followers are ordinarily unpleasant crackpots. The GDR's remaining proponents hope not for a return to the days of Honecker but to a revival of the original vision of socialism. Why did such enormous efforts to sway human attitudes have so little permanent effect? Let me begin by reviewing where and why the systems succeeded before turning to their ultimate failures.

Success

The primary success came in establishing the illusion, both at home and abroad, that National Socialism and Marxism-Leninism had a depth of support greater than they in fact had. Those who visited Nazi Germany in the 1930s returned with the impression of a country in which the vast majority of the population, if perhaps not 99 percent, supported the Führer. The Nuremberg rallies were persuasive spectacles both for participants and observers, as were the mass meetings and mass organizations. Germans themselves had difficulty determining how deep Hitler's support was. People knew their own attitudes and those of their close friends and family. Everyone knew that sensible souls were unlikely to express hostile views in public, but the appearance of unanimity that resulted from multiple pressures was persuasive.

The almost uniform mass media of the GDR, the well-organized mass gatherings, and the hulking apparatus of party and state presented a facade of a smoothly functioning system. There seemed little reason to believe that such an outwardly solid system was built on shifting sand. The GDR's sudden disappearance startled everyone, including scholars who predicted stability for the GDR even as it was collapsing.[1] The Stasi thought its state secure since there were only a handful of passionate dissidents. When visiting the GDR in 1988 and 1989, I told acquaintances that the GDR would have to make major changes within ten years. They replied that I was an American optimist and that it would take at least fifty years. We were both wrong by significant, if differing, margins.

In state religions, citizens generally at least go through the motions, making it difficult to be sure who believes and who does not. The same is true in political religions. Some citizens passionately believed in National Socialism or Marxism-Leninism. Both systems explained the world as it was and promised a better world to come. Many of the most dedicated believers had fought for their systems when they unpopular, often at personal cost. They had risked death and injury, endured scorn, lived in exile. Misguided they were, but many believed themselves fighting for noble causes.

Once their systems gained power, they were in an awkward rhetorical situation. Like Christians after the emperor Constantine's conversion, their once despised cause now controlled the state. Realizing their goals proved challenging. It is easier to attack than to build. Having sacrificed much, it was difficult to surrender belief; the pressures to keep believing were great. As Milovan Djilas wrote in the 1950s: "The world has seen few heroes as ready to sacrifice and suffer as the Communists were on the eve of and during the revolution. It has probably never seen such characterless wretches and stupid defenders of arid formulas as they became after attaining power."[2] Some dedicated to Hitler's cause before 1933 were not much different.

For the true believers, propaganda reinforced their beliefs. Since they accepted its premises, they were forgiving of its faults and eager to believe its claims. Having given much to win victory, admitting that they had fought for a dubious cause would have resulted in considerable dissonance. They *wanted* to believe, and propaganda gave them reason in full measure. Nazism or Marxism-Leninism became their de facto religion, the party group their congregation.

But true believers were the minority. The far greater percentage of the population was less committed. Hitler's best showing in a free election was 37 percent of the popular vote, and most of them were not true believers. Socialism came to the GDR with Russian troops and probably could never have won a majority in a free election. Propaganda was a critical element in maintaining the support of half-hearted believers.

Both systems, after all, claimed great goals. Few people supported Hitler in the hopes that he would bring world war or kill millions of Jews, nor did Nazi propaganda claim that he would. Rather, Hitler spoke of peace, national recovery, morality, even God. As Alan Bullock observed: "No man ever spoke with greater feeling of the horror and stupidity of war than Adolf Hitler."[3] He provided successes that a considerable majority of the German population welcomed: great reductions in unemployment, remilitarization, territorial conquest, a general brightening of mood. Marxism-Leninism did not win supporters by proposing a rigid bureaucracy, a ruined economy, and the Berlin Wall. Instead, it promised an egalitarian society free of exploitation, war, and misery. Its ability to provide social services and a dependable standard of living earned respect. Both systems took power from predecessors that had failed. After the great disaster of the Depression and the even greater disaster of World War II, Germans were willing to hope that a new system could at least make things better. It was hard to imagine them getting worse.

The evil of these two systems was both evident and hard to see at the same time. The great goals gave hope, the unpleasant elements could be ignored or explained away. When Germans claimed that they had known nothing about the Holocaust, they were engaging in a mixture of truth and self-deception. The evidence had been there, but most had not wanted to see it. J.P. Stern put it this way: "The people of the Reich, it seems, knew as much (for example about the killing of their German fellow citizens) or as little (for example about the killing of their Jewish fellow citizens) as they wanted to know. What they did not know, they did not want to know, for obvious reasons. But not wanting to know always means knowing enough to know that one doesn't want to know more."[4] There were reasons not to see what was unpleasant. Cowardice is one reason, but so is ordinary human nature. Few even in open societies go out of their way to encounter that which is unpleasant.

For those whose faith wavered, propaganda provided plausible reasons to believe. Reasons are important, even if they are not particularly good reasons. Ellen Langer's classic study had people ask to break into a line at a photocopy machine. Sixty percent of those who asked to break in without giving a reason succeeded. Ninety-four percent of those who gave a good reason ("I'm late for class") succeeded. A startling 93 percent of those who gave a poor reason ("Excuse me, may I use the Xerox machine, because I have to make some copies?") succeeded.[5] What was important was not the quality of the reason, rather that there was one. In a larger sense, propaganda also provided reasons, if often poor ones. World War II began, Germans were told, because the Western allies were trying to encircle Germany and because Poland attacked a German radio station. The Berlin Wall was built to keep Western fascists from destroying the GDR. These arguments were supported by a mass of evidence. Though the evidence was sometimes of poor quality, finding solid contrary evidence was usually difficult.

In opposing the system, one seemed to be opposing the vision of a better future. One could accept the inadequacies of the present in the hope of what would come. A frequent comment in Nazi Germany was: "If only the Führer knew." Hitler, despite his almost superhuman abilities, could not be expected to know everything. Such comments permitted people to view evil as peripheral to the system. Hans-Dieter Schütt, editor of *Junge Welt*, said after 1989: "My relationship with socialism was like that with a coat that one has buttoned wrongly from the first, but notices only with the last button. Still, the coat keeps one warm."[6] Another writer compared the view of many GDR intellectuals toward their state with that of parents toward a child with a disability: "a desperate, self-torturing love aware of the defect, hoping for improvement and filled with defensive rage when outsiders mention the problem."[7]

Moreover, propaganda presented facades of overwhelming public acceptance. The media, the arts, the schools, everyday activities—all suggested that nearly everyone else was in general sympathy with the state. Not only did such unanimity discourage actively hostile opinion and encourage ostentatiously approved behavior, the pressure it produced to conform led citizens gradually to shift their internal opinions to be consistent with their public behavior. One cannot say "Heil Hitler" a dozen times a day without being affected. Even in a democratic state repetition works, as advertisers know when they build frequency into their campaigns.

It was further impossible to live a normal life without regularly bending to the party. A socialist observer within Germany thought in 1937 that the Nazis had given up trying to persuade every citizen. Instead, their system was so extensive that "no one can get anything done in Germany without depending on some National Socialist organization."[8] Little happened in the GDR without some involvement or support from the party. To live a relatively normal life, people simply had to bow to the system, to say and do what was expected of them.

And the consequences of public disbelief were unpleasant. Life became more difficult. One's career—or worse, the future of one's children—could be damaged by opposing the massive structures of society. As Havel observes: "Most people are loath to spend their days in ceaseless conflict with authority, especially when it can only end in the defeat of the isolated individual. So why not do what is required of you? It costs nothing, and in time you cease to bother about it."[9] Both systems wanted to be taken for granted, to be seen as a realities that had to be accepted. One may not like a thunderstorm but still takes out the umbrella.

The mental processes are not unique to those living under totalitarian states. Pressures to conform are strong in any society. Timur Kuran's work on preference falsification argues that apparent public consensus encourages people to overdo their public performances as a way of demonstrating that they "really" believe.[10] Ellul argues: "The aim of modern propaganda is no longer to modify ideas, but to provoke action."[11] Actions change attitudes at least as much as attitudes change actions. Propaganda builds habits of belief and expression. Both Nazism and Marxism-Leninism worked mightily to get people to vote, to join the expected organizations, to say the right things, to avoid behaviors that might prove troublesome.

The sanctions for violating norms have power. GDR journalists later spoke of "the scissors in the head," or self-censorship. Authors noted that censorship stopped some books from being published, but self-censorship prevented even more from being written at all. Again, this is not limited to totalitarian states. A survey of American journalists published in 2000 found that a quarter of them had avoided newsworthy stories because they anticipated professional difficulties.[12] Whatever the merits of the brouhaha over "political correctness" in the United States, there is scarcely doubt that even in open societies many factors conjoin in ways leading to spirals of silence or prudence.

Looking around at the unrelenting propaganda surrounding them, it is not surprising that most citizens of National Socialist Germany or the GDR chose to live as peacefully as possible. Moreover, since to most of them politics was not as central as their leaders wanted it to be, the compromises that gradually bent their spines were relatively easy to make. A common rationalization in both systems was to believe that if one were not doing a particular job, he or she would likely be replaced by a hard-liner. Going part of the way prevented someone else from going all of the way. But going part of the way today makes it easier to go all the way tomorrow.

Both systems called for absolute commitment but settled for citizens who caused no trouble and made at least some public signs of holding the right attitudes and doing the right things. As long as the twin pillars of propaganda and force held, the Potemkin villages stood.

Failure

In a deeper sense, both propagandas failed catastrophically. Both claimed to tell the truth; neither was credible. Both demanded enthusiastic support but settled for public compliance. Both spoke of eternal values; neither had them. Both caused more misery than joy. Their failures are at root the same. Both asked propaganda to do more than it can do.

One must begin by remembering that both systems failed primarily for reasons that had little to do with propaganda. Despite the claims of Nazi propaganda, human will was not sufficient to overcome the overwhelming enemy advantage in men and matériel. Hitler's Reich collapsed under military force that no amount of propaganda could have withstood. The GDR imploded because the Soviet Union was no longer willing to support it militarily and because of its desolate economic condition. The best propaganda can only go so far in persuading people to ignore the evidence of their senses, particularly when Goebbels's sharp sword no longer is behind it.

Totalitarian propaganda fails for inherent reasons that over the long term (which may be generations) make it unable to achieve the goals its makers set. It fails because it is untruthful, because it encourages hypocrisy, and because it is in the biblical sense idolatrous, placing a human absolute in place of a divine absolute. The last is the worst. With the conviction that the Führer or the party is infallible, the way to evil is open.

Total claims to truth make propaganda deceitful. National Socialists and Marxist-Leninists ignored facts that were sometimes obvious. For systems that claim truth, reality is inconvenient. Things don't turn out the way the theory predicts they should. As Havel observes: "Reality does not shape theory, but rather the reverse. Thus power gradually draws closer to ideology than it does to reality; it draws its strength from theory and becomes entirely dependent on it."[13] Propaganda is forced into a shifting relationship with the world as it is. Since one cannot admit error, reality bends like spines to the requirements of ideology. A classic case for the Nazis was the German-Soviet pact of August 1939 that freed Germany to begin the war. It eliminated the prospect of a two-front war until Hitler thought he was ready for it two years later, but it was in ugly contradiction to everything the Nazis had said for years. The system was at a loss to explain it even to its propagandists.[14] Joseph Stalin, the great friend of the German people, became an unperson after his death. Observant GDR citizens noticed.

News determined by propaganda undermined confidence in the system. Ellul notes that propaganda needs to be consonant with the facts: it "cannot prevail against facts that are too massive and definite."[15] Goebbels recognized that news could not disagree with people's direct experiences, ordering, for example, that reports of bombing damage should be accurate in the affected area: "It is nonsense to distort facts which have taken place in front of everybody's eyes."[16] However, any observant citizen knew that the news was manipulated. As a 1942 SD report observed: "Citizens have the feeling that the public media always provide the 'official view' of negative events. The result is that wide circles of the public no longer see the press as the best source of information."[17]

People in these systems lived with the knowledge that news was not reliable, that the government would say what it needed to say to reach its ends. In 1965, as a draft of the forthcoming *Argument der Woche* (a pamphlet sent to agitators) dealing with Western television was being circulated around the Agitation Department for criticism, one staff member suggested: "I think the argument that opinion surveys have found that 75% don't believe Western television is *a* bad *one*. Would that it were so!"[18] Private disbelief had little direct impact on day-to-day life and could be more or less ignored, but it also left a nagging knowledge that there was a discrepancy between ideals and reality. Both citizens and leaders were engaged in public hypocrisy. The government told citizens things that were not true, and that citizens often knew to be untrue, but required them to behave in public as if they were true.

That was not in itself a critical problem. Even if citizens were not sure, they could not personally check out every story and every fact. The vast majority of the news in both systems had at least some basis in fact. More than that, the news set the agenda for public opinion. Citizens who read about the Night of the Long Knives in 1934 knew that Ernst Röhm was no longer a great hero of the movement and adopted their public statements accordingly. Citizens who read reports that people throughout the GDR welcomed the building of the Wall might not share those sentiments, but they knew what they should say to avoid difficulties. And people's daily lives were of more direct interest to them than the secondhand events reported by the press and broadcast media.

The larger problem was that propaganda could give neither system what it craved: a citizenry of one mind and one spirit. Instead, it promoted hypocrisy. A 1935 report from the Münster area noted that public enthusiasm was low. The signs were subtle: "Since people fear legal consequences, their true feelings seldom are expressed in public. But their true opinions are evident in the obvious passivity of the population with regards to the movement's meetings."[19] There are many similar comments in the files.

Citizens played the game, but many of them knew better. The Nazis satirized "the 110 percenters," citizens who tried too hard to wear the cloak of loyalty, but they also went after those whose commitment seemed less than 100 percent. It was hard to walk the line between over- and under-enthusiasm. As Politburo member Günter Schabowski noted, the SED knew that many who joined the mass organizations and said the expected things in public were not strong supporters. Leaders had to act in public as if they believed they had mass support, knowing that the support was shallower than they wished.

One way to see the problem is to recall Hitler's distinction between the members and followers of a political movement. The members were passionate, willing to risk all, true believers. The followers were those who voted for a party or made modest sacrifices in its cause but for whom it was not of life-forming significance. This is a useful distinction for a revolutionary movement, but when the movement gains power and insists that all share the passion of the few, difficulties inevitably come. It is no longer easy to tell the two groups apart. A citizen does not "suffer" for being a Nazi or a Communist. Now a citizen suffers for not being one. It becomes difficult to tell who really believes and who does not.

One cannot compel long-term passionate belief. It is relatively easy to make people act as if they believe. Most people will adjust outwardly to prevailing opinion. For a state that wants peace and order, that may be sufficient, but not for worldviews, whether religious or political. Both National Socialism and Marxism-Leninism produced citizens who merely went through the motions. People pretended to believe, and governments pretended to believe that people believed.

Internal GDR reports make the point. Shortly after the building of the Wall, a report on the medical profession noted that physicians were saying: "Particularly after 13.8. [1961], it is not good to say anything. It is best to say nothing. One does not always have the proper opinion, after all."[20] A summary of discussions with journalists two years later found that they were leery of any kind of criticism, particularly of functionaries: "It is best to keep away from it, since then at least nothing can happen to one."[21] One Soviet citizen told a Western journalist that he had six faces: "one for my wife; one, less candid, for my children, just in case they blurted out things heard at home; one for close friends; one for acquaintances; one for colleagues at work; and one for public display."[22] Citizens of the Third Reich and the GDR could say the same.

The majority of citizens in both states did not actively resist the propaganda they encountered. Much of it they even accepted, at least on a superficial level. A considerable majority of the citizens of Hitler's Reich would have voted for him even in a free election by 1938. At least a significant minority of the GDR's citizens favored the vision of socialism. But the roots were shallow. Most held the "right" views because such views were safe and easy and because they were outwardly plausible. Yet there was unease in the corners of their minds.

A 1984 report of the Institute for Youth Research in Leipzig found that 80 percent of the GDR's youth listened to or watched West German media. This had clear consequences on their attitude toward the GDR: "A central finding of previous research is the strong relationship between high consumption of Western media and lower political consciousness, lower societal activity, a lower significance of socialist values for one's life orientation, and so on."[23] These were still young people who were members of the FDJ, who served in the army, who joined the right organizations when they matured. They adapted to what was expected of them. Günter Gaus's classic description of the GDR as a "niche society" speaks to the same point. People found corners where they could do as they wished, relatively free of party or state coercion.[24] This, of course, contradicted the GDR's claim that there was no corner of life that was not political. Whereas religions tend to integrate belief and action, totalitarian systems tend to disintegrate people's thoughts and actions, no matter how much propaganda is poured into them.

Horst Sindermann, then head of the SED's Agitation Department, speaking to a propaganda conference in 1959, said clearly what was true for the entire history of the GDR: "Discussions with citizens clearly prove how unclear citizens still are even about the central questions of our policies."[25] In SED jargon, that meant disagreement. A report from the GDR's Academy of Sciences in the last months noted: "[T]he conviction that our era is characterized above all by the transition from capitalism to socialism has clearly weakened. A growing number of workers no longer accepts automatically our view that socialism is the historically necessary and socially desirable alternative to capitalism."[26] These are reports of what a church writer might call a "spiritual vacuum." The core beliefs of the system were evaporating.

Strong forces joined to keep those of little faith holding on to their little faith. Testifying to the Enquete Commission, Wolfgang Schuller outlined the fundamental repressive principles of the GDR system, principles that apply as well to the Third Reich:

- A broad, impenetrable and comprehensive network of measures that hindered any opposition;
- A "Mafia Principle," by which he means that both systems forced citizens to bend to their wills, to collaborate to a greater or lesser degree, to accomplish even life's ordinary purposes;
- An environment that seemed fixed and immovable;

The result of these principles was "a feeling of weakness, a feeling of subordination, a feeling of being at someone else's mercy, and, perhaps a little overstated, a feeling of anxiety, and that by intention."[27]

Although repression succeeded in keeping most people quiet, it did not make them true believers, only nervous ones. The fundamental problem is that the freedom to disbelieve is essential if one is to believe.[28] Both systems demanded belief, and made it unpleasant to disbelieve, at least outwardly. Citizens knew why they were doing what they were doing in public, and felt no pressure to internalize the demands of the system, to make them their own.

Not only ordinary citizens faced a dilemma between their private and public lives. Party members and functionaries were in a treacherous position. On the one hand, they were devoting their lives to a cause some thought had high and noble goals, or what at least could be thought to be such. On the other hand, they could see the failings of their system as clearly as anyone else yet were less free to admit it. With the decline in ideological fervor, the leadership's nature changed. Havel's 1987 description of Czechoslovakia also applies to the GDR: "We are no longer governed by fanatics, revolutionaries, or ideological zealots. The country is administered by faceless bureaucrats who profess adherence to a revolutionary ideology, but look out only for themselves, and no longer believe in anything."[29] The GDR produced a huge corps of functionaries who were "professional believers." Their livelihoods depended on saying and doing the right things. In the words of Jesus, many were "whited sepulchres," presenting a facade that concealed hypocrisy.

This situation had a critical role in the GDR's ultimate collapse. Lenin, Stalin, or even Ulbricht would not have stood by as the GDR disintegrated in 1989. They would have used state force. Earlier approaches to totalitarianism observed this clearly. Friedrich and Brzezinski's classic 1965 *Totalitarian Dictatorship and Autocracy,* for example, claimed: "The [totalitarian] system, because of the alleged ideological infallibility of its dogma, is continually tempted to increase terror by a violent passion for assent, for unanimity."[30] Jeane Kirkpatrick's *Dictatorships and Double Standards* made a similar argument in 1982.[31] The argument was reasonable, since in fact there were as yet no examples of totalitarian states fading away like Lewis Carroll's Cheshire Cat. The argument, however, assumed that new leaders of totalitarian states would maintain the same willingness to hold to power whatever the cost. This did not turn out to be true. When it came time to shoot, second- or third-generation Communist leaders across Europe who had lost the passion of the founders flinched. Their own faith in the systems was too weak to justify killing.

Nazism's leaders did not have sufficient time to reach such a state, though later generations of leaders would have lacked the passion of the first. Nonetheless, large numbers of bureaucrats and functionaries who adjusted to the advent of the new system did lack the revolutionary fervor Nazism demanded. This was a source of steady distress to the leadership.

Ironically, propaganda deceived its own leadership, eager to believe what it wished to believe. Besides, the systems were usually good to those who kept them functioning. Albert Speer surrounded the evening gathering of Nazi leaders during the Nuremberg rallies with the spectacular "dome of light," with scores of searchlights pointing upward, in part to conceal the growing paunches. Speer, a remarkable and able man, served the system with a passion that provided him with opportunity for a lifetime of reflection after 1945. Although the SED leadership suburb of Wandlitz did not rival the palaces of Nazi leaders, it was a pleasanter place to live than an apartment in a high-rise housing development.

The masses seemed to appreciate their leaders. Such support is satisfying. As Timothy Garton Ash observed, "the element of simple vanity should never be underrated in explaining the conduct of men and women in power."[32] Speer reported driving through a series of villages with Hitler. As word passed from one village to the next, the waiting crowds grew. Hitler remarked: "Heretofore only one German has been hailed like this: Luther. When he rode through the country, people gathered from far and wide to cheer him. As they do for me today!"[33] Erich Honecker, interviewed after the collapse of his state, simply could not understand what had happened. "My fall as chief of party and state was the result of a vast plot, the organizers of which are still hiding in the background," he said, utterly missing the fact that it was brought on by a massively disaffected citizenry.[34] A well-regulated system kept him supplied with good news and happy workers. He saw few signs of impending doom, at least few signs that he chose to see.

One reason there were few signs is that subordinates knew that forthrightness was not a good career move. Hitler told his followers that no one should complain to him about poor morale. It was their responsibility to produce good morale.[35] As a result, sanitized reports were passed up the line. Even those at the lower level who were relatively direct in their reports had their words toned down by their superiors.[36] Mary Fulbrook found the same phenomenon in the GDR: "Reports from the provinces were increasingly bland depictions of alleged popular support for the regime and its ruler; and those, such as Hans Modrow, First Secretary of Dresden, who sought to draw Honecker's attention to the social realities which lay below the mounting discontent, were disciplined for their pains."[37] The standard report from SED district first secretaries to Berlin began with a litany of successes, with cautious mention of real problems that might be solved with some extra resources toward the end. This, too, promoted internal hypocrisy. Leaders knew they were bending their spines to please their superiors. There was no space for critics and hence for truth. Sycophants replace prophets when leaders believe too strongly in their own greatness.

The same was true across public life. People grew used to what Eastern Europeans called "living the lie" or "breathing underwater." Such behavior can lead to relatively stable societies for a time, but it does not produce what both Nazism and the GDR wanted: new Nazi or socialist men and women committed passionately to a coming utopia. Instead, they got citizens who cheered on command, who said the right things in public, who even believed some or much of what propaganda told them, but superficially rather than deeply. They were like adherents to a state religion who do not quite disbelieve.

New societies are not built by people who do not disbelieve but by those with passion and a willingness to sacrifice. Both Nazism and socialism had such followers before they gained power. They may not have been the best, but, in Auden's words, they were filled with "passionate intensity." Nazism did not outlive its founders, but after forty-five years of Marxism, most GDR leaders were of the second or third generation. Some still had passion, but many were themselves half-hearted believers with a personal interest in the continuation of the system. They grew less willing to shoot their fellow citizens to defend the system.

National Socialism had a stronger base of support than Marxism-Leninism, but it faded quickly from Germany after 1945. It took courage to march in Leipzig on 9 October 1989, the night the East German revolution began. It was not at all clear that the GDR's leaders had lost the willingness to back propaganda with force. Once they failed to use power to stop that massive display of public dissatisfaction, the system crumbled within weeks. Those with less courage joined those with more until even those with no courage at all joined the throng.

The pressure for unanimity corrupted the systems. Too many people said too many things they did not believe too many times. Few raised in public problems that nearly all privately saw. That does not mean there was no disagreement. Hitler's henchmen and his generals could disagree with him—and sometimes persuade him. The GDR's citizens in private conversations (even at party meetings) spoke of the cracks in the system. But there was no public forum for significant criticism in either system. Propaganda and force saw to that. As Ellul claims: "Propaganda ceases where simple dialogue begins."[38] And evil begins where simple dialogue ends.

"The only person who likes change is a wet baby," as a recent phrase puts it. Without voices urging change, little changes. The Nazi system could not respond effectively to challenges that required more than order and obedience to resolve. It is interesting that some of its greatest successes came in areas where relative openness prevailed (for example, Albert Speer's ministry). The GDR's command economy functioned in jerks and starts. At the end of the GDR, Honecker was boasting of the enormous resources that had been sunk into producing a one megabyte computer chip that was outdated as he spoke. Meanwhile, the GDR's factories, despite talk of being the world's tenth leading industrial nation, had no hope of being competitive once the protections of the closed system vanished after 1989.

But worse than one-sided newspapers, economic failure, and corroded personalities, the propagandas of both systems called evil good and good evil, and few had the courage to say nay. The scale of evil perpetrated by German National Socialism dwarfs that caused by the GDR, but the GDR was part of a larger system that killed as many as 100 million people. The controversy occasioned by *The Black Book of Communism* is interesting evidence that, for some, the victims of Marxism-Leninism are more "acceptable" than the victims of National Socialism, that their deaths somehow are not as evil since, to their minds, Marxism-Leninism was pursuing noble goals; but it pursued those goals using many of the same methods as its competing worldview.[39]

Claiming to have the truth, each system was incapable of repairing the evil it produced. In the conviction that they could mold a new and uniform type of human being, they destroyed existing human beings. Pope John Paul II's 1993 encyclical letter *Veritatis Splendor* made the point precisely: "[T]he root of modern totalitarianism is to be found in the denial of the transcendent dignity of the human person who, as the visible image of the invisible God, is therefore by his very nature the subject of rights which no one may violate—no individual, group, class, nation or state." [40] Both systems evaluated individual human beings not as uniquely and inherently valuable, rather by their usefulness to the reigning creed. By failing to affirm both the mystery and intrinsic value of human life, they failed as substitute religions. In bending spines, the totalitarian systems misunderstood human nature and brought out the worst of old human beings rather than the best of new ones.

No one who attended the last Nuremberg rally in 1938 expected that the whole structure of National Socialism would vanish within seven years. When visiting Leipzig in July 1988, I was surprised by the energy with which people criticized the system to me in private conversation. Surely, I thought, I was only encountering those with enough courage to invite an American to dinner. They could not be typical of the population. I was not alone in my defective analysis.

Under both National Socialism and Marxism-Leninism, propaganda was powerful and persuasive. Spines bent. Ordinary human beings sometimes acted in ways that ranged from unpleasant to dreadful. Yet no matter how hard the dictatorships tried and how long they worked, it was not possible to produce nations of citizens committed passionately and unanimously to the reigning creed—a creed that at its core was rotten. Just as religions have found that forced adherence is shallow, the great dictatorships of the twentieth century, for all their sound and fury, failed to create new human beings capable of building a secular millennium. To use a biblical metaphor, they built houses upon sand that could not resist the storm.

Notes

Introduction

1. Cited by Victoria Barnett, *For the Soul of the People: Protestant Protest Against Hitler* (New York: Oxford University Press, 1992), 60.
2. Johannes R. Becher, "Gebranntes Kind," *Sinn und Form* 42 (2000): 343.
3. Cited by Stefan Wolle, *Die heile Welt der Diktatur: Alltag und Herrschaft in der DDR, 1971–1989*, 2nd ed. (Berlin: Ch. Links, 1998), 14.
4. Cited by Günter Heydemann and Christopher Beckmann, "Zwei Diktaturen in Deutschland: Möglichkeiten und Grenzen des historischen Diktaturvergleichs," *Deutschland Archiv* 30 (1997): 2.
5. For an interesting attempt to clarify the term, see Stanley B. Cunningham, *The Idea of Propaganda: A Reconstruction* (Westport, Conn.: Praeger, 2002).
6. Friedrich Schönemann, *Die Kunst der Massenbeeinflussung in den Vereinigten Staaten von Amerika* (Stuttgart: Deutsche Verlags-Anstalt, 1924), 9.
7. Myers Collection, University of Michigan Library, Kreisleitung Eisenach/56: Propaganda-Parole Nr. 7, 1942, 9.
8. Even Joseph Goebbels spoke of enemy propaganda in a June 1942 essay in which he argued that the only explanation for the fact that the Allied nations were still fighting was that "their powers of judgment have been blinded by unscrupulous and lying propaganda." See Joseph Goebbels, *Das eherne Herz: Reden und Aufsätze aus den Jahren 1941/42* (Munich: Franz Eher, 1943), 344.
9. *Kleines politisches Wörterbuch*, 7th ed. (Berlin: Dietz, 1988), 795. For the full definitions, see the German Propaganda Archive (GPA): http://www.calvin.edu/academic/cas/gpa/kpwb.htm. Future references to the GPA will take this form: GPA/title.htm.
10. Jacques Ellul, *Propaganda: The Formation of Men's Attitudes*, trans. Konrad Kellen and Jean Lerner (New York: Alfred A. Knopf, 1968), 61.
11. Ibid., 121.
12. Hitler was unhappy with the Peace of Westphalia for a variety of reasons and proposed to abolish it, although that would hardly have had

any practical consequences. See Elke Fröhlich, ed., *Die Tagebücher von Joseph Goebbels* (Munich: K. G. Sauer, 1997–2001), 7:33.

13. For an extended analysis of evildoers with good consciences in the context of the GDR, see Lothar Fritze, *Täter mit gutem Gewissen: Über menschliches Versagen im diktatorischen Sozialismus* (Cologne: Böhlau, 1998).

14. Kenneth Burke, "The Rhetoric of Hitler's 'Battle,'" in *The Philosophy of Literary Form* (New York: Vintage, 1957), 188.

15. Adolf Hitler, *Mein Kampf*, trans. Ralph Manheim (Boston: Houghton Mifflin, 1971), 379–380.

16. Ibid., 267.

17. Joseph Goebbels, *Signale der neuen Zeit: 25 ausgewählte Reden*, 5th ed. (Munich: Franz Eher, 1938), 44–45.

18. *Materialien der Enquete-Kommission "Aufarbeitung von Geschichte und Folgen der SED-Diktatur in Deutschland" (12. Wahlperiode des Deutschen Bundestages)*. vol. 3, book 2 (Frankfurt: Suhrkamp, 1995), p. 1416.

19. Hans-Joachim Maaz, *Behind the Wall: The Inner Life of Communist Germany*, trans. Margot Bettauer Dembo (New York: W. W. Norton, 1995), 2–3.

20. Czeslaw Milosz, *The Captive Mind*, trans. Jane Zielonko (New York: Octagon Books, 1981), xiii.

21. *Materialien der Enquete-Kommission*, vol. 3, bk. 3, p. 2077.

22. Erich Voegelin, *Political Religions*, trans. T. J. DeNapoli and E. S. Easterly III (Lewiston, N.Y.: Edwin Mellen Press, 1986), 59.

23. For two quite different examples, see Alan Bullock, *Hitler and Stalin: Parallel Lives* (New York: Alfred A. Knopf, 1992), and Aryeh Unger, *The Totalitarian Party: Party and People in Nazi Germany and Soviet Russia* (Cambridge: Cambridge University Press, 1974).

24. A British acquaintance tells of attending a conference on East Germany in the 1980s where leading scholar David Childs gave a critical account of conditions in the GDR, including the system's inability to meet consumer expectations. He mentioned shortages of vegetables as an example. The audience of academics, predominately sympathetic with the GDR project, responded with vigor. One professor rose, shaking with anger, to say: "I did not come to this conference to hear anecdotes about vegetables!" But the GDR's inability to provide consumers with what they wanted was, of course, a major reason for its collapse.

25. Michael Ruck, *Bibliogaphie zum Nationalsozialismus*, 2nd ed. (Darmstadt: Wissenschaftliche Buchgesellschaft, 2000).

26. A bibliography published in 2000 listed 5,800 books published between 1990 and 2000. See Hendrick Berth and Elmar Brähler, *Zehn Jahre Deutsche Einheit: Die Bibliographie* (Berlin: Verlag für Wissenschaft und Forschung, 2000). The associated on-line database listed 46,000 items in December 2003, although many items in the bibliography and database concern what happened after 1989. See http://www.wiedervereinigung.de/.

27. Having asked people to write to me, I could hardly ignore their letters, but neither was I capable of corresponding with that many people. I therefore responded to the first 1,800 of them with a lengthy form letter in June 1989. I made the letter as innocuous as possible, since I knew that such a mass of letters arriving from the United States would attract the interest of the State Security officers that inspected incoming international mail. I expected either that all of the letters would be blocked or none. As it turned out, there were ten regional postal districts in the GDR. Four of them delivered the letters. The other six districts delivered none of them.

Chapter 1

1. Schriftsteller Verband der DDR, *X. Schriftstellerkongreß der Deutschen Demokratischen Republik: Arbeitsgruppen.* (Cologne: Pahl-Rugenstein, 1988), 24.

2. Fröhlich, *Die Tagebücher von Joseph Goebbels,* 7:293.

3. See Hans Maier, ed., *"Totalitarismus" und "politische Religionen": Konzepte des Diktaturvergleichs,* 2 vols., (Paderborn: Ferdinand Schöningh, 1996); Michael Burleigh, *The Third Reich: A New History* (New York: Hill and Wang, 2000); and Claus-Ekkehard Bärsch, *Die politische Religion des Nationalsozialismus: Die religiöse Dimension der NS-Ideologie in den Schriften von Dietrich Eckardt, Joseph Goebbels, Alfred Rosenberg und Adolf Hitler* (Munich: Wilhelm Fink, 1998). Earlier studies of Nazi political religion include Hans-Jochen Gamm, *Der braune Kult: Das Dritte Reich und seine Ersatzreligion: Ein Beitrag zur politischen Bildung* (Hamburg: Rütten & Loening, 1962) and Klaus Vondung, *Magie und Manipulation: Ideologischer Kult und politische Religion des Nationalsozialismus* (Göttingen: Vandenhoeck & Ruprecht, 1971).

4. For a good general history of the term, see Abbott Gleason, *Totalitarianism: The Inner History of the Cold War* (New York: Oxford University Press, 1995). For a good review of the applicability of the term

"totalitarian" to the GDR, see Corey Ross, *The East German Dictatorship: Problems and Perspectives in the Interpretation of the GDR* (London: Arnold, 2002), 19–43. He finds the term substantially less useful than I do.

5. This follows the standard classic definitions of totalitarianism and is a slightly altered version of that proposed by Norbert Kapferer, *Der Totalitarismusbegriff auf dem Prüfstand* (Dresden: Hannah-Arendt-Institut für Totalitarismusforschung, 1995).

6. Otto Zander, ed., *Weimar: Bekenntnis und Tat: Kulturpolitisches Arbeitslager der Reichsjugendführung, 1938* (Berlin: Wilhelm Limpert, 1938), 63.

7. Wolfgang Schultz, "Auch an seinem Heim erkennt man den Nationalsozialisten!" *Der Hoheitsträger* 3, no. 8 (1939): 17.

8. *Kleines politisches Wörterbuch* (1988), 1077–1079.

9. Heinrich Gemkow, ed., *Der Sozialismus—Deine Welt* (Berlin: Neues Leben, 1975), 477.

10. A. Hempel, "Zuviel Politik," *Trommel,* 18/1980, 1.

11. Landesarchiv Berlin, BPA/SED IV—2/9.01/894, Wochenbericht (5.2.1958), 2.

12. Hermann Göring, untitled editorial, *Sommerlager- und Heimabendmaterial für die Schulungs- und Kulturarbeit,* summer 1941, 2.

13. See GPA/posters/hitler1.jpg.

14. Gunter d'Alquen, *Das ist der Sieg! Briefe des Glaubens in Aufbruch und Krieg* (Berlin: Franz Eher, 1941), 42. See GPA/sieg.htm.

15. Baldur von Schirach, ed., *Das Lied der Getreuen: Verse ungennanter österreichischer Hitler-Jugend aus den Jahren der Verfolgung, 1933–37* (Leipzig: Philipp Reclam jun., 1938), 12. For more examples, see GPA/hit-poet.htm. A similar book with a wider range of authors is Karl Hans Bühner, ed., *Dem Führer: Gedichte für Adolf Hitler* (Stuttgart: Georg Truckenmüller, 1939).

16. Helmut Heiber, *Goebbels Reden, 1932–1945,* 2 vols. (Munich: Wilhelm Heyne, 1971), 2:455.

17. The texts of many of them are available on the GPA.

18. For examples, see GPA/ah-art.htm.

19. *Adolf Hitler: Bilder aus dem Leben des Führers* (Hamburg: Cigaretten/ Bilderdienst Hamburg-Bahrenfeld, 1936). Parts of the book are available in GPA/ah.htm.

20. For material from this book, see GPA/hitler2.htm.

21. Rudolf Herz, *Hoffmann & Hitler: Fotographie als Medium des Führer-Mythos* (Munich: Klinkhardt & Biermann, 1994), 329.

22. William Uricchio, "Rituals of Reception, Patterns of Neglect: Nazi Television and Its Postwar Representation," *Wide Angle* 11 (1989): 51.

23. Partei Kanzlei, *Verfügungen/Anordnungen Bekanntgaben* (Munich: Franz Eher, 1943), 1:2.

24. Bundesarchiv Berlin, NS 22/904: Anordnung Nr. 93/39 (1939).

25. Hugo Ringler, "Die Arbeit des Propagandisten im nationalsozialistischen Staat," *Unser Wille und Weg* 4 (1934): 297. The NSDAP's publishing house referred to it as the *Standardwerk* of the movement.

26. George L. Mosse, *The Nationalization of the Masses: Political Symbolism and Mass Movements in Germany from the Napoleonic Wars Through the Third Reich* (New York: Howard Fertig, 1975), 10.

27. Gaupropagandaamt Oberdonau, "Parteigenossen!" *Front der Heimat* (1939). For the full text, see GPA/heimat.htm.

28. See GPA/images/hitler/hoyer.jpg.

29. Marie Harm and Hermann Wieble, *Lebenskunde für Mittelschulen: Fünfter Teil, Klasse 5 für Mädchen* (Halle: Hermann Schroedel, 1942), 168–173. See GPA/textbk01.htm.

30. This is based on a figure in "Die Arbeit der Partei-Propaganda im Kriege," *Unser Wille und Weg* 11 (1941), which claims that 32.5 million copies of the weekly quotation posters had been printed since the beginning of the war. For examples, see GPA/ws.htm.

31. "Wie reimt sich das zusammen?" *Der Stürmer*, 24/1936, 10.

32. "Zum Geburtstag des Führers," *Deutsche Kinderwelt*, 9/1936, 71.

33. Henry Albert Phillips, *Germany Today and Tomorrow* (New York: Dodd, Mead, 1935), 59.

34. Cornelia Schmitz-Berning, *Vokabular des Nationalsozialismus* (Berlin: Walter De Gruyter, 1998), 143.

35. Ian Kershaw, *The "Hitler Myth": Image and Reality in the Third Reich* (Oxford: Oxford University Press, 1987), 189.

36. For material from the 1936 rally, see GPA/pt36.htm. The best general treatment of Nazism's cult of the dead is Jay W. Baird, *To Die for Germany: Heroes in the Nazi Pantheon* (Bloomington: Indiana University Press, 1990).

37. Bundesarchiv Berlin, NS 22/227: Teilnehmerzahlen für den Reichsparteitag (1940). The party was planning for an attendance of 199,500 as late as July 1940.

38. Hauptkulturamt der NSDAP, *Deutsche Kriegsweihnacht* (Munich: Franz Eher, 1944). For a 1937 discussion of Christmas, see Hannes Kremer,

"Neuwertung 'überlieferter' Brauchformen?" *Die neue Gemeinschaft* 3 (1937): 3005a–c, available in GPA/feier37.jpg.

39. *New York Times,* 10 November 1935, 42.

40. Taken from a recommended program for 9 November 1942 ceremonies in *Die neue Gemeinschaft* 8 (1942): 493–498. For additional material, see GPA/99feier.htm.

41. Max Domarus, *Hitler: Speeches and Proclamations, 1932–1945,* trans. Mary Fran Gilbert (Wauconda, Ill.: Bolchazy-Carducci Publishers, 1990–2002), 1:542.

42. Ewin Hilbig, "Sind Feierstunden notwendig?" *Unser Wille und Weg* 9 (1939): 164–165.

43. "9 November," *Völkischer Beobachter,* 8 November 1935.

44. *Fränkische Tageszeitung* (Nuremberg), 24, 29, and 31 October 1935. The *Völkischer Beobachter* also carried the series.

45. See GPA/stamps.htm and GPA/9nov.htm.

46. Carl Schütte, *Schulfeiern im Geist der neuen Zeit* (Langensalza: Verlag von Julius Beltz, 1937), 137.

47. *Völkischer Beobachter,* 10 November 1936.

48. Personal communication, 11 February 2002.

49. Robert Gellately, *Backing Hitler: Consent and Coercion in Nazi Germany* (Oxford: Oxford University Press, 2001), 259.

50. Helmut Stellrecht, *Glauben und Handeln: Ein Bekenntnis der jungen Nation* (Berlin: Franz Eher, 1943). See GPA/glauben.htm.

51. Review of *Glauben und Handeln* by Helmut Stellrecht, *Unser Wille und Weg* 8 (1938): 349.

52. Werner von Hofe, "Mein Junge," *NS Frauen Warte* 7, no. 4 (1938): 97.

53. Domarus, *Hitler: Speeches,* 1:452.

54. Hans Weberstedt and Kurt Langner, *Gedenkhalle für die Gefallenen des Dritten Reiches* (Munich: Franz Eher, 1938), 9.

55. Joseph Goebbels, "Das Jahr 2000," *Das Reich,* 25 February 1945, 2. The full article is available in GPA/goeb49.htm.

56. *Der Stürmer,* 9/1943. See GPA/images/sturmer/ds9–43.jpg.

57. Marx-Engels-Lenin-Institut, *J. Stalin: Kurze Lebensbeschreibung* (Berlin: Verlag der Sowjetischen Militärverwaltung in Deutschland, 1945), 81.

58. Alan L. Nothnagle, *Building the East German Myth: Historical Mythology and Youth Propaganda in the German Democratic Republic, 1945–1989* (Ann Arbor: University of Michigan Press, 1999), 159.

59. This story comes from Pfarrer Helmut Hasse in Wittenberg.

60. Nothnagle, *Building the East German Myth,* 121.

61. The subtitle was common. An illustrated volume with the same title, for example, was published in Hindenburg's honor in 1934.

62. See GPA/images/hitler/ah.jpg.

63. See GPA/images/ulbr/ulbrcov.jpg.

64. *Walter Ulbricht—Ein Leben für Deutschland* (Leipzig: VEB E. A. Seemann, 1968), 10. For more material from the book, see GPA/ulbricht.htm.

65. See GPA/posters/ahsieg.jpg.

66. Stiftung Archiv der Parteien und Massenorganizationen der DDR im Bundesarchiv, DY 30/IV 2/9.03/22: Beschluß des Sekretariats des Zentralrats der Freien Deutschen Jugend über die propagandistische Arbeit im Verband unter der Jugend, 1961. Future references will be to SAPMO.

67. See GPA/images/honecker.jpg.

68. Manfred Uschner, *Die zweite Etage: Funktionsweise eines Machtapparates* (Berlin: Dietz, 1993), 88.

69. *Kleines politisches Wörterbuch* (1988), 880.

70. Götz Scharf, *Über den moralischen Faktor im modernen Krieg* (Berlin: Verlag des Ministeriums für nationale Verteidigung, 1959), 110.

71. *Feierstunde zum 40. Jahrestag der Gründung der Kommunistischen Partei Deutschlands* (Berlin: Zentralvorstand der Gewerkschaft Unterricht und Erziehung, 1958). The full text is available in GPA/kpd40.htm.

72. Cited by Nothnagle, *Building the East German Myth,* 16.

73. Monika Gibas and Rainer Gries, "Die Inszenierung des sozialistischen Deutschland: Geschichte und Dramaturgie der Dezennienfeiern in der DDR," in *Wiedergeburten: Zur Geschichte der runden Jahrestage der DDR,* ed. Monika Gibas et al. (Leipzig: Leipziger Universitätsverlag, 1999), 12–17.

74. Günter Schabowski, "Ihr Vermächtnis ist unser Kampf für Arbeit, Brot und Völkerfrieden," *Neues Deutschland,* 13 January 1986, 2.

75. For a detailed discussion of 7 October festivities, see Gibas et al., *Wiedergeburten.*

76. Nothnagle, *Building the East German Myth,* 66.

77. *Gedenkstätten: Arbeiterbewegung, Antifaschistischer Widerstand, Aufbau des Sozialismus* (Jena: Urania, 1974).

78. Annadora Miethe, ed., *Buchenwald* (N.p., 1983), 4.

79. Rudolf Fischer, Ursula Langspach, and Johannes Schellenberger, eds., *Sieh, das ist unser Tag! Lyrik und Prosa für sozialistische Gedenk- und Feierstunden* (Berlin: Tribüne, 1961), 6. For a similar volume, see Heinz

Czechowski, ed., *Unser der Tag unser das Wort: Lyrik und Prosa für Gedenk-und Feiertage* (Halle: Mitteldeutscher, 1966).

80. Dieter Vorsteher, ed., *Parteiauftrag: Ein neues Deutschland: Bilder, Rituale und Symbole der früheren DDR* (Munich: Koehler & Amelang, 1997), 37. This book provides a remarkable range of other illustrations of early GDR rituals and symbols.

81. Ernst Z. Ichenhäuser, *Erziehung zum guten Benehmen,* 3rd ed. (Berlin: Volk und Wissen, 1983), 11–12.

82. Poster in the author's collection.

83. Gerhart Neuner, *Politisch-ideologische Arbeit und Erziehung.* (Berlin: Akademie, 1978), 9/G:4.

84. Ernst Hampf, *Weil die Partei führt, ist unser Sieg gewiß* (Berlin: Militärverlag der DDR, 1973), 35.

85. *Kleines politisches Wörterbuch* (1988), 474.

86. Václav Havel, "The Power of the Powerless," in *The Power of the Powerless: Citizens Against the State in Central-Eastern Europe,* ed. John Keane (Armonk, N.Y.: M. E. Sharpe, 1985), 25.

87. Scholle, "Vom Ortsgruppenleiter," *Der Hoheitsträger* 6, no. 9 (1942): 29.

88. Joseph Goebbels, *Joseph Goebbels Tagebücher, 1924–1945,* ed. Ralf Georg Reuth (Munich: Piper, 1999), 5:1927.

89. Heinz Boberach, ed., *Meldungen aus dem Reich: Die geheimen Lageberichte des Sicherheitsdienstes der SS, 1938–1945* (Herrsching: Pawlak, 1984), 7:2522.

90. See, for example, a typical 1953 cartoon in GPA/images/wind/windd.jpg.

91. Cited by John Rodden, *Repainting the Little Red Schoolhouse: A History of East German Education, 1945–1995* (New York: Oxford University Press, 2002), 260.

92. Hannah Arendt, *The Origins of Totalitarianism* (New York: Harcourt Brace, 1951), xxiii.

93. Cornelius Plantinga Jr., *Not the Way It's Supposed to Be: A Breviary of Sin* (Grand Rapids, Mich.: William B. Eerdmans, 1995), 98.

Chapter 2

1. Joseph Goebbels, *Kampf um Berlin: Der Anfang* (Munich: Franz Eher, 1934), 18. See also Goebbels's 1928 speech to party members on propaganda, *Signale der neuen Zeit,* 41. The full text of this speech is translated in GPA/goeb54.htm.

2. Schulze-Wechsungen, "Politische Propaganda," *Unser Wille und Weg* 4 (1934): 323–332. See GPA/polprop.htm.

3. Ringler, "Die Arbeit des Propagandisten," 297.

4. See Haig A. Bosmajian, "The Sources and Nature of Adolf Hitler's Techniques of Persuasion," *Central States Speech Journal* 25 (1974): 240–248.

5. Hitler, *Mein Kampf,* 115. See Jeane J. Kirkpatrick, *Dictatorships and Double Standards: Rationalism and Reason in Politics* (New York: Simon and Schuster, 1982), 106–109, for a discussion of Hitler's views of the German masses.

6. Hitler, *Mein Kampf,* 99.

7. Ibid., 173.

8. Goebbels, *Kampf um Berlin,* 191.

9. Hitler, *Mein Kampf,* 107.

10. Ibid., 106–107.

11. Ibid., 231.

12. Ibid., 177.

13. *Der Kongress zu Nürnberg vom 5. bis 10. September 1934: Offizieller Bericht über den Verlauf des Reichsparteitages mit sämtlichen Reden* (Munich: Franz Eher, 1934), 134. For the full speech, see GPA/goeb59.htm.

14. Hitler, *Mein Kampf,* 183.

15. Goebbels, *Kampf um Berlin,* 200.

16. Hitler, *Mein Kampf,* 180–181. All italics in original.

17. Ibid., 185.

18. Ibid., 338.

19. Ibid., 492.

20. Ibid., 593.

21. Ibid., 171, 152, 114, 459.

22. Ibid., 455.

23. Alfred Rosenberg and Wilhelm Weiß, *Der Reichsparteitag der National-sozialistischen Deutschen Arbeiterpartei Nürnberg: 19./21. August 1927* (Munich: Franz Eher, 1927), 42.

24. Hitler, *Mein Kampf,* 352, 580.

25. Adolf Raskin, "Dramaturgie der Propaganda," in *Handbuch des deutschen Rundfunks, 1939/40,* ed. Hans-Joachim Weinbrenner (Heidelberg: Kurt Vowinkel, 1939), 84.

26. Hitler, *Mein Kampf,* 595.

27. Ibid., p. 581 (italics in original).

28. "Schrifttum über Propaganda," *Zeitschriften-Dienst,* 28 October 1939. See GPA/biblio.htm.

29. Eugen Hadamovsky, *Propaganda und nationale Macht: Die Organisation der öffentlichen Meinung für die nationale Politik* (Oldenburg: Gerhard Stalling, 1933).

30. See, for example, Gerhard Baumann, *Grundlagen und Praxis der internationalen Propaganda* (Essen: Essener Verlagsanstalt, 1941), 18–48.

31. See, for example, Josef H. Krumbach, *Grundfragen der Publizistik: Die Wesenselemente des publizistischen Prozesses: Seine Mittel und Ergebnisse* (Berlin: Walter de Gruyter, 1935). This journalism textbook begins with an unenlightening chapter on propaganda.

32. Willi Münzenberg, *Propaganda als Waffe* (Paris: Éditions du Carrefour, 1937), 11.

33. W. I. Lenin, *Über Agitation und Propaganda* (Berlin: Dietz, 1974). The book was translated from the 1969 Russian edition.

34. *Die Aufgaben der Agitation und Propaganda bei der weiteren Verwirklichung der Beschlüsse des VIII. Parteitages der SED* (Berlin: Dietz, 1972), 87.

35. Ibid.

36. A. S. Wischnjakov et al., *Methodik der politischen Bildung,* trans. Intertext (Berlin: Dietz, 1974), 20, 45.

37. David Wedgwood Benn, *Persuasion and Soviet Politics* (London: Basil Blackwell, 1989), 41.

38. William McGuire, "Resistance to Persuasion Conferred by Active and Passive Prior Refutation of the Same and Alternative Counterargument," *Journal of Abnormal and Social Psychology* 63 (1961): 326–332.

39. Benn, *Persuasion and Soviet Politics,* 166.

40. Georg Klaus, *Die Macht des Wortes: Ein erkenntnistheoretisch-pragmatisches Traktat,* 4th ed. (Berlin: VEB Deutscher Verlag der Wissenschaften, 1968), and Georg Klaus, *Sprache der Politik* (Berlin: VEB Deutscher Verlag der Wissenschaften, 1971).

41. *Kleines politisches Wörterbuch* (Berlin: Dietz, 1967), 369.

42. Günter Herlt, *Sendeschluß: Ein Insider des DDR-Fernsehens berichtet* (Berlin: edition ost, 1995), 73.

43. For one of many examples, see the speech by Fred Oelßner to the IV. Party Congress in 1954, *Über die allseitige Verbesserung unserer politisch-ideologischen Massenarbeit: Diskussionsrede auf dem IV. Parteitag der Sozialistischen Einheitspartei Deutschlands* (Berlin: Dietz, 1954). The speech is translated in GPA/oelsner1.htm.

44. SAPMO, DY 30/IV 2/2.033/37: Zu Problemen der ideologischen Arbeit unter Jugendlichen (1972), 26.

45. *Kleines politisches Wörterbuch* (1988), 795. For the full text, see GPA/kpwb.htm.

46. Ibid., 17.

47. Ibid., 62.

48. Klaus, *Sprache der Politik*, 49.

49. Wischnjakov, *Methodik der politischen Bildung*, 313.

50. Fred Oelßner, *Über die Verbesserung der Arbeit der Presse und des Rundfunks* (Berlin: Dietz, 1953), 3. The text was originally delivered as a speech to the Central Committee, but 35,000 copies were printed. He made the same comment six months later at the IV. Party Congress. See Oelßner, *Über die allseitige Verbesserung*, 10.

51. SAPMO, vorl.SED/11527: Stenographisches Niederschrift der Konferenz der Zentralkomitees der SED über die Aufgaben der Agitation und Propaganda bei der weitern Verwirklichung der Beschlüsse des VIII. Parteitages der SED am 16. und 17. November 1972, 201.

52. K. Kalaschnikow, *Die Grundsätze der bolschewistischen Agitation* (Berlin: Dietz, 1951), 37.

53. Wischnjakov, *Methodik der politischen Bildung*, 285.

54. Klaus, *Sprache der Politik*, 15–21.

55. Cited by Enquete-Kommission, *Materialien der Enquete-Kommission*, vol. 3, bk. 3, p. 2038.

Chapter 3

1. Joseph Goebbels, *Final Entries, 1945: The Diaries of Joseph Goebbels*, trans. Richard Barry (New York: G. P. Putnam's Sons, 1978), 277–278.

2. Dietrich Orlow, *The History of the Nazi Party, 1933–1945* (Pittsburgh: University of Pittsburgh Press, 1973), 74.

3. Jay W. Baird, *The Mythical World of Nazi War Propaganda, 1939–1945* (Minneapolis: University of Minnesota Press, 1974), 9.

4. Michael Balfour, *Propaganda in War, 1939–1945: Organisations, Policies and Publics in Britain and Germany* (London: Routledge & Kegan Paul, 1979), 104.

5. Arvid Fredborg, *Behind the Steel Wall: A Swedish Journalist in Berlin, 1941–43* (New York: Viking, 1944), 17–18.

6. Horst J. P. Bergmeier and Rainer E. Lotz, *Hitler's Airwaves: The Inside Story of Nazi Radio Broadcasting and Propaganda Swing* (New Haven, Conn.: Yale University Press, 1997), 170.

7. See Baird, *The Mythical World,* and Robert Edwin Herzstein, *The War That Hitler Won: The Most Infamous Propaganda Campaign in History* (New York: G. P. Putnam's Sons, 1978).

8. Balfour, *Propaganda in War,* 468.

9. Paul Oestreich, *Walther Funk: Ein Leben für die Wirtschaft* (Munich: Franz Eher, 1940), 92.

10. Herzstein, *The War That Hitler Won,* 134.

11. Heiber, *Goebbels Reden,* 1:250.

12. Herzstein, *The War That Hitler Won,* 120. Goebbels himself fit this profile.

13. Ibid., 123.

14. Goebbels had announced in 1933 that radio revenues should in general be put back into radio or else serve the broader cultural needs of the nation. See Goebbels, *Signale der neuen Zeit,* 205.

15. David Welch, *The Third Reich: Politics and Propaganda* (London: Routledge, 1993), 138.

16. Ibid., 28–29. For a Nazi account, see Karl-Friedrich Schrieber, *Die Reichskulturkammer* (Berlin: Junker und Dünhaupt, 1934).

17. "Die Reichspropagandaleitung der NSDAP," *Unser Wille und Weg* 6 (1936): 6–11. A translation is available in GPA/rpl.htm.

18. "1. Lehrgang der Gau- und Kreispropagandaleiter der NSDAP," *Unser Wille und Weg* 9 (1939): 126.

19. Walter Tießler, "Der Reichsring für nat.-soz. Propaganda und Volksaufklärung," *Unser Wille und Weg* 5 (1935): 412–416.

20. Herzstein, *The War That Hitler Won,* 148.

21. Heiber, *Goebbels Reden,* 1:252.

22. Fröhlich, *Die Tagebücher von Joseph Goebbels,* 7:182.

23. Peter Longerich, *Propagandisten im Krieg: Die Presseabteilung des Auswärtigen Amtes unter Ribbentrop* (Munich: R. Oldenbourg, 1987), 117.

24. See, for example, Alfred Rosenberg, *Lehrstoffsammlung und Grundplan für die weltanschauliche Schulung der Nationalsozialistischen Deutschen Arbeiterpartei* (Munich: Beauftragten des Führers für die gesamte geistige und weltanschauliche Schulung und Erziehung der NSDAP, 1939).

25. For the details, see Longerich, *Propagandisten im Krieg.*

26. Fröhlich, *Die Tagebücher von Joseph Goebbels,* 9:387–388.

27. Glenn R. Cuomo, ed., *National Socialist Cultural Policy* (New York: St. Martin's, 1995), 171.

28. Fröhlich, *Die Tagebücher von Joseph Goebbels,* 9:388.

29. Ernest K. Bramsted, *Goebbels and National Socialist Propaganda, 1925–1945* (East Lansing: Michigan State University Press, 1965), 111–113.

30. Carl Röver, *Gauleiter* of Weser-Ems, wrote a memo in 1942 that went into some detail on Nazi organizational confusion. He urged that propaganda be entirely the province of the party. He viewed the Propaganda Ministry as a mistake. See Michael Rademacher, *Carl Röver: Der Bericht des Reichsstatthalters von Oldenburg und Bremen und Gauleiter des Gaues Weser-Ems über die Lage der NSDAP: Eine Denkschrift aus dem Jahr 1942* (Vechta: Selbstverlag des Verfassers, 2000), 74–80.

31. Ian Kershaw, "'Working toward the Führer': Reflections on the Nature of the Hitler Dictatorship," in *Stalinism and Nazism: Dictatorships in Comparison,* ed. Ian Kershaw and Moshe Lewin (Cambridge: Cambridge University Press, 1997), 104.

32. Gunter Holzweißig, *Zensur ohne Zensor: Die SED-Informationsdiktatur* (Bonn: Bouvier, 1997), 13.

33. For full details of the various rearrangements within the ZK's departments, see Andreas Herbst, Gerd-Rüdiger Stephan, and Jürgen Winkler, *Die SED: Geschichte, Organisation, Politik: Ein Handbuch* (Berlin: Dietz, 1997), 878–884.

34. SAPMO, DY 30/IV 2/2.037/24: Bericht über die Prüfung in der Abteilung Propaganda des ZK der SED (1983).

35. SAPMO, DY 30/IV 2/2.037/24: Bericht über die Prüfung in der Abteilung Agitation des ZK der SED (1987).

36. Holzweißig, *Zensur ohne Zensor,* 9.

37. Herlt, *Sendeschluß,* 74.

38. Wilfried Poßner, *Immer bereit! Parteiauftrag: kämpfen, spielen, fröhlich sein* (Berlin: edition ost, 1995), 128.

39. Holzweißig, *Zensur ohne Zensor,* 29.

40. Ibid., 75.

41. Renate Schubert, *Ohne größeren Schaden? Gespräche mit Journalistinnen und Journalisten der DDR* (Munich: Ölschläger, 1992), 51–52.

42. From the SED's viewpoint, the Protestant Church was the numerically stronger and more troublesome entity. For a discussion of the Catholic Church, see Bernd Schäfer, *Staat und katholische Kirche in der DDR* (Cologne: Böhlau, 1998).

43. Holzweißig, *Zensur ohne Zensor,* 82.
44. Schubert, *Ohne größeren Schaden,* 38.

Chapter 4

1. Fritz Mehnert, "Die Statistik der NSDAP," *Der Hoheitsträger* 3, no. 7 (1939): 10–12. Local groups were supposed to have no more than 1,500 households.
2. Orlow, *The History of the Nazi Party,* 92.
3. Curt Belling, *Der Film in Staat und Partei* (Berlin: "Der Film," 1936), 72.
4. For details of these functionaries, see Detlef Schmiechen-Ackermann, "Der 'Blockwart': Die unteren Parteifunktionäre im nationalsozialistischen Terror- und Überwachungsapparat," *Vierteljahrshefte für Zeitgeschichte* 48 (2000): 575–602. There were 204,359 block wardens alone in 1935. See Reichsorganisationsleiter, *Partei-Statistik: Stand: 1935* (Munich: Reichsorganisationsleiter, 1935), 2:7.
5. See Herwart Vorländer, *Die NSV: Darstellung und Dokumentation einer nationalsozialistischen Organisation* (Boppard am Rhein: Harald Boldt, 1988). Although this was a tangled enterprise involving both party and state, Goebbels headed each annual campaign, evidence of its significance as propaganda. For more on the functioning of local groups, see Carl-Wilhelm Reibel, *Das Fundament der Diktatur: Die NSDAP-Ortsgruppen 1932–1945* (Paderborn: Ferdinand Schöningh, 2002).
6. *Sozialisten der Tat: Das Buch der unbekannten Kämpfer der N.S.V. Gau Groß-Berlin* (Berlin: N.S.D.A.P. Amt für Volkswohlfahrt, Gau Groß-Berlin, 1934), 66.
7. Myers Collection, Kreisleitung Eisenach/11a: Bericht über die Tätigkeit eines Blockleiters (1939).
8. Joachim Kuropka, ed., *Meldungen aus Münster, 1924–1944* (Münster: Regensberg, 1992), 668. For an example of the detailed form used by block leaders to keep track of their neighbors, see *Deutschland-Berichte der Sozialdemokratischen Partei Deutschlands (Sopade), 1934–1940* (Salzhausen: Petra Nettelbeck, 1980), 3:1644–1645.
9. Boberach, *Meldungen aus dem Reich,* 8:3020.
10. See two articles by Ross Scanlan for more details of the system: "The Nazi Party Speaker System," *Speech Monographs* 16 (1949): 82–97, and "The Nazi Party Speaker System, II," *Speech Monographs* 17 (1950): 134–148.
11. "Reichsredner der NSDAP," *Unser Wille und Weg* 6 (1936): 222–223.

12. Fröhlich, *Die Tagebücher von Joseph Goebbels,* 7:309.

13. Hugo Ringler, "Der Rednerstoßtrupp der Reichspropagandaleitung," *Unser Wille und Weg* 5 (1935): 154. Forty were under consideration in 1936.

14. Herzstein, *The War That Hitler Won,* 144.

15. Hugo Ringler, "Neuordnung des politischen Rednerstabes," *Unser Wille und Weg* 5 (1935): 30.

16. "Die Arbeit der Partei-Propaganda im Kriege," 1. The text is available in GPA/warprop.htm.

17. Kurt Sperber, "Die Versammlungswelle," *Der Hoheitsträger* 3, no. 1 (1939): 27–28. The text is available in GPA/breslau.htm.

18. "Die Versammlungen der NSDAP: Eine Uebersicht über das Winter-halbjahr 1943/44," *Die Lage,* Folge 116 B (1944), 5.

19. See, for example, Schulze-Wechsungen, "Politische Propaganda," available in GPA/polprop.htm. See also GPA/dietz.htm.

20. For examples, see GPA/rim1.htm and GPA/rim2.htm.

21. Bundesarchiv Berlin, NS 22/894: "Der Hoheitsträger" Verteilerliste Folge 1/1942.

22. For details, see Herzstein, *The War That Hitler Won,* 156–157. Two examples are available in GPA/hsa01.htm and GPA/hsa02.htm.

23. See, for example, issues of *Gau* Thuringia's propaganda newsletters in the Myers Collection, Kreis Eisenach/56.

24. *Die Lage,* 31 May 1944.

25. Goebbels often spoke to propagandists at the Nuremberg rally, for example. Two translations are available in GPA/goeb41.htm and GPA/goeb59.htm.

26. Forty separate organizations were part of the Propaganda Circle in *Gau* Weser-Ems in 1942, according to "Merkblatt für den Propagandisten im Gau Weser-Ems," *Monatsblätter der Gaupropagandaleitung Weser-Ems der NSDAP* 7, no. 3 (1942). They included all party entities but also such organizations as gardeners' societies and singing clubs. See GPA/weserems.htm.

27. *Organisationsbuch der NSDAP,* 5th ed. (Munich: Franz Eher, 1938), 8.

28. Hans Hackl, "Die Partei hat in allem Vorbild zu sein!" *Die Lage,* September 1943, 4.

29. Eugen Hadamovsky, *Hilfsarbeiter Nr. 50 000* (Munich: Franz Eher, 1938), 21.

30. See, for example, Ross Scanlan, "The Nazi Speakers' Complaints," *Quarterly Journal of Speech* 40 (1954): 1–14.

31. "Qualitative Stärkung der Reihen der SED fortgesetzt," *Neues Deutschland,* 11 January 1989, 3.
32. *Über die Verbesserung der Parteipropaganda: Entschließung des Parteivorstandes der SED vom 2. und 3. Juni 1950* (Berlin: Parteivorstand der SED, Abteilung Propaganda, 1950), 6.
33. Heinz Puder, "Zu den Aufgaben der marxistisch-leninistischen Bildung und Erziehung sowie zu den Anforderungen an die Propagandisten des Parteilehrjahres," in *Beiträge zur Methodik im Parteilehrjahr* (Berlin: ZK der SED, 1988), 7–8.
34. SAPMO, Bericht über die Prüfung in der Abteilung Propaganda.
35. Cited by Ernst Richert, *Agitation und Propaganda: Das System der publizistischen Massenführung in der Sowjetzone* (Berlin: Franz Vahlen, 1958), 218–219.
36. Landesarchiv Berlin, BPA/SED IV/A-4/06/097: Agitationsarbeit in den Wohngebieten (1963).
37. Landesarchiv Berlin, BPA/SED 005725: Information über Ergebnisse und Erfahrungen in der Arbeit der Agitatoren der Partei (1986).
38. Bezirksleitung Cottbus, *Erfahrungen Formen Methoden der Parteiarbeit: 3. Agitatorenkonferenz der Bezirksleitung Cottbus der SED, 13.12.1976* (Cottbus: Bezirksleitung Cottbus der SED, Abteilung Agitation/ Propaganda, 1977), 14.
39. SAPMO, DY 30/vorl.SED 33899: Zur politischen Massenarbeit im Centrum-Warenhaus Leipzig (1980).
40. SAPMO, DY 30/IV 2/9.03/15: Bericht über die Auswertung der Propagandistenkonferenz des ZK im Bezirk Neubrandenburg (1961), 134. There are numerous similar complaints in the SED files.
41. Politburo member Fred Oelßner noted in 1954, for example, that, in Halle, meetings of the *Bezirk* staff lasted from 10 A.M. to 5 or 6 the next morning. "Not much good can come of such meetings," he sensibly observed. See Oelßner, *Über die allseitige Verbesserung,* 23.
42. SAPMO, DY 30/IV 2/9.02/159: Darüber muß man offen reden! (1961).
43. Hermann von Berg, *Marxismus-Leninismus: Das Elend der halb deutschen, halb russischen Ideologie* (Cologne: Bund, 1986), 19.
44. SAPMO, DY 30/IV 2/9.02/14: Vorlage für das Sekretariat des ZK zur Verbesserung einiger Seiten der Agitationsarbeit der Partei (1957).
45. SAPMO, DY 30/IV 2/9.03/15: Bericht über Einsatz im Kreis Prenzlau (April 1961).

46. SAPMO, DY 30/IV A2/9.02/39: Bericht über eine Aussprache mit Kreiszeitungsredakteuren der Gebietsgruppe Karl-Marx-Stadt des VDJ am 25. Juni 1963. Holzweißig, *Zensur ohne Zensor,* suggests that another reason for people's reluctance to serve in this capacity was the understandable concern that they would be serving as informants by passing on the remarks of their coworkers (102).

47. SAPMO, DY 30/vorl.SED 18300: Information über den Erfahrungsaustausch zu Fragen der Agitation auf dem 1. Weiterbildungslehrgang mit den Sekretären für Agit/Prop an der Sonderschule des ZK in Kleinmachnow (1976), 1.

48. SAPMO, DY 30/vorl.SED 12885/2: Arbeitsgruppe: Welche Anforderungen müssen heute an die theoretischen und pädagogischen Fähigkeiten der Propagandisten gestellt werden? (1972), 1. In 1988, 110,000 propagandists were involved in the *Parteilehrjahr.* See Puder, "Zu den Aufgaben," 7.

49. SAPMO, DY 30/IV 2/2.037/14: Information über die Auflagenentwicklung von "Was und Wie" nach Bezirken (1980). This means that about 3 percent of the population were agitators. A 1965 study estimated that the comparable figure for the Soviet Union was 1 percent. See Carl J. Friedrich and Zbigniew K. Brzezinski, *Totalitarian Dictatorship and Autocracy* (Cambridge: Harvard University Press, 1965), 145.

50. *Bilanz zwischen zwei Parteitagen: Fakten und Ergebnisse der Agitation und Propaganda der Kreisparteiorganisation Weißenfels* (Weißenfels: Kreisleitung Weißenfels der SED, Abteilung Agitation und Propaganda, 1976), 13, 15.

51. Kalaschnikow, *Die Grundsätze der bolschewistischen Agitation,* 37.

52. "Warum ist die Oder-Neiße-Grenze die Friedensgrenze?" *Frage und Antwort: Argumente für die tägliche Diskussion,* no. 6 (1950), 3–4. See GPA/oder.htm for a translation.

53. Michael Heiss, "'Gegen Dummheit gibt's kein Mittel!'" *Neuer Weg,* December 1949, 31.

54. SAPMO, DY 30/IV 2/9.03/5: Wie erfüllt der "Neuen Weg" seine Aufgaben zur Vermittlung und Verallgemeinerung der besten Erfahrungen der Arbeit der Grundorganisationen und der Führungstätigket der Kreisleitungen (1962), 249.

55. Heinz Geggel, "Jederzeit aktiv und überzeugend die Politik der Partei vertreten," *Neuer Weg* 44 (1989): 197.

56. Ernst Becker, "Staatsterrorismus—warum und wie wird er verstärkt von den USA praktiziert?" *Neuer Weg* 41 (1986): 236–238.

57. For examples, see GPA/notiz1.htm and GPA/notiz2.htm.
58. "In eigener Sache," *WAS und WIE,* December 1989, 4–5.
59. For a translation of parts of the material, see GPA/nva01.htm and GPA/radar1.htm.
60. SAPMO, DY 30/IV 2/9.03/14: Jochen Eichstädt to Abt. Propaganda on 5 September 1961.
61. Monika Deutz-Schroeder and Jochen Staadt, *Teurer Genosse! Briefe an Erich Honecker* (Berlin: Transit Buchverlag, 1994), 49.
62. SAPMO, DY 30/IV A 2/9.02/169: Horst Bredereck to Kurt Seibert on 17 June 1962, 6.
63. SAPMO, DY 30/IV 2/2.037/24: Bericht über die Prüfung Die Herausgabe, den Betrieb und die Nutzung von Agitations- und Anschauungsmitteln (1982).
64. The challenges are discussed by Richert, *Agitation und Propaganda,* 219–221.
65. For one of numerous examples, see SAPMO, DY 30/vorl.SED 18300: Information über den Erfahrungsaustausch (zur Leitung der Agitationsarbeit der Partei) auf dem Lehrgang mit den Sekretären für Agitation und Propaganda der Kreisleitungen der SED (1974), 4. This is the report of a conference of county heads for agitation and propaganda.
66. Oelßner, *Über die allseitige Verbesserung,* 8. See GPA/oelsner1.htm.
67. SAPMO, DY 30/IV 2/9.02/92: Bezirksleitung Cottbus to Walter Ulbricht on 8 March 1961.
68. The reference is to Goebbels's weekly articles in *Das Reich.*
69. "Alles nur für den Sieg, der Sieg allein entscheidet!" *Monatsblätter der Gaupropagandaleitung Weser-Ems der NSDAP,* 7, no. 3 (1942): 19. See GPA/weserems.htm.
70. *Plan der massenpolitischen Arbeit der Kreisparteiorganisation Rochlitz für das Jahr 1982* (Rochlitz: SED Kreisleitung Rochlitz, 1982). See GPA/rochlitz.htm.

Chapter 5

1. The literature on Nazi journalism is substantial. A good place to start is Norbert Frei and Johannes Schmitz, *Journalismus im dritten Reich,* 2nd ed. (Munich: C. H. Beck, 1989). The best analyses of the content of Nazi media are in Herzstein, *The War That Hitler Won;* Baird, *The Mythical World;* and Bramsted, *Goebbels and National Socialist Propaganda.* The literature on GDR media is smaller but growing. Holzweißig's two

books on the GDR media are the best place to start, *Die schärfste Waffe der Partei: Eine Mediengeschichte der DDR* (Cologne: Böhlau, 2002) and *Zensur ohne Zensor.* For an English summary of the GDR media system, see Simone Barck, Christoph Classen, and Thomas Heimann, "The Fettered Media: Controlling Public Debate," in *Dictatorship as Experience: Towards a Socio-Cultural History of the GDR*, ed. Konrad H. Jarausch (New York: Berghahn Books, 1999), 213–240.

2. Hadamovsky, *Propaganda und nationale Macht*, 100.
3. Frei and Schmitz, *Journalismus im Dritten Reich*, 99.
4. Welch, *The Third Reich*, 36.
5. Frei and Schmitz, *Journalismus im Dritten Reich*, 122.
6. Welch, *The Third Reich*, 144.
7. Samples are available in Joseph Wulf, *Presse und Funk im Dritten Reich: Eine Dokumentation* (Gütersloh: Sigbert Mohn, 1964), 90–110. The full versions are available in Hans Bohrmann, ed., *NS-Presseanweisungen der Vorkriegszeit: Edition und Dokumentation*, 7 vols. (Munich: K. G. Saur, 1984–2001).
8. Frei and Schmitz, *Journalismus im Dritten Reich*, 34.
9. Gabriele Toepser-Ziegert, *NS-Presseanweisungen der Vorkriegszeit: Eine Einführung in ihre Edition* (Munich: K. G. Saur, 1984), 13.
10. Bohrmann, *NS-Presseanweisungen*, 7:382, 399, 556, 624–625.
11. Robert G. Young, "'Not This Way Please!' Regulating the Press in Nazi Germany," *Journalism Quarterly* 64 (1988): 787–792.
12. Karl-Heinz Reuband, "'Schwarzhören' im Dritten Reich: Verbreitung, Erscheinungsformen und Kommunikationsmuster beim Umgang mit verbotenen Sendern," in *Archiv für Sozialgeschichte*, vol. 41 (Bonn: J.H.W. Dietz Nachf., 2001), 245–262.
13. Hans Fritzsche commented on the problem during the Nuremberg trials. See Hildegard Springer, ed., *Es sprach Hans Fritzsche* (Stuttgart: Thield, 1949), 225–226.
14. See Uricchio, "Rituals of Reception," and Heiko Zeutschner, *Die braune Mattscheibe: Fernsehen im Nationalsozialismus* (Hamburg: Rotbuch, 1995).
15. Hilmar Hoffman, *The Triumph of Propaganda: Film and National Socialism, 1933–1945*, trans. John A. Broadwin and V. R. Berghahn (Providence, R.I.: Berghahn Books, 1996), 211.
16. Herzstein, *The War That Hitler Won*, 225.
17. Fröhlich, *Die Tagebücher von Joseph Goebbels*, 9:426.

18. Fritz Hippler, *Die Verstrickung: Einstellungen und Rückblenden von Fritz Hippler ehem. Reichsfilmintendant unter Josef Goebbels,* 2nd ed. (Düsseldorf: MEHR WISSEN, 1982), 143.

19. For the best discussion of World War II newsreels, see Herzstein, *The War That Hitler Won,* 223–258.

20. Boberach, *Meldungen aus dem Reich,* 1:27.

21. Bloc parties were officially allowed parties for Christians, farmers, and the middle class that followed the SED line but allowed citizens to express slightly different shades of opinion.

22. Holzweißig, *Zensur ohne Zensor,* 129.

23. See Ulrich Bürger, *Das sagen wir natürlich so nicht! Donnerstag-Argus bei Herrn Geggel* (Berlin: Dietz, 1990), a pseudonym, according to Holzweißig, for Ulrich Ginolas. Other examples survive in Günter Schabowski's files. See SAPMO, DY 30/IV 2/2.040/16.

24. For examples, see Holzweißig, *Die schärfste Waffe,* 243–246.

25. Holzweißig, *Zensur ohne Zensor,* 99.

26. Reinhold Andert and Wolfgang·Herzberg, *Der Sturz: Erich Honecker im Kreuzverhör,* 3rd ed. (Berlin: Aufbau, 1991), 325.

27. SAPMO, DY 30/IV 2/2.040/16.

28. Michael Meyen, "Ein Stück Privatleben: Die Anfänge des Fernsehens in der DDR," *Deutschland Archiv* 33 (2000): 209.

29. For somewhat biased accounts of GDR television written by people involved, see Erich Selbmann, *DFF Aldershof: Wege übers Fernsehland: Zur Geschichte des DDR-Fernsehens* (Berlin: edition ost, 1998), and Herlt, *Sendeschluß.*

30. For an example, see "Lügensender am Pranger," *Frau von Heute,* 29 September 1961, 7.

31. The GDR also chose the SECAM television system in contrast to the PAL norm followed by West Germany. It was easy to add a converter to a SECAM receiver, but the necessity of doing so made receiving Western television a little harder.

32. Selbmann, *DFF Aldershof,* 457.

33. SAPMO, DY 30/IV 2/2.037/16: E. Fensch to Joachim Herrmann on 6 January 1982. There were occasional exceptions. When Chancellor Helmut Schmidt visited the GDR in 1982, the audience reached an unprecedented 50 percent, since the GDR's journalists were in a better position to provide coverage.

34. Selbmann, *DFF Aldershof,* 309.

35. For a summary of propaganda about Stalingrad, see Baird, *The Mythical World*, 175–190.

36. Ibid., 177.

37. Willy Beer, "Das Schlacht um Stalingrad," *Das Reich*, 18 October 1942, 4.

38. Cited by Baird, *The Mythical World*, 177.

39. See the SD Report for 19 November 1942 in Boberach, *Meldungen aus dem Reich*, 12:4484.

40. Joseph Goebbels, *The Goebbels Diaries, 1942–1943*, trans. Louis P. Lochner (Garden City, N.J.: Doubleday, 1948), 239.

41. Baird, *The Mythical World*, 179.

42. Boberach, *Meldungen aus dem Reich*, 12:4537.

43. Ibid., 12:4630.

44. Joseph Goebbels, *Joseph Goebbels Tagebücher*, 5:1879. Goebbels's lack of regular access to Hitler was a source of steady complaint.

45. Baird, *The Mythical World*, 182.

46. Boberach, *Meldungen aus dem Reich*, 12:4761.

47. Goebbels, *Joseph Goebbels Tagebücher*, 5:1890.

48. Cited by Baird, *The Mythical World*, 184.

49. Hans Schwarz van Berk, "Die offenen Verlustlisten," *Das Reich*, 14 February 1943, 3. The text is in GPA/dr03.htm. The SD report found that this essay was well received.

50. The printed text, which does not fully follow the oral version, is in Joseph Goebbels, *Der steile Aufstieg: Reden und Aufsätze aus den Jahren 1942/43* (Munich: Franz Eher, 1944), 167–204. For a translation of the printed text, see the GPA/goeb36.htm.

51. Boberach, *Meldungen aus dem Reich*, 12:4831.

52. The text of the speech is available in Goebbels, *Der steile Aufstieg*, 287–306, and a translation in GPA/goeb40.htm.

53. SAPMO, DY 30/IV 2/9.02/95: Informationsbericht über Lage und Stimmung in Bezirk Dresden (1961), 90–93.

54. SAPMO, DY 30/IV 2/9.02/18: Bericht über die bisherige Durchführung des Politbürobeschlusses vom 13.6.61 und die Vorbereitung der Wahlen zu den Gemeindevertretungen und Kreistagen entsprechend den Beschluß des Politbüros vom 20.6.1961, 148.

55. SAPMO, DY 30/IV 2/9.02/159: Argumentation 46: Menschenhandel und Kopfprämien in Westberlin! (1961).

56. Herbst, Stephan, and Winkler, *Die SED*, 57.

57. *Neues Deutschland*, 14 August 1961, 1.

58. *Junge Generation,* 16/1961, 1.
59. "Der Frieden ist stärker geworden," *Frau von Heute,* 25 August 1961, 2.
60. *Eulenspiegel,* 34/1961, 2.
61. "Zum 13. August," *Neues Deutschland,* 13 August 1962, 1.
62. Balfour, *Propaganda in War,* 34–35.
63. Goebbels, *The Goebbels Diaries,* 327.
64. Günter Simon, *Tischzeiten: Aus den Notizen eines Chefredakteurs 1981 bis 1989* (Berlin: Tribüne, 1990), 92–93.
65. Roland Reck, *Wasserträger des Regimes: Rolle und Selbstverständnis von DDR-Journalisten vor und nach der Wende, 1989/90* (Münster: Lit, 1996), 158.
66. "Nie wieder Journalisten!" *Das Schwarze Korps,* 3 March 1938, 6.
67. SAPMO, DY 30/IV A2/9.02/39: Harry Tisch to Werner Lamberz on 5.6.1969.
68. See the Propaganda Ministry activity report for 24 January 1945, National Archives microfilm series T-580, roll 1037, frame 6500428.
69. Ellul, *Propaganda,* 102–117.

Chapter 6

1. Domarus, *Hitler: Speeches,* 2:695.
2. For a good study of Nazi art policy, see Jonathan Petropoulos, *Art as Politics in the Third Reich* (Chapel Hill: University of North Carolina Press, 1995).
3. Cited by Igor Golomstock, *Totalitarian Art in the Soviet Union, the Third Reich, Fascist Italy and the People's Republic of China,* trans. Robert Chandler (New York: IconEditions, 1990), 97.
4. For a full treatment of the exhibition, including reproductions of many of the art works pilloried, see Stephanie Barron, ed., *"Degenerate Art": The Fate of the Avant-Garde in Nazi Germany* (Los Angeles: Los Angeles County Museum of Art, 1991).
5. For more information on the magazine, see Otto Thomae, *Die Propaganda-Maschinerie: Bildende Kunst und Öffentlichkeitsarbeit im Dritten Reich* (Berlin: Gebr. Mann, 1978), 201–209.
6. Hitler, *Mein Kampf,* 264.
7. Albert Speer, *Inside the Third Reich,* trans. Richard Winston and Clara Winston (New York: Macmillan, 1970), 56.
8. Hanns Johst, *Ruf des Reiches—Echo des Volkes!* (Munich: Franz Eher, 1940), 80.

9. Hanns Johst, *Requiem* (Munich: Franz Eher, 1943), 13.

10. For a summary of Nazi literary policy, see Jan-Pieter Barbian, "Literary Policy in the Third Reich," in *National Socialist Cultural Policy*, ed. Glenn R. Cuomo (New York: St. Martin's, 1995), 121–154.

11. Alfred Karrasch, *Parteigenosse Schmiedecke* (Berlin: "Zeitgeschichte," 1934). At least 40,000 copies were printed.

12. *Deutsches Bühnen-Jahrbuch, 1940* (Berlin: Buchdruckerei und Verlag Albert May, 1939), 1.

13. Eugen Hadamovsky, *Dein Rundfunk: Das Rundfunkbuch für alle Volksgenossen* (Munich: Franz Eher, 1934), 72.

14. Heiber, *Goebbels Reden*, 1:87,

15. Gerhard Eckert, *Der Rundfunk als Führungsmittel: Studien zum Weltrundfunk and Fernsehrundfunk* (Heidelberg: Kurt Vowinkel, 1941), 243.

16. For general surveys of Nazi film, see David Welch, *Propaganda and the German Cinema, 1933–1945* (Oxford: Clarendon Press, 1983), and Hoffman, *The Triumph of Propaganda*.

17. The post was held by the less than competent Willi Krause until April 1936, when he was replaced by Jürgen Nierentz. Fritz Hippler took over in 1939.

18. Goebbels, *Joseph Goebbels Tagebücher*, 3:1112.

19. Eric Rentschler, *The Ministry of Illusion: Nazi Cinema and Its Afterlife* (Cambridge: Harvard University Press, 1996), 2.

20. For another view of Nazi film, see Sabine Hake, *Popular Cinema of the Third Reich* (Austin: University of Texas Press, 2001).

21. Belling, *Der Film in Staat und Partei*, 143.

22. George L. Mosse, *Nazi Culture: Intellectual, Cultural and Social Life in the Third Reich*, trans. Salvator Attanasio et al. (New York: Grosset & Dunlap, 1968), 162.

23. Wulf, *Presse und Funk*, 85.

24. Henrik Eberle, *Kopfdressur: Zur Propaganda der SED in der DDR* (Asendorf: MUT, 1994), 101.

25. Landesarchiv Berlin, BPA/SED IV B 2/9.01/615: Warum bauen wir das Zentrum der sozialistischen Hauptstadt konzentriert auf? 5, 8.

26. Barck, Classen, and Heimann, "The Fettered Media," 217.

27. Manfred Jäger, *Kultur und Politik in der DDR, 1945–1990* (Cologne: Wissenschaft und Politik, 1995), 87–92.

28. Cited by Anne McElvoy, *The Saddled Cow: East Germany's Life and Legacy* (London: Faber and Faber, 1992), 11.

29. Jäger, *Kultur und Politik*, 103.

30. McElvoy, *The Saddled Cow*, 156.

31. Robert Von Hallberg, *Literary Intellectuals and the Dissolution of the State: Professionalism and Conformity in the GDR*, trans. Kenneth J. Northcott (Chicago: University of Chicago Press, 1996), 239.

32. Viewership for the program, never high, was about 7 percent in 1980. See SAPMO, DY 30/IV 2/2.037/41: Information über wichtige Ergebnisse der Fernseharbeit im I. Quartal 1980.

33. Holzweißig, *Zensur ohne Zensor*, 42.

34. Seán Allen and John Sandford, eds., *DEFA: East German Cinema, 1946–92* (New York: Berghahn Books, 1999).

35. Kurt Hager, *Beiträge zur Kulturpolitik: Reden und Aufsätze 1972 bis 1981* (Berlin: Dietz, 1981), 224.

36. Fröhlich, *Die Tagebücher von Joseph Goebbels*, 9:39, 42.

37. Peter Jelavich, *Berlin Cabaret* (Cambridge: Harvard University Press, 1993), 228.

38. Ibid.

39. Bohrmann, *NS-Presseanweisungen*, 7:313.

40. A letter from Goebbels on the matter is in Wulf, *Presse und Funk*, 136–137.

41. Jelavich, *Berlin Cabaret*, 245.

42. SAPMO, DY 30/vorl.SED 32727: Zu ausgewählten Tendenzen und Problemen bei der Entwicklung des politisch satirischen Berufskabaretts in der DDR in Auswertung der 3. Werkstatttage der Berufskabaretts vom 14. bis 18. Januar 1983 in Gera.

43. According to a 1965 report by Peter Nelken, there were 1,000 amateur cabarets. See SAPMO, DY 30/IV A2/2.028/64: Thesen zur Aufgabenstellung und den Formen der sozialistischen Satire.

44. Maja Lopatta, "Von der Hochschulbank? Zur Aus- und Weiterbildung von Kabarettisten: Gespräch mit Dr. Gisela Oechelhaeuser," *Unterhaltungskunst*, April 1987, 7–9.

45. SAPMO, DY 30/vorl.SED 32727: Kurzinformation zur Situation der Berufskabaretts in der DDR (1983).

46. SAPMO, DY 30/IV 2/9.02/21: Information an Genossen Norden (1961).

47. See SAPMO, DY 30/IV A2/2.028/64: Nelken to Norden on 15 September 1964 and Nelken's Thesen zur Aufgabenstellung.

48. SAPMO, DY 30/vorl.SED 32727: Kurzinformation zur Situation.

49. For examples of *Lustige Blätter* during the war, see GPA/lustige.htm.

50. For examples of cartoons from *Brennessel*, see GPA/brenn1.htm and GPA/brenn2.htm.

51. For *Eulenspiegel* cover cartoons, see GPA/spieg.htm.

52. Peter Nelken, "Die Satire—Waffe der sozialistischen Erziehung: Ein Diskussionsbeitrag," *Einheit* 16 (1962): 107.

53. See *Eulenspiegel* 13/1985, 22/1985, and 25/1985 for the examples cited.

54. For examples, see caricatures of Churchill (12 November 1935, 691), Dolfuß (27 February 1934, 29), and Stalin (2 July 1935, 405).

55. For details, see Scanlan, "The Nazi Party Speaker System."

56. *Brennessel*, 23 October 1934, 677.

57. *Brennessel*, 3 December 1935, 725.

58. *Brennessel*, 30 October 1934, 689.

59. *Brennessel*, 6 November 1934, 710.

60. Nelken, "Die Satire," 108.

61. *Eulenspiegel*, 5/1985, 8–9.

62. *Eulenspiegel*, 8/1985, 13; 43/1985, 8–9; 20/1985, 4.

63. *Eulenspiegel*, 22/1985, 13.

64. *Eulenspiegel*, 6/1986, 4.

65. *Eulenspiegel*, 35/1985, 4.

66. *Eulenspiegel*, 4/1985, 7.

67. *Eulenspiegel*, 22/1985, 16.

68. *Eulenspiegel*, 34/1985, 16.

69. *Eulenspiegel*, 33/1985, 10.

70. Karl Kultzscher, *Links und rechts der Dumme: Lebensdatenverarbeitung eines DDR-Satirikers* (Cologne: Tiberius, 1993), 28.

71. SAPMO, DY 30/IV A2/2.028/64: Nelken to Norden on 27 June 1963. The joke appears on the cover of *Eulenspiegel*, 26/1963. An article in the same issue is titled "How Do We Write about Walter Ulbricht?" It concluded that since Ulbricht was a statesman of stature, the task of satire was to help him achieve his goals, not poke fun at him. Yet another article responded to a West German journalist's comment that Ulbricht never laughed with fourteen photographs of Ulbricht laughing in various situations (8–10).

72. See, for example, SAPMO, NY 4182/921/Bl. 55–58: Über die ideologische Schwankungen im "Eulenspiegel" (1957).

73. *Brennessel*, 31 December 1934, 840.

74. *Brennessel*, 8 May 1934, 294.

75. *Brennessel*, 19 November 1935, 705.

76. *Eulenspiegel*, 29/1986, 13.
77. *Brennessel*, 4 June 1935, 341.
78. *Brennessel*, 12 February 1935, 82.
79. *Eulenspiegel*, 41/1985, 3.
80. *Eulenspiegel*, 6/1986, 13.
81. *Brennessel*, 20 December 1938, 695.
82. These figures are based on the circulation guaranteed advertisers.
83. Speer, *Inside the Third Reich*, 125.
84. Nelkcn "Die Satire," 103.
85. Von Hallberg, *Literary Intellectuals*, 317.

Chapter 7

1. Ellul, *Propaganda*, 11.
2. Goebbels, *Signale der neuen Zeit*, 34.
3. Partei Kanzlei, *Verfügungen/Anordnungen Bekanntgaben*, 1:18.
4. Balfour, *Propaganda in War*, 50.
5. Dmitri Volkogonov, *Autopsy for an Empire: The Seven Leaders Who Built the Soviet Regime*, trans. Harold Shukman (New York: Free Press, 1998), 280.
6. Günter Schabowski, *Das Politbüro: Ende eines Mythos: Eine Befragung* (Reinbek: Rowohlt, 1990), 20.
7. SAPMO, DY 30/NL 4182/29: Honecker to Ulbricht on 22 October 1962.
8. *Kleines politisches Wörterbuch* (1988), 179–180.
9. *Statut der Sozialistischen Einheitspartei Deutschlands* (Berlin: Dietz, 1975), 16.
10. *Materialien der Enquete-Kommission*, vol. 3, bk. 1, p. 322.
11. Wolfgang Leonhard, *Child of the Revolution*, trans. C. M. Woodhouse (London: Collins, 1957), 373.
12. Landolf Scherzer, *Der Erste: Protokoll einer Begegnung* (Rudolstadt: Greifenverlag zu Rudolstadt, 1988), 205.
13. Heiber, *Goebbels Reden*, 1:93.
14. Cited by Baumann, *Grundlagen und Praxis*, 44.
15. Alfred Dietz, "Das Wesen der heutigen Propaganda," *Unser Wille und Weg* 4 (1934): 300.
16. Peter Joachim Lapp, "Wahlen und Wahlfälschungen in der DDR," *Deutschland Archiv* 29 (1996), 92–93.
17. See the 1961 election reports in SAPMO, DY 30/IV A2/9.02/191.

18. Eberle, *Kopfdressur,* 92. According to the accompanying propaganda directive, this was to be used as an expression of the will of the population, not an order, though it is hard to imagine it being taken by the audience as anything but a threat.
19. See the police report in Kuropka, *Meldungen aus Münster,* 153.
20. Ellul, *Propaganda,* 11.
21. Malcolm Gladwell, *The Tipping Point: How Little Things Can Make a Big Difference* (Boston: Little, Brown, 2000). This is not a new argument. Gustav Le Bon made the same point in 1895: "Ideas, sentiments, emotions and beliefs possess in crowds a contagious power as intense as that of microbes." See Gustav Le Bon, *The Crowd: A Study of the Popular Mind* (New York: Viking, 1960), 126.
22. Gerhard Paul, *Staatlicher Terror und gesellschaftliche Verrohung: Die Gestapo in Schleswig-Holstein* (Hamburg: Ergebnisse, 1996), 333.
23. Elisabeth Noelle-Neumann, *Die Schweigespirale: Öffentliche Meinung—unsere soziale Haut* (Frankfurt: Ullstein Sachbuch, 1982).
24. Timur Kuran, *Private Truths, Public Lies: The Social Consequences of Preference Falsification* (Cambridge: Harvard University Press, 1995), 113.
25. Anton Lingg, *Die Verwaltung der Nationalsozialistischen Deutschen Arbeiterpartei,* 3rd ed. (Munich: Franz Eher, 1940), 163.
26. Jost Dülffer, *Nazi Germany, 1933–1945: Faith and Annihilation,* trans. Dean Scott McMurray (London: Arnold, 1996), 103.
27. *Dein Brief eine scharfe Waffe der Aufklärung im Kampfe für Einheit und Frieden* (Berlin: Büro des Präsidiums des Nationalrates des Nationalen Front des demokratischen Deutschland, 1952).
28. Lutz Niethammer, Alexander von Plato, and Dorothee Wierling, *Die Volkseigene Erfahrung: Eine Archäologie des Lebens in der Industrieprovinz der DDR: 30 biographische Eröffnungen* (Berlin: Rowohlt, 1991), 330.
29. *Materialien der Enquete-Kommission,* vol. 7, bk. 1, p. 210.
30. *Materialien der Enquete-Kommission,* vol. 2, bk. 1, p. 322.
31. Ellul, *Propaganda,* 9.
32. William Sheridan Allen, *The Nazi Seizure of Power: The Experience of a Single German Town, 1922–1945,* rev. ed. (New York: Franklin Watts, 1984), 217–232.
33. SAPMO, DY 30/J IV 2/3/999: Verbesserung der weltanschaulich-atheistischen Propaganda (1964), 28.
34. For an excellent account of the GDR education system, see Rodden, *Repainting the Little Red Schoolhouse.*

35. Cited by Heinz Elmar Tenorth, Sonja Kudella, and Andreas Paetz, *Politisierung im Schulalltag der DDR: Durchsetzung und Scheitern einer Erziehungsambition* (Weinheim: Deutscher Studien, 1996), 155.

36. Poßner, *Immer bereit*, 14–19.

37. There were areas of trouble even at the end of the GDR, usually in rural areas where the hold of the church remained strong. In the village of Motzlar, 85 percent of the youth avoided the *Jugendweihe* as late as 1987, for example, but this was unusual. See Scherzer, *Der Erste*, 63.

38. *Materialien der Enquete-Kommission*, vol. 2, bk. 2, pp. 1268–1273.

39. Alison Owings, *Frauen: German Women Recall the Third Reich* (New Brunswick, N.J.: Rutgers University Press, 1993), 202.

40. Helmut Behrens, *Wissenschaft in turbulenter Zeit: Erinnerungen eines Chemikers an die Technische Hochschule München, 1933–1953* (Munich: Institut für Geschichte der Naturwissenschaften, 1998), 48.

41. Robert Gellately, *The Gestapo and German Society* (Oxford: Oxford University Press, 1990).

42. Randall Bytwerk, *Julius Streicher: Nazi Editor of the Notorious Anti-Semitic Newspaper* Der Stürmer, 2nd ed. (New York: Cooper Square, 2001), 199.

43. *Materialien der Enquete-Kommission*, vol. 6, bk. 1, p.373.

44. SAPMO, DY 30/vorl.SED 33899: Aktennotiz über eine Aussprache im Centrum-Warenhaus Berlin, Alexanderplatz, 14.2.1980.

45. Landesarchiv Berlin, BPA/SED IV/4/06/261: Bericht zur Lage: 29.8.1962, 3–3a.

46. Eric A. Johnson, *Nazi Terror: The Gestapo, Jews, and Ordinary Germans* (New York: Basic Books, 1999), 367.

47. Charles S. Maier, *Dissolution: The Crisis of Communism and the End of East Germany* (Princeton, N.J.: Princeton University Press, 1997), 173.

48. Dirk Philipsen, *We Were the People: Voices from East Germany's Revolutionary Autumn of 1989* (Durham, N.C.: Duke University Press, 1993), 49.

49. Christoph Kaufmann, Doris Mundis, and Kurt Nowak, *Sorget nicht, was Ihr reden werdet: Kirche und Staat in Leipzig im Spiegel kirchlicher Gesprächsprotokolle (1977–1989): Dokumentation* (Leipzig: Evangelische Verlagsanstalt, 1993), 203. Christian students about the same time jokingly cited I Mielke 2:1: "Where two or three are gathered together against my will, there am I in midst of them." This is a parody of Christ's statement in Matthew 18:20: "For where two or three come

together in my name, there am I with them." See Hanalore Klein-schmid, "Der Mut zum Nein: Ein Bericht über Menschen, die sich der Stasi verweigerten," *Deutschland Archiv* 28 (1995): 355.

50. Christian Dietrich and Uwe Schwabe, *Freunde und Feinde. Friedensgebete in Leipzig zwischen 1981 und dem 9. Oktober 1989. Dokumentation* (Leipzig: Evangelische Verlagsanstalt, 1994), 198. An account from a participant in the march reports that it had more public visibility than the Stasi report suggests (ibid., 198–199).

51. *Materialien der Enquete-Kommission,* vol. 6, bk. 1, p. 274.

52. *Materialien der Enquete-Kommission,* vol. 3, bk. 1, p. 87.

53. Hermann Weber, *Geschichte der DDR* (Munich: Deutsche Taschenbuch, 1999), 16.

54. Domarus, *Hitler: Speeches,* 1:347.

55. Johnson, *Nazi Terror,* 270.

56. Boberach, *Meldungen aus dem Reich,* 4:1217.

57. Myers Collection, Kreisleitung Eisenach/56: Propaganda-Parole Nr. 3 (1942).

58. See many reports from 1942–1943 in National Archives microfilm series T-81, roll 176. These are the files of the Gauschulungsamt Baden.

59. Marlis G. Steinert, *Hitler's War and the Germans: Public Mood and Attitude during the Second World War,* ed. and trans. Thomas E. J. de Witt (Athens: Ohio University Press, 1977), 53. Steinert provides many details on Nazi surveillance of the churches.

60. Boberach, *Meldungen aus dem Reich,* 15:6114–6118.

61. Manfred Gailus, "Die andere Seite des 'Kirchenkampfes': Nazifizierte Kirchengemeinden und 'braune' Pfarrer in Berlin, 1933–1945," in *Berlin in Geschichte und Gegenwart: Jahrbuch des Landesarchivs Berlin, 1995,* ed. Sigurd-H. Schmidt (Berlin: Gebr. Mann, 1995), 150–151.

62. Kuropka, *Meldungen aus Münster,* 537.

63. *Kleines politisches Wörterbuch* (1988), 828. For a comprehensive study of the relations between church and state in the GDR, see three books by Gerhard Besier: *Der SED-Staat und die Kirche: Der Wege in die Anpassung* (Munich: C. Bertelsmann, 1993); *Der SED-Staat und die Kirche, 1969–1990: Die Vision vom "Dritten Weg"* (Berlin: Propyläen, 1995); and *Der SED-Staat und die Kirche, 1983–1991: Höhenflug und Absturz* (Frankfurt: Propyläen, 1999).

64. See, for example, Mark Allinson, *Politics and Popular Opinion in East Germany, 1945–68* (Manchester: Manchester University Press, 2000),

87–112, for the SED's efforts to reduce the hold of the church in Thuringia.

65. *Materialien der Enquete-Kommission,* vol. 3, bk. 1, p. 87.

66. Gerhard Besier and Stephan Wolf, *Pfarrer, Christen und Katholiken: Das Ministerium für Staatsicherheit der ehemaligen DDR und die Kirchen* (Neukirchen: Neukirchener, 1991), 183.

67. Ehrhart Neubert, "Meister der Legende: Ein Kommentar zum Text des 'Insider-Komitees,'" *Deutschland Archiv* 27 (1994): 395.

68. For details, see SAPMO, DY 30/vorl.SED 33276: Ordnung für die Ko-ordenierung von Maßnahmen der kultur-politischen Propaganda, Agitation und Öffentlichkeitsarbeit anläßlich der Martin-Luther-Ehrung der Deutschen Demokratischen Republik 1983.

69. SAPMO, DY 30/vorl.SED 42314/2: Hager to Honecker on 29 January 1988.

70. John P. Burgess, *The East German Church and the End of Communism: Essays on Religion, Democratization and Christianity* (New York: Oxford University Press, 1997), 45.

71. Mary Fulbrook, *Anatomy of a Dictatorship: Inside the GDR, 1949–1989* (Oxford: Oxford University Press, 1995), 116.

72. Burgess, *The East German Church,* 48.

73. *Deutschland-Berichte,* 4:322.

74. *Materialien der Enquete-Kommission,* vol. 2, bk. 1, p. 146.

75. Hadamovsky, *Propaganda und nationale Macht,* 22.

76. *Deutschland-Berichte,* 3:543.

77. Martin Hirsch, Diemut Majer, and Jürgen Meinck, eds., *Recht, Verwaltung und Justiz im Nationalsozialismus: Ausgewählte Schriften, Gesetze und Gerichtsentscheidungen von 1933 bis 1945* (Cologne: Bund, 1984), 328–329.

78. "Rücksicht am falschen Platz," *Das Schwarze Korps,* 2 September 1943, 2. For the full text, see GPA/sk02.htm.

79. "Stasi-Dokumente, 1989," *Deutschland Archiv* 23 (1990): 613–614.

80. Havel, "The Power of the Powerless," 27–28.

81. Havel, *Open Letters,* 53–54.

82. My response to Goldhagen is "Is It Really That Simple? A Response to Goldhagen (and Newman)," *Rhetoric and Public Affairs* 1 (1998): 425–438.

83. Stéphane Courtois, ed., *The Black Book of Communism: Crimes, Terror, Repression* (Cambridge: Harvard University Press, 1999).

Chapter 8

1. Norman Naimark, for example, an outstanding historian, wrote a report for the West German government in July 1989 that said: "One can only imagine the Berlin Wall being removed under several specific conditions: the East German regime would earn the full trust and respect of its own population; or the Western Powers would decide, with or without Bonn's initiative, to abandon West Berlin; or Bonn would grant the GDR its Gera demands, especially the full recognition by the West Germans of separate GDR citizenship. [The "Gera demands" were made by Honecker in 1980.] Although the third condition has a greater chance of being met than the other two . . . the contemporary situation—as Gorbachev and his advisors consistently reiterate—does not lend itself to eliminating the Berlin Wall.] See Norman Naimark, *Soviet-GDR Relations: An Historical Overview* (Bonn: Bundesinstitut für ostwissenschaftliche Studien, 1989), 26.

2. Milovan Djilas, *The New Class: An Analysis of the Communist System* (New York: Frederick A. Praeger, 1957), 155.

3. Cited by Timothy Garton Ash, *In Europe's Name: Germany and the Divided Continent* (New York: Random House, 1993), 20.

4. J. P. Stern, *Hitler: The Führer and the People* (Berkeley: University of California Press, 1975), 215.

5. Ellen Langer, A. Blank, and B. Chanowitz, "The Mindlessness of Ostensibly Thoughtful Action: The Role of 'Placebic' Information in Interpersonal Interaction," *Journal of Personality and Social Psychology* 36 (1978): 635–642.

6. Poßner, *Immer bereit,* 221.

7. Heinz Niemann, *Hinterm Zaun: Politische Kultur und Meinungsforschung in der DDR—die geheimen Berichte an das Politbüro der SED* (Berlin: edition ost, 1995), 45.

8. *Deutschland-Berichte,* 4:300.

9. Havel, *Open Letters,* 58.

10. Kuran, *Private Truths,* 61.

11. Ellul, *Propaganda,* 25.

12. Andrew Kohut, "Self-Censorship: Counting the Ways," *Columbia Journalism Review* (May/June 2000): 42–43.

13. Havel, *The Power of the Powerless,* 33.

14. See, for example, a September 1939 note to party officials titled "Reich und Sowjetunion," *Der Hoheitsträger* 3, no. 9 (1939): 52. It briefly notes

the economic and military advantages of the treaty and suggests that it was proof of the superiority of authoritarian systems to democratic ones.

15. Ellul, *Propaganda,* 295.

16. Willi A. Boelcke, *The Secret Conferences of Dr. Goebbels: The Nazi Propaganda War, 1939–43,* trans. Ewald Osers (New York: E. P. Dutton, 1970), 81.

17. Boberach, *Meldungen aus dem Reich,* 9:3195.

18. SAPMO, DY 30/IV A2/9.02/45: To Rudi Singer on 28.1.1965.

19. Kuropka, *Meldungen aus Münster,* 162.

20. SAPMO, DY 30/IV 2/9.03/22: Argumente der Intelligenz—Stichtag 1. Dez. 1961, 166.

21. SAPMO, DY 30/IV A2/9.02/39: Bericht über eine Aussprache mit Kreiszeitungsredakteuren der Gebietsgruppe Karl-Marx-Stadt des VDJ am 25. Juni 1963.

22. Cited by Kuran, *Private Truths,* 39.

23. Dieter Wiedemann and Hans-Jörg Stiehler, *Die Funktion der Massenmedien bei der kommunistischen Erziehung der Jugend,* (Leipzig: Zentralinstitut für Jugendforschung, 1984), 90–91.

24. Günter Gaus, *Wo Deutschland liegt: Eine Ortsbestimmung* (Hamburg: Hoffmann und Campe, 1983).

25. Horst Sindermann, "Über die Änderung der Arbeitsweise der Agitation und Propaganda," in *Die Agitation und Propaganda ganz dem neuen Leben und dem Sieg des Sozialismus zuwenden* (Berlin: Abteilung Agitation und Propaganda beim Zentralkomitee der SED, 1959).

26. SAPMO, DY 30/vorl.SED 42224/1, "Resümee der Studie: Ausgewählte Probleme der Entwicklung des sozialistischen Bewußtseins in der DDR" (June 1989).

27. *Materialien der Enquete-Kommission,* vol. 2, bk. 1, pp. 220–228.

28. The SED leadership always reacted vehemently to those who cited Rosa Luxemburg's familiar statement that "freedom is only freedom if it makes room for those who think differently."

29. Havel, *Open Letters,* 334.

30. Friedrich and Brzezinski, *Totalitarian Dictatorship and Autocracy,* 163.

31. Kirkpatrick, *Dictatorships and Double Standards.* At the time she wrote, it was still accurate to say: "[T]he history of this century provides no grounds for expecting that radical totalitarian regimes will transform themselves" (51).

32. Ash, *In Europe's Name,* 199.

33. Speer, *Inside the Third Reich,* 65.

34. Andert and Herzberg, *Der Sturz,* 19–21.

35. See his speech at the outbreak of the war, Domarus, *Hitler: Speeches,* 3:1755. Hitler's injunction was quoted regularly in material for propagandists. See, for example, Fritz Krammer, "Haltung und Mundpropaganda," *Der Hoheitsträger* 6, no. 10 (1942): 11.

36. For examples, see Unger, *The Totalitarian Party,* 233–236.

37. Fulbrook, *Anatomy of a Dictatorship,* 27.

38. Ellul, *Propaganda,* 6.

39. For an illuminating discussion of the book's reception in Germany, see John Rodden, "'It Should Have Been Written Here': Germany and *The Black Book," Human Rights Review* 2 (2001): 144–164.

40. Siegfried Mampel makes a similar point in his study of the Stasi as an ideological police force. See his *Das Ministerium für Staatssicherheit der ehemaligen DDR als Ideologiepolizei: Zur Bedeutung einer Heilslehre als Mittel zum Griff auf das Bewußtsein für das Totalitarismusmodell* (Berlin: Duncker & Humblot, 1996), 368.

Selected Bibliography

Archival Sources

Bundesarchiv Berlin: Records in NS 22. These are files of Robert Ley's *Reichsorganisationsleitung.*

Landesarchiv Berlin: Records of *Bezirk* Berlin of the SED.

Myers Collection, University of Michigan Library: Records of NSDAP *Kreis* Eisenach.

Stiftung Archiv der Parteien und Massenorganisationen der DDR im Bundesarchiv (SAPMO): The Foundation for the Archives of the Parties and Mass Organizations of the GDR under the German Federal Archives holds the records of the Socialist Unity Party of Germany (SED), the four bloc parties, and the mass organizations of the GDR. A useful brief guide to its collections is Elrun Dolatowski, Anette Meiburg, and Sigrun Mühl-Benninghaus, *Die Bestände der Stiftung Archiv der Parteien und Massenorganisationen der DDR im Bundesarchiv: Kurzübersicht* (Berlin: Edition Colloquium, 1996).

U.S. National Archives, Captured German Records: Microfilm series T-81 and T-580.

Published Sources

Adolf Hitler: Bilder aus dem Leben des Führers. Hamburg: Cigaretten/Bilderdienst Hamburg-Bahrenfeld, 1936.

Allen, Seán, and John Sandford, eds. *DEFA: East German Cinema, 1946–92.* New York: Berghahn Books, 1999.

Allen, William Sheridan. *The Nazi Seizure of Power: The Experience of a Single German Town, 1922–1945.* Rev. ed. New York: Franklin Watts, 1984.

"'Alles nur für den Sieg, der Sieg allein entscheidet!'" *Monatsblätter der Gaupropagandaleitung Weser-Ems der NSDAP* 7, no. 3 (1942): 18–19.

Allinson, Mark. *Politics and Popular Opinion in East Germany, 1945–68.* Manchester: Manchester University Press, 2000.

Andert, Reinhold, and Wolfgang Herzberg. *Der Sturz: Erich Honecker im Kreuzverhör.* 3rd ed. Berlin: Aufbau, 1991.

Arendt, Hannah. *The Origins of Totalitarianism*. New York: Harcourt Brace, 1951.

Ash, Timothy Garton. *In Europe's Name: Germany and the Divided Continent*. New York: Random House, 1993.

Baird, Jay W. *The Mythical World of Nazi War Propaganda, 1939–1945*. Minneapolis: University of Minnesota Press, 1974.

_____. *To Die for Germany: Heroes in the Nazi Pantheon*. Bloomington: Indiana University Press, 1990.

Balfour, Michael. *Propaganda in War, 1939–1945: Organisations, Policies and Publics in Britain and Germany*. London: Routledge & Kegan Paul, 1979.

Barbian, Jan-Pieter. "Literary Policy in the Third Reich." In *National Socialist Cultural Policy*, ed. Glenn R. Cuomo, 121–154. New York: St. Martin's, 1995.

Barck, Simone, Christoph Classen, and Thomas Heimann. "The Fettered Media: Controlling Public Debate." In *Dictatorship as Experience: Towards a Socio-Cultural History of the GDR*, ed. Konrad H. Jarausch, 213–240. New York: Berghahn Books, 1999.

Barnett, Victoria. *For the Soul of the People: Protestant Protest Against Hitler*. New York: Oxford University Press, 1992.

Barron, Stephanie, ed. *"Degenerate Art": The Fate of the Avant-Garde in Nazi Germany*. Los Angeles: Los Angeles County Museum of Art, 1991.

Bärsch, Claus-Ekkehard. *Die politische Religion des Nationalsozialismus: Die religiöse Dimension der NS-Ideologie in den Schriften von Dietrich Eckardt, Joseph Goebbels, Alfred Rosenberg und Adolf Hitler*. Munich: Wilhelm Fink, 1998.

Baumann, Gerhard. *Grundlagen und Praxis der internationalen Propaganda*. Essen: Essener Verlagsanstalt, 1941.

Becher, Johannes R. "Gebranntes Kind." *Sinn und Form* 42 (2000): 343.

Becker, Ernst. "Staatsterrorismus—warum und wie wird er verstärkt von den USA praktiziert?" *Neuer Weg* 41 (1986): 236–238.

Beer, Willy. "Das Schlacht um Stalingrad." *Das Reich*, 18 October 1942, 4–5.

Behrens, Helmut. *Wissenschaft in turbulenter Zeit: Erinnerungen eines Chemikers an die Technische Hochschule München, 1933–1953*. Studien zur Geschichte der Mathematik und der Naturwissenschaften, ed. Menso Folkerts, no. 25. Munich: Institut für Geschichte der Naturwissenschaften, 1998.

Belling, Curt. *Der Film in Staat und Partei*. Berlin: "Der Film," 1936.

Benn, David Wedgwood. *Persuasion and Soviet Politics*. London: Basil Blackwell, 1989.

Berg, Hermann von. *Marxismus-Leninismus: Das Elend der halb deutschen, halb russischen Ideologie.* Cologne: Bund, 1986.

Bergmeier, Horst J. P., and Rainer E. Lotz. *Hitler's Airwaves: The Inside Story of Nazi Radio Broadcasting and Propaganda Swing.* New Haven, Conn.: Yale University Press, 1997.

Berth, Henrik, and Elmar Brähler. *Zehn Jahre Deutsche Einheit: Die Bibliographie.* Berlin: Verlag für Wissenschaft und Forschung, 2000.

Besier, Gerhard. *Der SED-Staat und die Kirche: Der Wege in die Anpassung.* Munich: C. Bertelsmann, 1993.

———. *Der SED-Staat und die Kirche, 1969–1990: Die Vision vom "Dritten Weg."* Berlin: Propyläen, 1995.

———. *Der SED-Staat und die Kirche, 1983–1991: Höhenflug und Absturz.* Frankfurt: Propyläen, 1999.

Besier, Gerhard, and Stephan Wolf. *Pfarrer, Christen und Katholiken: Das Ministerium für Staatssicherheit der ehemaligen DDR und die Kirchen.* Neukirchen: Neukirchener, 1991.

Bezirksleitung Cottbus. *Erfahrungen Formen Methoden der Parteiarbeit: 3. Agitatorenkonferenz der Bezirksleitung Cottbus der SED 13.12.1976.* Cottbus: Bezirksleitung Cottbus der SED, Abteilung Agitation/Propaganda, 1977.

Bilanz zwischen zwei Parteitagen: Fakten und Ergebnisse der Agitation und Propaganda der Kreisparteiorganisation Weißenfels. Weißenfels: Kreisleitung Weißenfels der SED, Abteilung Agitation und Propaganda, 1976.

Boberach, Heinz, ed. *Meldungen aus dem Reich: Die geheimen Lageberichte des Sicherheitsdienstes der SS, 1938–1945.* 17 vols. Herrsching: Pawlak, 1984.

Boelcke, Willi A. *The Secret Conferences of Dr. Goebbels: The Nazi Propaganda War, 1939–43.* Trans. Ewald Osers. New York: E. P. Dutton, 1970.

Bohrmann, Hans, ed. *NS-Presseanweisungen der Vorkriegszeit: Edition und Dokumentation.* 7 vols. Munich: K. G. Saur, 1984–2001.

Bosmajian, Haig A. "The Sources and Nature of Adolf Hitler's Techniques of Persuasion." *Central States Speech Journal* 25 (1974): 240–248.

Bramsted, Ernest K. *Goebbels and National Socialist Propaganda, 1925–1945.* East Lansing: Michigan State University Press, 1965.

Bühner, Karl Hans, ed. *Dem Führer: Gedichte für Adolf Hitler.* Stuttgart: Georg Truckenmüller, 1939.

Bullock, Alan. *Hitler and Stalin: Parallel Lives.* New York: Alfred A. Knopf, 1992.

Bürger, Ulrich [Ulrich Ginolas]. *Das sagen wir natürlich so nicht! Donnerstag-Argus bei Herrn Geggel.* Berlin: Dietz, 1990.

Burgess, John P. *The East German Church and the End of Communism: Essays on Religion, Democratization and Christianity.* New York: Oxford University Press, 1997.

Burke, Kenneth. "The Rhetoric of Hitler's 'Battle.'" In *The Philosophy of Literary Form,* 164–189. New York: Vintage, 1957.

Burleigh, Michael. *The Third Reich: A New History.* New York: Hill and Wang, 2000.

Bytwerk, Randall. "Is It Really That Simple? A Response to Goldhagen (and Newman)." *Rhetoric and Public Affairs* 1 (1998): 425–438.

_____. *Julius Streicher: Nazi Editor of the Notorious Anti-Semitic Newspaper* Der Stürmer. 2nd ed. New York: Cooper Square, 2001.

Courtois, Stéphane, ed. *The Black Book of Communism: Crimes, Terror, Repression.* Cambridge: Harvard University Press, 1999.

Cunningham, Stanley B. *The Idea of Propaganda: A Reconstruction.* Westport, Conn.: Praeger, 2002.

Cuomo, Glenn R., ed. *National Socialist Cultural Policy.* New York: St. Martin's, 1995.

Czechowski, Heinz, ed. *Unser der Tag unser das Wort: Lyrik und Prosa für Gedenk- und Feiertage.* Halle: Mitteldeutscher, 1966.

d'Alquen, Gunter. *Das ist der Sieg! Briefe des Glaubens in Aufbruch und Krieg.* Berlin: Franz Eher, 1941.

Dein Brief eine scharfe Waffe der Aufklärung im Kampfe für Einheit und Frieden. Berlin: Büro des Präsidiums des Nationalrates des Nationalen Front des demokratischen Deutschland, 1952.

"Der Frieden ist stärker geworden." *Frau von Heute,* 25 August 1961, 2–3, 14.

Der Kongress zu Nürnberg vom 5. bis 10. September 1934: Offizieller Bericht über den Verlauf des Reichsparteitages mit sämtlichen Reden. Munich: Franz Eher, 1934.

Deutsches Bühnen-Jahrbuch, 1940. Berlin: Buchdruckerei und Verlag Albert May, 1939.

Deutschland-Berichte der Sozialdemokratischen Partei Deutschlands (Sopade), 1934–1940. 7 vols. Salzhausen: Petra Nettelbeck, 1980.

Deutz-Schroeder, Monika, and Jochen Staadt. *Teurer Genosse! Briefe an Erich Honecker.* Berlin: Transit Buchverlag, 1994.

"Die Arbeit der Partei-Propaganda im Kriege." *Unser Wille und Weg* 11 (1941): 1–12.

Die Aufgaben der Agitation und Propaganda bei der weiteren Verwirklichung der Beschlüsse des VIII. Parteitages der SED. Berlin: Dietz, 1972.

"Die Reichspropagandaleitung der NSDAP." *Unser Wille und Weg* 6 (1936): 6–11.

Dietrich, Christian, and Uwe Schwabe. *Freunde und Feinde: Friedensgebete in Leipzig zwischen 1981 und dem 9. Oktober 1989: Dokumentation.* Leipzig: Evangelische Verlagsanstalt, 1994.

Dietz, Alfred. "Das Wesen der heutigen Propaganda." *Unser Wille und Weg* 4 (1934): 299–301.

"Die Versammlungen der NSDAP: Eine Uebersicht über das Winterhalbjahr 1943/44." *Die Lage,* Folge 116 B (1944): 5.

Djilas, Milovan. *The New Class: An Analysis of the Communist System.* New York: Frederick A. Praeger, 1957.

Domarus, Max. *Hitler: Reden und Proklamationen, 1932–1945.* 4 vols. Munich: Süddeutscher, 1965.

———. *Hitler: Speeches and Proclamations, 1932–1945.* Trans. Mary Fran Gilbert. 4 vols. Wauconda, Ill.: Bolchazy-Carducci, 1990–2002.

Dülffer, Jost. *Nazi Germany, 1933–1945: Faith and Annihilation.* Trans. Dean Scott McMurray. London: Arnold, 1996.

Eberle, Henrik. *Kopfdressur: Zur Propaganda der SED in der DDR.* Blaue Aktuelle Reihe, no. 26. Asendorf: MUT, 1994.

Eckert, Gerhard. *Der Rundfunk als Führungsmittel: Studien zum Weltrundfunk and Fernsehrundfunk.* Heidelberg: Kurt Vowinkel, 1941.

Ellul, Jacques. *Propaganda: The Formation of Men's Attitudes.* Trans. Konrad Kellen and Jean Lerner. New York: Alfred A. Knopf, 1968.

Enquete-Kommission. *Materialien der Enquete-Kommission "Aufarbeitung von Geschichte und Folgen der SED-Diktatur in Deutschland" (12. Wahlperiode des Deutschen Bundestages),* 9 vols. Frankfurt: Suhrkamp, 1995.

Feierstunde zum 40. Jahrestag der Gründung der Kommunistischen Partei Deutschlands. Berlin: Zentralvorstand der Gewerkschaft Unterricht und Erziehung, 1958.

Fischer, Rudolf, Ursula Langspach, and Johannes Schellenberger, eds. *Sieh, das ist unser Tag! Lyrik und Prosa für sozialistische Gedenk- und Feierstunden.* Berlin: Tribüne, 1961.

Fredborg, Arvid. *Behind the Steel Wall: A Swedish Journalist in Berlin, 1941–43.* New York: Viking, 1944.

Frei, Norbert, and Johannes Schmitz. *Journalismus im Dritten Reich.* 2nd ed. Munich: C. H. Beck, 1989.

Friedrich, Carl J., and Zbigniew K. Brzezinski. *Totalitarian Dictatorship and Autocracy.* Cambridge: Harvard University Press, 1965.

Fritze, Lothar. *Täter mit gutem Gewissen: Über menschliches Versagen im diktatorischen Sozialismus.* Schriften des Hannah-Arendt-Instituts, vol. 8. Cologne: Böhlau, 1998.

Fröhlich, Elke, ed. *Die Tagebücher von Joseph Goebbels.* 15 vols. Munich: K. G. Sauer, 1997–2001.

Fulbrook, Mary. *Anatomy of a Dictatorship: Inside the GDR, 1949–1989.* Oxford: Oxford University Press, 1995.

Gailus, Manfred. "Die andere Seite des 'Kirchenkampfes': Nazifizierte Kirchengemeinden und 'braune' Pfarrer in Berlin, 1933–1945." In *Berlin in Geschichte und Gegenwart: Jahrbuch des Landesarchivs Berlin, 1995,* ed. Sigurd-H. Schmidt, 149–170. Berlin: Gebr. Mann, 1995.

Gamm, Hans-Jochen. *Der braune Kult: Das Dritte Reich und seine Ersatzreligion: Ein Beitrag zur politischen Bildung.* Hamburg: Rütten & Loening, 1962.

Gaupropagandaamt Oberdonau, Linz. "Parteigenossen!" *Front der Heimat* 1939, 1.

Gaus, Günter. *Wo Deutschland liegt: Eine Ortsbestimmung.* Hamburg: Hoffmann und Campe, 1983.

Gedenkstätten: Arbeiterbewegung, Antifaschistischer Widerstand, Aufbau des Sozialismus. Jena: Urania, 1974.

Geggel, Heinz. "Jederzeit aktiv und überzeugend die Politik der Partei vertreten." *Neuer Weg* 44 (1989): 195–200.

Gellately, Robert. *Backing Hitler: Consent and Coercion in Nazi Germany.* Oxford: Oxford University Press, 2001.

———. *The Gestapo and German Society.* Oxford: Oxford University Press, 1990.

Gemkow, Heinrich, ed. *Der Sozialismus—Deine Welt.* Berlin: Neues Leben, 1975.

Gibas, Monika, and Rainer Gries. "Die Inszenierung des sozialistischen Deutschland: Geschichte und Dramaturgie der Dezennienfeiern in der DDR." In *Wiedergeburten: Zur Geschichte der runden Jahrestage der DDR,* ed. Monika Gibas, Rainer Gries, Barbara Jakoby, and Doris Müller, 11–40. Leipzig: Leipziger Universitätsverlag, 1999.

Gibas, Monika, Rainer Gries, Barbara Jakoby, and Doris Müller, eds. *Wiedergeburten: Zur Geschichte der runden Jahrestage der DDR.* Leipzig: Leipziger Universitätsverlag, 1999.

Gladwell, Malcolm. *The Tipping Point: How Little Things Can Make a Big Difference.* Boston: Little, Brown, 2000.

Gleason, Abbott. *Totalitarianism: The Inner History of the Cold War.* New York: Oxford University Press, 1995.

Goebbels, Joseph. *Das eherne Herz: Reden und Aufsätze aus den Jahren 1941/42.* Munich: Franz Eher, 1943.

———. "Das Jahr 2000." *Das Reich,* 25 February 1945, 1–2.

———. *Der steile Aufstieg: Reden und Aufsätze aus den Jahren 1942/43.* Munich: Franz Eher, 1944.

———. *Final Entries, 1945: The Diaries of Joseph Goebbels.* Trans. Richard Barry. New York: G. P. Putnam's Sons, 1978.

———. *The Goebbels Diaries: 1942–1943.* Trans. Louis P. Lochner. Garden City: Doubleday, 1948.

———. *Joseph Goebbels Tagebücher, 1924–1945.* Ed. Ralf Georg Reuth. Erweiterte Sonderausgabe. 5 vols. Munich: Piper, 1999.

———. *Kampf um Berlin: Der Anfang.* Munich: Franz Eher, 1934.

———. *Signale der neuen Zeit: 25 ausgewählte Reden.* 5th ed. Munich: Franz Eher, 1938.

Golomstock, Igor. *Totalitarian Art in the Soviet Union, the Third Reich, Fascist Italy and the People's Republic of China.* Trans. Robert Chandler. New York: IconEditions, 1990.

Göring, Hermann. Untitled editorial. *Sommerlager- und Heimabendmaterial für die Schulungs- und Kulturarbeit,* summer 1941, 2.

Hackl, Hans. "Die Partei hat in allem Vorbild zu sein!" *Die Lage,* September 1943, 1–7.

Hadamovsky, Eugen. *Dein Rundfunk: Das Rundfunkbuch für alle Volksgenossen.* Munich: Franz Eher, 1934.

———. *Hilfsarbeiter Nr. 50 000.* Munich: Franz Eher, 1938.

———. *Propaganda und nationale Macht: Die Organisation der öffentlichen Meinung für die nationale Politik.* Oldenburg: Gerhard Stalling, 1933.

Hager, Kurt. *Beiträge zur Kulturpolitik: Reden und Aufsätze 1972 bis 1981.* Berlin: Dietz, 1981.

Hake, Sabine. *Popular Cinema of the Third Reich.* Austin: University of Texas Press, 2001.

Hampf, Ernst. *Weil die Partei führt, ist unser Sieg gewiß.* Wissen und Kämpfen. Berlin: Militärverlag der DDR, 1973.

Harm, Marie, and Hermann Wieble. *Lebenskunde für Mittelschulen: Fünfter Teil, Klasse 5 für Mädchen.* Halle: Hermann Schroedel, 1942.

Hauptkulturamt der NSDAP. *Deutsche Kriegsweihnacht.* Munich: Franz Eher, 1944.

Havel, Václav. *Open Letters: Selected Writings, 1965–1990.* Trans. Paul Wilson. New York: Alfred A. Knopf, 1991.

———. "The Power of the Powerless." In *The Power of the Powerless. Citizens Against the State in Central-Eastern Europe,* ed. John Keane, 23–97. Armonk, N.Y.: M. E. Sharpe, 1985.

Heiber, Helmut. *Goebbels Reden, 1932–1945.* 2 vols. Munich: Wilhelm Heyne, 1971.

Heiss, Michael. "'Gegen Dummheit gibt's kein Mittel!'" *Neuer Weg,* December 1949, 31.

Hempel, A. "Zuviel Politik." *Trommel,* 18/1980, 1.

Herbst, Andreas, Gerd-Rüdiger Stephan, and Jürgen Winkler. *Die SED: Geschichte, Organisation, Politik: Ein Handbuch.* Berlin: Dietz, 1997.

Herlt, Günter. *Sendeschluß: Ein Insider des DDR-Fernsehens berichtet.* Berlin: edition ost, 1995.

Herz, Rudolf. *Hoffmann & Hitler: Fotographie als Medium des Führer-Mythos.* Munich: Klinkhardt & Biermann, 1994.

Herzstein, Robert Edwin. *The War That Hitler Won: The Most Infamous Propaganda Campaign in History.* New York: G. P. Putnam's Sons, 1978.

Heydemann, Günter, and Christopher Beckmann. "Zwei Diktaturen in Deutschland: Möglichkeiten und Grenzen des historischen Diktaturvergleichs." *Deutschland Archiv* 30 (1997): 12–39.

Hilbig, Ewin. "Sind Feierstunden notwendig?" *Unser Wille und Weg* 9 (1939): 164–165.

Hippler, Fritz. *Die Verstrickung: Einstellungen und Rückblenden von Fritz Hippler ehem. Reichsfilmintendant unter Josef Goebbels.* 2nd ed. Düsseldorf: MEHR WISSEN, 1982.

Hirsch, Martin, Diemut Majer, and Jürgen Meinck, eds. *Recht, Verwaltung und Justiz im Nationalsozialismus: Ausgewählte Schriften, Gesetze und Gerichtsentscheidungen von 1933 bis 1945.* Cologne: Bund, 1984.

Hitler, Adolf. *Mein Kampf.* Trans. Ralph Manheim. Boston: Houghton Mifflin, 1971.

Hofe, Werner von. "Mein Junge." *NS Frauen Warte* 7, no. 4 (1938): 97.

Hoffman, Hilmar. *The Triumph of Propaganda: Film and National Socialism, 1933–1945.* Trans. John A. Broadwin and V. R. Berghahn. Providence, R.I.: Berghahn Books, 1996.

Holzweißig, Gunter. *Die schärfste Waffe der Partei: Eine Mediengeschichte der DDR.* Cologne: Böhlau, 2002.

———. *Zensur ohne Zensor: Die SED-Informationsdiktatur.* Bonn: Bouvier, 1997.

Ichenhäuser, Ernst Z. *Erziehung zum guten Benehmen.* 3rd ed. Berlin: Volk und Wissen, 1983.

"In eigener Sache." *WAS und WIE,* December 1989, 4–5.

Jäger, Manfred. *Kultur und Politik in der DDR, 1945–1990.* Cologne: Wissenschaft und Politik, 1995.

Jelavich, Peter. *Berlin Cabaret.* Cambridge: Harvard University Press, 1993.

Johnson, Eric A. *Nazi Terror: The Gestapo, Jews, and Ordinary Germans.* New York: Basic Books, 1999.

Johst, Hanns. *Requiem.* Munich: Franz Eher, 1943.

———. *Ruf des Reiches—Echo des Volkes!* Munich: Franz Eher, 1940.

Kalaschnikow, K. *Die Grundsätze der bolschewistischen Agitation.* Bibliothek des Agitators. Berlin: Dietz, 1951.

Kapferer, Norbert. *Der Totalitarismusbegriff auf dem Prüfstand.* Dresden: Hannah-Arendt-Institut für Totalitarismusforschung, 1995.

Karrasch, Alfred. *Parteigenosse Schmiedecke.* Berlin: "Zeitgeschichte," 1934.

Kaufmann, Christoph, Doris Mundis, and Kurt Nowak. *Sorget nicht, was Ihr reden werdet: Kirche und Staat in Leipzig im Spiegel kirchlicher Gesprächsprotokolle (1977–1989): Dokumentation.* Leipzig: Evangelische Verlagsanstalt, 1993.

Kershaw, Ian. *The 'Hitler Myth': Image and Reality in the Third Reich.* Oxford: Oxford University Press, 1987.

———. "'Working toward the Führer': Reflections on the Nature of the Hitler Dictatorship." In *Stalinism and Nazism: Dictatorships in Comparison,* ed. Ian Kershaw and Moshe Lewin, 88–106. Cambridge: Cambridge University Press, 1997.

Kirkpatrick, Jeane J. *Dictatorships and Double Standards: Rationalism and Reason in Politics.* New York: Simon and Schuster, 1982.

Klaus, Georg. *Die Macht des Wortes: Ein erkenntnistheoretisch-pragmatisches Traktat.* 4th ed. Berlin: VEB Deutscher Verlag der Wissenschaften, 1968.

———. *Sprache der Politik.* Berlin: VEB Deutscher Verlag der Wissenschaften, 1971.

Kleines politisches Wörterbuch. Berlin: Dietz, 1967.

Kleines politisches Wörterbuch. 7th ed. Berlin: Dietz, 1988.

Kleinschmid, Hanalore. "Der Mut zum Nein: Ein Bericht über Menschen, die sich der Stasi verweigerten." *Deutschland Archiv* 28 (1995): 348–359.

Kohut, Andrew. "Self-Censorship: Counting the Ways." *Columbia Journalism Review* (May/June 2000): 42–43.

Krammer, Fritz. "Haltung und Mundpropaganda." *Der Hoheitsträger* 6, no. 10 (1942): 11–12.

Kremer, Hannes. "Neuwertung 'überlieferter' Brauchformen?" *Die neue Gemeinschaft* 3 (1937): 3005 a-c.

Krumbach, Josef H. *Grundfragen der Publizistik: Die Wesenselemente des publizistischen Prozesses: Seine Mittel und Ergebnisse.* Berlin: Walter de Gruyter, 1935.

Kultzscher, Karl. *Links und rechts der Dumme: Lebensdatenverarbeitung eines DDR-Satirikers.* Cologne: Tiberius, 1993.

Kuran, Timur. *Private Truths, Public Lies: The Social Consequences of Preference Falsification.* Cambridge: Harvard University Press, 1995.

Kuropka, Joachim, ed. *Meldungen aus Münster, 1924–1944.* Münster: Regensberg, 1992.

Langer, Ellen, A. Blank, and B. Chanowitz. "The Mindlessness of Ostensibly Thoughtful Action: The Role of 'Placebic' Information in Interpersonal Interaction." *Journal of Personality and Social Psychology* 36 (1978): 635–642.

Lapp, Peter Joachim. "Wahlen und Wahlfälschungen in der DDR." *Deutschland Archiv* 29 (1996): 92–106.

Le Bon, Gustav. *The Crowd: A Study of the Popular Mind.* New York: Viking, 1960.

Lenin, W. I. *Über Agitation und Propaganda.* Berlin: Dietz, 1974.

Leonhard, Wolfgang. *Child of the Revolution.* Trans. C. M. Woodhouse. London: Collins, 1957.

Lingg, Anton. *Die Verwaltung der Nationalsozialistischen Deutschen Arbeiterpartei.* 3rd ed. Munich: Franz Eher, 1940.

Longerich, Peter. *Propagandisten im Krieg: Die Presseabteilung des Auswärtigen Amtes unter Ribbentrop.* Studien zur Zeitgeschichte, no. 33. Munich: R. Oldenbourg, 1987.

Lopatta, Maja. "Von der Hochschulbank? Zur Aus- und Weiterbildung von Kabarettisten: Gespräch mit Dr. Gisela Oechelhaeuser." *Unterhaltungskunst,* April 1987, 7–9.

"Lügensender am Pranger." *Frau von Heute,* 29 September 1961, 7.

Maaz, Hans-Joachim. *Behind the Wall: The Inner Life of Communist Germany.* Trans. Margot Bettauer Dembo. New York: W. W. Norton, 1995.

Maier, Charles S. *Dissolution: The Crisis of Communism and the End of East Germany.* Princeton, N.J.: Princeton University Press, 1997.

Maier, Hans. "Deutungen totalitärer Herrschaft, 1919–1989." *Vierteljahrshefte für Zeitgeschichte* 50 (2002): 349–366.

———, ed. *'Totalitarismus' und 'politische Religionen': Konzepte des Diktaturvergleichs.* 2 vols. Politik- und Kommunikationswissenschaftliche

Veröffentlichungen der Görres-Gesellschaft. Paderborn: Ferdinand Schöningh, 1996.

Mampel, Siegfried. *Das Ministerium für Staatssicherheit der ehemaligen DDR als Ideologiepolizei: Zur Bedeutung einer Heilslehre als Mittel zum Griff auf das Bewußtsein für das Totalitarismusmodell.* Schriftenreihe der Gesellschaft für Deutschlandforschung, no. 50. Berlin: Duncker & Humblot, 1996.

Marx-Engels-Lenin-Institut. *J. Stalin: Kurze Lebensbeschreibung.* Berlin: Verlag der Sowjetischen Militärverwaltung in Deutschland, 1945.

McElvoy, Anne. *The Saddled Cow: East Germany's Life and Legacy.* London: Faber and Faber, 1992.

McGuire, William. "Resistance to Persuasion Conferred by Active and Passive Prior Refutation of the Same and Alternative Counterargument." *Journal of Abnormal and Social Psychology* 63 (1961): 326–332.

Mehnert, Fritz. "Die Statistik der NSDAP." *Der Hoheitsträger* 3, no. 7 (1939): 10–12.

"Merkblatt für den Propagandisten im Gau Weser-Ems." *Monatsblätter der Gaupropagandaleitung Weser-Ems der NSDAP.* 7, no 3 (1942): 10–13.

Meyen, Michael. "Ein Stück Privatleben: Die Anfänge des Fernsehens in der DDR." *Deutschland Archiv* 33 (2000): 207–216.

Miethe, Annadora, ed. *Buchenwald.* N.p., 1983.

Milosz, Czeslaw. *The Captive Mind.* Trans. Jane Zielonko. New York: Octagon Books, 1981.

Mosse, George L. *The Nationalization of the Masses: Political Symbolism and Mass Movements in Germany from the Napoleonic Wars through the Third Reich.* New York: Howard Fertig, 1975.

———. *Nazi Culture: Intellectual, Cultural and Social Life in the Third Reich.* Trans. Salvator Attanasio et al. New York: Grosset & Dunlap, 1968.

Münzenberg, Willi. *Propaganda als Waffe.* Paris: Éditions du Carrefour, 1937.

Naimark, Norman. *Soviet-GDR Relations: An Historical Overview.* Bonn: Bundesinstitut für ostwissenschaftliche Studien, 1989.

Nelken, Peter. "Die Satire—Waffe der sozialistischen Erziehung: Ein Diskussionsbeitrag." *Einheit* 16 (1962): 103–113.

Neubert, Ehrhart. "Meister der Legende: Ein Kommentar zum Text des 'Insider-Komitees.'" *Deutschland Archiv* 27 (1994): 391–407.

Neuner, Gerhart. *Politisch-ideologische Arbeit und Erziehung.* Sitzungsberichte der Akademie der Wissenschaften der DDR. Vol. 9/G. Berlin: Akademie, 1978.

Niemann, Heinz. *Hinterm Zaun: Politische Kultur und Meinungsforschung in der DDR—die geheimen Berichte an das Politbüro der SED.* Berlin: edition ost, 1995.

Niethammer, Lutz, Alexander von Plato, and Dorothee Wierling. *Die Volkseigene Erfahrung: Eine Archäologie des Lebens in der Industrieprovinz der DDR: 30 biographische Eröffnungen.* Berlin: Rowohlt, 1991.

"Nie wieder Journalisten!" *Das Schwarze Korps,* 3 March 1938, 6.

"9 November." *Völkischer Beobachter,* 8 November 1935.

Noelle-Neumann, Elisabeth. *Die Schweigespirale: Öffentliche Meinung—unsere soziale Haut.* Frankfurt: Ullstein Sachbuch, 1982.

Nothnagle, Alan L. *Building the East German Myth: Historical Mythology and Youth Propaganda in the German Democratic Republic, 1945–1989.* Social History, Popular Culture, and Politics in Germany. Ann Arbor: University of Michigan Press, 1999.

Oelßner, Fred. *Über die allseitige Verbesserung unserer politisch-ideologischen Massenarbeit: Diskussionsrede auf dem IV. Parteitag der Sozialistischen Einheitspartei Deutschlands.* Berlin: Dietz, 1954.

_____. *Über die Verbesserung der Arbeit der Presse und des Rundfunks.* Berlin: Dietz, 1953.

Oestreich, Paul. *Walther Funk: Ein Leben für die Wirtschaft.* Munich: Franz Eher, 1940.

"1. Lehrgang der Gau- und Kreispropagandaleiter der NSDAP." *Unser Wille und Weg* 9 (1939): 124–139.

Organisationsbuch der NSDAP. 5th ed. Munich: Franz Eher, 1938.

Orlow, Dietrich. *The History of the Nazi Party: 1933–1945.* Pittsburgh: University of Pittsburgh Press, 1973.

Owings, Alison. *Frauen: German Women Recall the Third Reich.* New Brunswick, N.J.: Rutgers University Press, 1993.

Partei Kanzlei. *Verfügungen/Anordnungen Bekanntgaben.* 4 vols. Munich: Franz Eher, 1943.

Paul, Gerhard. *Staatlicher Terror und gesellschaftliche Verrohung. Die Gestapo in Schleswig-Holstein.* Hamburg: Ergebnisse, 1996.

Petropoulos, Jonathan. *Art as Politics in the Third Reich.* Chapel Hill: University of North Carolina Press, 1995.

Philipsen, Dirk. *We Were the People: Voices from East Germany's Revolutionary Autumn of 1989.* Durham, N.C.: Duke University Press, 1993.

Phillips, Henry Albert. *Germany Today and Tomorrow.* New York: Dodd, Mead, 1935.

Plan der massenpolitischen Arbeit der Kreisparteiorganisation Rochlitz für das Jahr 1982. Rochlitz: SED Kreisleitung Rochlitz, 1982.

Plantinga, Cornelius, Jr. *Not the Way It's Supposed to Be: A Breviary of Sin.* Grand Rapids, Mich.: William B. Eerdmans, 1995.

Poßner, Wilfried. *Immer bereit! Parteiauftrag: kämpfen, spielen, fröhlich sein.* Berlin: edition ost, 1995.

Puder, Heinz. "Zu den Aufgaben der marxistisch-leninistischen Bildung und Erziehung sowie zu den Anforderungen an die Propagandisten des Parteilehrjahres." In *Beiträge zur Methodik im Parteilehrjahr,* 3–15. Berlin: ZK der SED, 1988.

"Qualitative Stärkung der Reihen der SED fortgesetzt." *Neues Deutschland,* 11 January 1989, 3.

Rademacher, Michael. *Carl Röver: Der Bericht des Reichsstatthalters von Oldenburg und Bremen und Gauleiter des Gaues Weser-Ems über die Lage der NSDAP: Eine Denkschrift aus dem Jahr 1942.* Vechta: Selbstverlag des Verfassers, 2000.

Raskin, Adolf. "Dramaturgie der Propaganda." In *Handbuch des deutschen Rundfunks, 1939/40,* ed. Hans-Joachim Weinbrenner, 83–90. Heidelberg: Kurt Vowinkel, 1939.

Reck, Roland. *Wasserträger des Regimes: Rolle und Selbstverständnis von DDR-Journalisten vor und nach der Wende, 1989/90.* Medien und Kommunikation, ed. Hans-Dieter Küberl, vol. 24. Münster: Lit, 1996.

Reibel, Carl-Wilhelm. *Das Fundament der Diktatur: Die NSDAP-Ortsgruppen 1932–1945.* Paderborn: Ferdinand Schöningh, 2002.

Reichsorganisationsleiter. *Partei-Statistik: Stand: 1935.* Munich: Reichsorganisationsleiter, 1935.

"Reichsredner der NSDAP." *Unser Wille und Weg* 6 (1936): 222–223.

"Reich und Sowjetunion." *Der Hoheitsträger* 3, no. 9 (1939): 52.

Rentschler, Eric. *The Ministry of Illusion: Nazi Cinema and Its Afterlife.* Cambridge: Harvard University Press, 1996.

Reuband, Karl-Heinz. "'Schwarzhören' im Dritten Reich: Verbreitung, Erscheinungsformen und Kommunikationsmuster beim Umgang mit verbotenen Sendern." In *Archiv für Sozialgeschichte,* vol. 41, 245–262. Bonn: J.H.W. Dietz Nachf., 2001.

Review of *Glaube und Handeln* by Hellmut Stellrecht. *Unser Wille und Weg* 8 (1938): 349.

Richert, Ernst. *Agitation und Propaganda: Das System der publizistischen Massenführung in der Sowjetzone.* Schriften des Instituts für politische Wissenschaft, no. 10. Berlin: Franz Vahlen, 1958.

Ringler, Hugo. "Der Rednerstoßtrupp der Reichspropagandaleitung." *Unser Wille und Weg* 5 (1935): 154–156.

———. "Die Arbeit des Propagandisten im nationalsozialistischen Staat." *Unser Wille und Weg* 4 (1934): 293–299.

———. "Neuordnung des politischen Rednerstabes." *Unser Wille und Weg* 5 (1935): 30–33.

Rodden, John. "'It Should Have Been Written Here': Germany and *The Black Book*." *Human Rights Review* 2 (2001): 144–164.

———. *Repainting the Little Red Schoolhouse: A History of East German Education, 1945–1995.* New York: Oxford University Press, 2002.

Rosenberg, Alfred. *Lehrstoffsammlung und Grundplan für die weltanschauliche Schulung der Nationalsozialistischen Deutschen Arbeiterpartei.* Munich: Beauftragten des Führers für die gesamte geistige und weltanschauliche Schulung und Erziehung der NSDAP, 1939.

Rosenberg, Alfred, and Wilhelm Weiß. *Der Reichsparteitag der Nationalsozialistischen Deutschen Arbeiterpartei Nürnberg, 19./21. August 1927.* Munich: Franz Eher, 1927.

Ross, Colin. *The East German Dictatorship: Problems and Perspectives in the Interpretation of the GDR.* London: Arnold, 2002.

Ruck, Michael. *Bibliogaphie zum Nationalsozialismus.* 2nd ed. Darmstadt: Wissenschaftliche Buchgesellschaft, 2000.

"Rücksicht am falschen Platz." *Das Schwarze Korps,* 2 September 1943, 2.

Scanlan, Ross. "The Nazi Party Speaker System." *Speech Monographs* 16 (1949): 82–97.

———. "The Nazi Party Speaker System, II." *Speech Monographs* 17 (1950): 134–148.

———. "The Nazi Speakers' Complaints." *Quarterly Journal of Speech* 40 (1954): 1–14.

Schabowski, Günter. *Das Politbüro: Ende eines Mythos. Eine Befragung.* Reinbek: Rowohlt, 1990.

———. "Ihr Vermächtnis ist unser Kampf für Arbeit, Brot und Völkerfrieden." *Neues Deutschland,* 13 January 1986, 2.

Schäfer, Bernd. *Staat und katholische Kirche in der DDR.* Schriften des Hannah-Arendt-Instituts für Totalitarismusforschung, no. 8. Cologne: Böhlau, 1998.

Scharf, Götz. *Über den moralischen Faktor im modernen Krieg.* Schriftenreihe zur Diskussion über militärwissenschaftliche Fragen, no. 19. Berlin: Verlag des Ministeriums für nationale Verteidigung, 1959.

Scherzer, Landolf. *Der Erste: Protokoll einer Begegnung.* Rudolstadt: Greifen-verlag zu Rudolstadt, 1988.

Schirach, Baldur von, ed. *Das Lied der Getreuen: Verse ungennanter österreich-ischer Hitler-Jugend aus den Jahren der Verfolgung, 1933–37.* Leipzig: Philipp Reclam jun., 1938.

Schmiechen-Ackermann, Detlef. "Der 'Blockwart': Die unteren Parteifunk-tionäre im nationalsozialistischen Terror- und Überwachungsapparat." *Vierteljahrshefte für Zeitgeschichte* 48 (2000): 575–602.

Schmitz-Berning, Cornelia. *Vokabular des Nationalsozialismus.* Berlin: Walter De Gruyter, 1998.

Scholle. "Vom Ortsgruppenleiter." *Der Hoheitsträger* 6, no. 9 (1942): 29–30.

Schönemann, Friedrich. *Die Kunst der Massenbeeinflussung in den Vereinigten Staaten von Amerika.* Stuttgart: Deutsche Verlags-Anstalt, 1924.

Schrieber, Karl-Friedrich. *Die Reichskulturkammer.* Berlin: Junker und Dün-haupt, 1934.

Schriftsteller Verband der DDR. *X. Schriftstellerkongreß der Deutschen Demokratischen Republik: Arbeitsgruppen.* Cologne: Pahl-Rugenstein, 1988.

"Schrifttum über Propaganda." *Zeitschriften-Dienst,* 28 October 1939, 20–21.

Schubert, Renate. *Ohne größeren Schaden? Gespräche mit Journalistinnen und Journalisten der DDR.* Munich: Ölschläger, 1992.

Schultz, Wolfgang. "Auch an seinem Heim erkennt man den National-sozialisten!" *Der Hoheitsträger* 3, no. 8 (1939): 16–18.

Schulze-Wechsungen. "Politische Propaganda." *Unser Wille und Weg* 4 (1934): 323–334.

Schütte, Carl. *Schulfeiern im Geist der neuen Zeit.* Langensalza: Verlag von Julius Beltz, 1937.

Schwarz van Berk, Hans. "Die offenen Verlustlisten." *Das Reich,* 14 Febru-ary 1943: 3.

Selbmann, Erich. *DFF Aldershof: Wege übers Fernsehland: Zur Geschichte des DDR-Fernsehens.* Berlin: edition ost, 1998.

Simon, Günter. *Tischzeiten: Aus den Notizen eines Chefredakteurs 1981 bis 1989.* Berlin: Tribüne, 1990.

Sindermann, Horst. "Über die Änderung der Arbeitsweise der Agitation und Propaganda." In *Die Agitation und Propaganda ganz dem neuen Leben und dem Sieg des Sozialismus zuwenden.* Berlin: Abteilung Agitation und Propaganda beim Zentralkomitee der SED, 1959.

Sozialisten der Tat: Das Buch der unbekannten Kämpfer der N.S.V. Gau Groß-Berlin. Berlin: N.S.D.A.P. Amt für Volkswohlfahrt, Gau Groß-Berlin, 1934.

Speer, Albert. *Inside the Third Reich.* Trans. Richard Winston and Clara Winston. New York: Macmillan, 1970.

Sperber, Kurt. "Die Versammlungswelle." *Der Hoheitsträger* 3, no. 1 (1939): 27–28.

Springer, Hildegard, ed. *Es sprach Hans Fritzsche.* Stuttgart: Thield, 1949.

"Stasi-Dokumente, 1989." *Deutschland Archiv* 23 (1990): 612–622.

Statut der Sozialistischen Einheitspartei Deutschlands. Berlin: Dietz, 1975.

Steinert, Marlis G. *Hitler's War and the Germans: Public Mood and Attitude during the Second World War.* Ed. and trans. Thomas E. J. de Witt. Athens: Ohio University Press, 1977.

Stellrecht, Helmut. *Glauben und Handeln: Ein Bekenntnis der jungen Nation.* Berlin: Franz Eher, 1943.

Stern, J. P. *Hitler: The Führer and the People.* Berkeley: University of California Press, 1975.

Tenorth, Heinz Elmar, Sonja Kudella, and Andreas Paetz. *Politisierung im Schulalltag der DDR: Durchsetzung und Scheitern einer Erziehungsambition.* Bibliothek für Bildungsforschung, no. 2. Weinheim: Deutscher Studien, 1996.

Thomae, Otto. *Die Propaganda-Maschinerie: Bildende Kunst und Öffentlichkeitsarbeit im Dritten Reich.* Berlin: Gebr. Mann, 1978.

Tießler, Walter. "Der Reichsring für nat.-soz. Propaganda und Volksaufklärung." *Unser Wille und Weg* 5 (1935): 412–416.

Toepser-Ziegert, Gabriele. *NS-Presseanweisungen der Vorkriegszeit: Eine Einführung in ihre Edition.* Munich: K. G. Saur, 1984.

Über die Verbesserung der Parteipropaganda: Entschließung des Parteivorstandes der SED vom 2. und 3. Juni 1950. Berlin: Parteivorstand der SED, Abteilung Propaganda, 1950.

Unger, Aryeh. *The Totalitarian Party: Party and People in Nazi Germany and Soviet Russia.* Cambridge: Cambridge University Press, 1974.

Uricchio, William. "Rituals of Reception, Patterns of Neglect: Nazi Television and Its Postwar Representation." *Wide Angle* 11 (1989): 48–66.

Uschner, Manfred. *Die zweite Etage: Funktionsweise eines Machtapparates.* Berlin: Dietz, 1993.

Voegelin, Erich. *Political Religions.* Trans. T. J. DeNapoli and E. S. Easterly III. Toronto Studies in Theology. Lewiston, N.Y.: Edwin Mellen Press, 1986.

Volkogonov, Dmitri. *Autopsy for an Empire: The Seven Leaders Who Built the Soviet Regime.* Trans. Harold Shukman. New York: Free Press, 1998.

Vondung, Klaus. *Magie und Manipulation: Ideologischer Kult und politische Religion des Nationalsozialismus.* Göttingen: Vandenhoeck & Ruprecht, 1971.

Von Hallberg, Robert. *Literary Intellectuals and the Dissolution of the State: Professionalism and Conformity in the GDR.* Trans. Kenneth J. Northcott. Chicago: University of Chicago Press, 1996.

Vorländer, Herwart. *Die NSV: Darstellung und Dokumentation einer nationalsozialistischen Organisation.* Schriften des Bundesarchivs, no. 35. Boppard am Rhein: Harald Boldt, 1988.

Vorsteher, Dieter, ed. *Parteiauftrag: Ein neues Deutschland: Bilder, Rituale und Symbole der früheren DDR.* Munich: Koehler & Amelang, 1997.

Walter Ulbricht—Ein Leben für Deutschland. Leipzig: VEB E. A. Seemann, 1968.

"Warum ist die Oder-Neiße-Grenze die Friedensgrenze?" *Frage und Antwort: Argumente für die tägliche Diskussion,* no. 6 (1950): 3–4.

Weber, Hermann. *Geschichte der DDR.* Aktualisierte und erweiterte Neuausgabe. Munich: Deutsche Taschenbuch, 1999.

Weberstedt, Hans, and Kurt Langner. *Gedenkhalle für die Gefallenen des Dritten Reiches.* Munich: Franz Eher, 1938.

Welch, David. *Propaganda and the German Cinema, 1933–1945.* Oxford: Clarendon Press, 1983.

———. *The Third Reich: Politics and Propaganda.* London: Routledge, 1993.

Wiedemann, Dieter, and Hans-Jörg Stiehler. "Die Funktion der Massenmedien bei der kommunistischen Erziehung der Jugend." Leipzig: Zentralinstitut für Jugendforschung, 1984.

"Wie reimt sich das zusammen?" *Der Stürmer,* 24/1936, 10.

Wischnjakov, A. S., et al. *Methodik der politischen Bildung.* Trans. Intertext. Berlin: Dietz, 1974.

Wolle, Stefan. *Die heile Welt der Diktatur: Alltag und Herrschaft in der DDR, 1971–1989.* 2nd ed. Berlin: Ch. Links, 1998.

Wulf, Joseph. *Presse und Funk im Dritten Reich: Eine Dokumentation.* Gütersloh: Sigbert Mohn, 1964.

Young, Robert G. "'Not This Way Please!' Regulating the Press in Nazi Germany." *Journalism Quarterly* 64 (1988): 787–792.

Zander, Otto, ed. *Weimar: Bekenntnis und Tat: Kulturpolitisches Arbeitslager der Reichsjugendführung, 1938.* Berlin: Wilhelm Limpert, 1938.

Zeutschner, Heiko. *Die braune Mattscheibe: Fernsehen im Nationalsozialismus.* Hamburg: Rotbuch, 1995.

"Zum Geburtstag des Führers." *Deutsche Kinderwelt* 9/1936, 71.

"Zum 13. August." *Neues Deutschland,* 13 August 1962, 1.

Index